D1712838

The Education of a Survivor

The Education of a Survivor

FROM THE SCHOOL OF HARD KNOCKS
TO A DOCTORAL DEGREE

Arthur Goodfriend

With sketches from the author's journals

Published by
University of Hawaii Foundation

Library of Congress Cataloging-in-Publication Data

Goodfriend, Arthur, 1907–
    The education of a survivor / Arthur Goodfriend.
        p.   cm.
    Includes index.
    ISBN 0–8248–1222–0 (alk. paper)
    1. Comparative education.   2.   Education—Aims and objectives.
    3. Goodfriend, Arthur, 1907–   . I. Title.
    LB43.G66   1989
    370.19'5—dc20   89–5052
                                                                                CIP

∞™ The paper used in this publication meets
the minimum requirements of American National Standard for Information Sciences—Perma-
nence of Paper for Printed Library Materials
                              ANSI Z39.48-1984

Design and manufacture of this book was
through the production services program of the
University of Hawaii Press.

Distributed by
University of Hawaii Press
Order Department
2840 Kolowalu Street
Honolulu, Hawaii 96822

To members of humankind's noblest profession

TEACHERS

*with heartfelt sympathy, deep resentment,
and great regret*

CONTENTS

PREFACE

Colleges of Education almost everywhere are housed at a considerable distance from the university campus core. According to one dean of a different faculty, the reason is that education is not a discipline. "It is a mishmash of sociology, psychology, political science, and other studies taught by people who, having failed in their professions, find refuge in a hodgepodge misentitled 'Education'. We keep as distant from it as we can to avoid contamination."

Be that as it may, Wist Hall, where the College of Education at the University of Hawaii is quartered, shares the wrong side of University Avenue with a Pizza Hut, a Burger King, the Moiliili Hongwanji Buddhist Center, and the University High School. A sunny stucco facade hides a sepulchral inner ambience relieved by a lovely Japanese lady who guards the office of Educational Foundations. Inside Dr. Melvin Ezer, the chairperson, tall, gaunt, grizzled, greeted me warmly and asked what I had in mind.

I explained that I had just finished the last lap of a globe-girdling marathon studying school systems in America, Europe, Asia, Africa, and the South Pacific. My purpose was to find out why education is accused widely of failure to fulfill its function, however differently defined. Beginning with the school wars waged in New York City early in the century, my concerns about education intensified in prewar encounters with German and Japanese pedagogy, with the onset of World War II, and, as a soldier, in my role as a trainer of a largely illiterate American army.

Dr. Ezer seemed interested.

Before World War II, I went on, schooling was something to be suffered because society so ordered. Not until the indelible sight and stench of Dachau, Belsen, and Buchenwald overwhelmed my senses did I associate such evil with education. As editor of the army's newspaper *The Stars and Stripes* in Europe and China I became increasingly concerned about the connection of education with war and peace.

And so, to study schooling at its source, I was drawn to the great universities of the world, from whose heights doctrine descends to lower levels of education. I examined the American system at Harvard's Graduate School of Education, the British system at Cambridge, the Japanese at Kyoto University, and those of Australia and New Zealand at the Universities of Sydney and Canterbury. Investing a year in each country, I audited classes, interviewed students, teachers, parents, politicians, administrators, and others involved in the teaching-learning process, and traced the impact of higher education on secondary, primary, and preschool curricula.

Dr. Ezer was impressed.

Visits to the Soviet Union and China afforded insights on communist schooling from Stalin and Mao to Gorbachev and Deng. As a Rockefeller Fellow in Indonesia, a foreign service officer in India and Africa, and a Peace Corps volunteer in the Philippines, I participated in the Third World's efforts to educate its peoples. Finally, service as assistant chancellor of the East-West Center, as chairperson of a second culture course at the University of Hawaii, and as a lecturer aboard the University of Colorado's

Semester-at-Sea familiarized me with problems that beset echelons of education from its kindergartens to its ivory towers.

"Okay," said Dr. Ezer, "come to the point."

The point, I said, was that since school systems are often managed or otherwise influenced by PhDs and EdDs, I wanted to undergo the rigors of the paperchase for a doctoral degree. Unlike probes of scholars, national commissions, and private foundations whose reports highlight education's ills from elevated vantage points, I sought simply to relate one individual's experience in several school systems to that unmapped expanse variously called "life," "reality," "the world out there," perhaps thereby identifying some essentials in the absence of which education was unlikely to answer mankind's aspirations for peaceful resolutions of its problems.

Dr. Ezer asked that I submit official copies of my academic record and publications on which credit might be given in lieu of course work, enabling me to complete my doctoral work without delay. I complied and, after a week of consultation with his colleagues, Dr. Ezer advised that, in consideration of my age, eighty, and of my experience, my application was accepted, with requirements reduced to core courses in the history, sociology, and philosophy of education, an examination, and a dissertation.

Herewith, an account of the consequences—a collision between an eighty-year-old survivor of the school of hard knocks, and the theories, methods, manners, and scruples of the academy. Except for the last two chapters, it represents my dissertation for a doctoral degree. As episodes alternate between life's lessons and college course work, readers who pursue the quest vicariously in these pages may agree that, just as war cannot be entrusted to generals, education cannot be left to pedants.

I

Schooling Sets Off to a Rocky Start

P.S. 171, New York City
September 1912

I was a robust little boy—not a crybaby, bed-wetter, thumbsucker, or otherwise neurotic—but, aged five, scared witless on my first day at school, I soiled my knickers. Buckled below the knees, my corduroy pants formed twin pockets into which the feces fell, to the teacher's disgust and my classmates' derision. Humiliated, ostracized, and frantic with fear, I was sent home with a note to my mother. "Your child has socially unacceptable bowel control. Please report to the principal."

Being sent home from school became something of a habit. School was P.S. 171, an architectural calamity that, seventy-five years later, still stands on the upper east side of New York's Man-

hattan. It was visited each month by a matron who inspected the
children, mainly of German, Slavic, and Sicilian descent, for con-
tagious diseases, caries, ear wax, and lice. Not long after my earlier expulsion nits were found in my hair. Summoned to school for
a second time, my mother—a woman, if anything, obsessively
sanitary—suggested that the matron's comb had transferred nits
from another child's head to mine. The matron reminded my
mother of my earlier transgression, warned her against child
neglect, and added pediculosis to the encopresis already on my
record.

My mother, over time, became as much a fixture of the school
as chalk dust and disinfectant. Gross misconduct overtook hygiene as the reason for her visits. Pointing one day to the American
flag, the teacher told the class that it was every American's duty to
love it. In proof thereof each child was ordered to stand, salute,
and pledge allegiance to it. I refused, explaining that the flag had
too many stars and stripes. The French flag was simpler, I said,
and I liked it better. Outraged, the teacher packed me off to the
principal's office. Called once again on the carpet, my mother
vowed that I loved America with all my heart and that I was
merely expressing my preference for a less busy banner. "My son,"
she said, "is something of an artist." "Artist!" the principal
exploded, aiming a rigid finger at the diminutive Benedict Arnold.
"Your son, madam, is not an artist but a traitor to his country!"

My mother hadn't lied. One day, chalking pictures on the pave-
ment outside our house, I was watched by a stranger who scribbled a note to my parents. "Your son," he wrote, "has talent. Cultivate it." They did, providing me with pencils, paper, and paints.
Studying the structure of tulips, daffodils, and other flowers, I
became adept at rendering the curves and colors of their petals.
And so, at Easter, when the teacher told us to cut out tulips to
adorn the windows and walls, I felt sure of earning her approval.
Rather than cropping the standard silhouette, I painted a tulip in
the Monet manner. The teacher praised each child's production
until she came to mine. Frowning at my failure to follow instructions, she tore up my tulip. "You stupid, stubborn little boy, why
don't you ever do what you're told?"

Doubtless I was stupid and stubborn. But little we were supposed to learn had what today is termed relevance. Rather than
treasured tools, reading, writing, and arithmetic became obstacles

to be overcome on the track to dreaded tests. Reading began with flash cards rapidly shuffled from a deck on the teacher's lap. CAT, DOG, RAT chased each other faster than my eyes and mind could catch. To me a cat was a kitten to be stroked, a Krazy Kat in the comics. Suddenly, in the classroom, a cat became a cryptic code I had an instant to crack. Speed was the spur. Competitive kids, quick on the abecedarian draw, thrust up their hands, cried "cat!" and left me lost in feline revery. Except to go to the toilet, I rarely raised my hand. Remembered as I was for erratic elimination, I was never refused, but added to my offenses was "apathetic."

Once a little literacy was achieved we were plunged into *Rhymes and Fables,* a Golden Rod Book compiled by a pedant with a rather lethal outlook.

> There was a little man,
> And he had a little gun,
> And his bullets were made of lead, lead, lead.
> He went to a brook,
> And fired at a duck,
> And shot it through the head, head, head.

Arithmetic turned out to be tables taught by rote, a litany monotonously intoned in sing-song cadence. Rather than pennies, nickels, and dimes that bought candy, cookies, or any other commodity that gave import to integers, numbers merely equalled more numbers. History too—a blur of Christopher Columbus landing on Plymouth Rock and eating turkey with savage redskins —had no hooks on which my interest could be hung. Geography divided the world into numerous nations inhabited by wops, krauts, kikes, greasers, spicks, micks, and chinks—nomenclature not taught in texts but easily assimilated in the slang of the streets. To cast off the alien umbra of our origins and assert our American identity in ethnic slurs animated many first generation youngsters like myself.

At the core of the primary curriculum was a principle applied to every subject: in terms of time, place, character, occurrence, and applicability, take it as far from the child as one possibly can. It was as though some omnipotent tyrant deliberately decreed ends and means contrary to his vassals' abilities and ambitions. Some kids, competitive achievers, cottoned to the system. Rewarded with A's on their report cards—monthly indictments I dreaded taking home as evidence of my amentia—they were promoted and even skipped to higher grades. Left back were dullards, dreamers, delinquents like me who counted on their fingers and saw cats and dogs as pets rather than as letters locked into words, words parsed into sentences, sentences processed into paragraphs, and paragraphs fractured into parts of speech. That grammar might be the archenemy of reading and writing was as much a heresy as making a map of the world without America in the middle.

School notwithstanding, I learned. When my father came home with the evening's *Journal,* I seized the cartoons. What the Rosetta Stone was to archaeologists, comics were to me. The mouths of Krazy Kat, the Katzenjammer Kids, Maggie and Jiggs emitted bubbles filled with cyphers I loved to decode. Visualization led to verbalism, promoting the process of Americanization. America was Uncle Sam. Freedom was the Statue of Liberty. Courage was Jack Dempsey. Sinister Japanese whose almond eyes leered across the Pacific at achromatic America taught me to spell "The Yellow Peril." The creative spark quenched in classrooms was ignited by the illuminated manuscripts of medieval monks in the Metropolitan Museum of Art. Enraptured by their elegant calligraphy, I embarked on a series of illustrated journals, emulating their intricate initials, weaving letters into words, authoring words and pictures, and binding them into books—doing, in short, not what I was told but what welled up within me.

From cartoons to penny dreadfuls was a simple step. Horatio Alger, Frank Merriwell, the Rover Boys, became constant companions. So did the lady in the Carnegie Library who laid down her due-date stamp and led me to a shelf of lavishly illustrated books about King Arthur, Treasure Island, and Huckleberry Finn —a threshold once crossed that opened endless realms of adventure, relaxation, and self-instruction. No day ended without a bedtime tale by my mother who read to me, not to test my syntax, but to augment my enjoyment. Pleasure opened avenues to wherever it was that my expanding interests beckoned—nowhere better satisfied than in books.

Like reading, arithmetic came alive outside the classroom. When grapes were in season, my mother tore off as many from their stems as I could count. Given such stimuli, adding ten or more was easy. As each grape was eaten, I learned to subtract.

Nothing was so rewarding as the magic of multiplication. To double or triple a given number of grapes by so many times two or three awakened the Einstein within me. But school problems remained riddles resisting resolution. Typically, at what point two trains rushing toward each other on a single track at a mile a minute would collide lay beyond my ability to reckon. Not even my mother, however, could overcome my aversion to arithmetic. Her method failed when applied to brussel sprouts which I detested.

To imply that P.S. 171 was a total loss would be unjust. Somehow, something was grafted on unwilling stock—spelling, telling time, not picking our noses. The problem, in part, was the difficulty a teacher faced in ascertaining the aptitudes and responding to the interests of thirty-five or forty budding identities. Endless, almost, were the inclinations of the boys on my block. One could prick a piece of crystal with a needle and produce a primitive radio. Another could build cantilever and suspension bridges with a Meccano. Others played the piano and balanced aquaria. One boy, not yet ten, was already into masturbation while, to me, a penis had no purpose but to pee. Potential doctors, lawyers, thespians, thieves early exhibited talents that foretold their future. Individually, some were slow, impaired, at the bottom of bell curves, destined to become the infantry of the war our generation was fated to fight. Collectively we comprised the vibrant society of the street. Only when homogenized in school did so many diverse personalities become a problem. To understand, to control, to civilize such diversity lay beyond the abilities of women—ill paid, overworked, poorly prepared, and prey to political pressures about to erupt in New York City.

And so it was that my education as a child came mainly from my parents, my peers, and from the pages of the *New York Evening Journal*. From its headlines I learned about Pancho Villa who invaded Texas, an event given meaning by maps, cartoons, and photographs of swarthy bandits in sombreros. Soldiers from the Squadron A cavalry on Madison Avenue marshaled below my bedroom window and trotted off to war—a skirmish overtaken by Kaiser Bill, U-boats, Big Berthas, and Huns who ravished Belgian nuns. Bloody battles on the Western Front drove Mother Goose, Puss-in-Boots, and Simple Simon into limbo. The Russian Revolution revived interest in Little Red Riding Hood but only for the time it took to discredit her communist credentials. To me, aged

nine, trench warfare in Flanders meant more than bleeding feet at
Valley Forge. Beside the drum-beat of the daily press, school
seemed archaic, teachers pedantic, textbooks obsolete.

Vying with the war waged overseas was a local struggle of
which I was but dimly aware. It engaged my parents in dinner-
table discussion almost acrimonious in the passion the issue
aroused. Something called "the Gary Plan" centered attention on
New York City's schools. It appeared that I was not alone in my
dissatisfaction with the system. All the city's problems were
blamed on education—unemployment, poverty, crime, malnutri-
tion, child labor, and other abuses that festered in the slums.

Seething as she was from insults suffered at the principal's
hands, my mother saw the Gary Plan as his comeuppance. The
fact that it was favored by the Vanderbilts, Astors, and other blue-
stockings assured her that, at long last, my problems at P.S. 171
would be addressed and alleviated.

My father was of an opposite opinion. Less assimilated than my
mother, he clung to the prejudices of the European working class.
To him the Gary Plan augured manipulation of the schools by rob-
ber barons out to turn slum children into slaves of a capitalist
economy. In protest he joined the Anti-Gary League. Tempers
flared, a strike was declared, and ten days before the municipal
election of 1917 mobs milled around P.S. 171 bearing banners
"Can the Gary System!" and "Save the City's Schools!"

The kids in my class were caught up in the frenzy. With them I
raced past the police, picked up a rock, and aimed it at my classroom window. Consistent with all my other efforts in elementary
education, I missed.

2

New York City's "School Wars"

Wist Hall, University of Hawaii
Honolulu, January 1987

Classes begin at the College of Education. I take two courses, one on American education from Puritan times to the present, the other on higher education in the United States. Both require extensive reading, and the anecdotal nature of my narrative takes on a deeper dimension. Diane Ravitch's *The Great School Wars* and Theodore Sizer's *Horace's Compromise* both touch on P.S. 171, rounding out my recollections of the Gary Plan uproar, and revealing that my elementary alma mater may still make history.

Ravitch writes that Tammany Hall had lost the 1913 election to a Fusion candidate, John Purroy Mitchell. As mayor, Mitchell's aim was to eliminate the congestion, irrelevance, and waste that disgraced the city's public school system. Searching the nation for a paradigm of pedagogic perfection, he found it in Gary, Indiana, a company town named after Elbert Gary, chairman of United States Steel. Under Dr. William Wirt, a disciple of John Dewey, Gary had integrated work, study, and play into a program fulfilling Dewey's theories of democratic education in an industrial society. Each Gary school spread over ten to twenty acres of abundant land provided by the corporation at little cost. Playgrounds, pools, art and music studios, science labs, machine shops abounded. Publicized as "Schools of Utopia," they sought to "educate the whole child physically, artistically, manually, scientifically as well as intellectually." School buildings were used eight hours a day by two shifts or, as the system came to be called, "platoons." Stretching the school year from forty to forty-four weeks without additional compensation for teachers, the Gary Plan was said to save taxpayers a lot of money.

Mayor Mitchell induced Wirt to come to New York for one week a month as an adviser to the superintendent of schools at a salary of $10,000 per annum, a sum matching that received by the superintendent for full-time service. P.S. 171 was one of the first schools to feel the Gary Plan's impact, but because neither space, facilities, population factors, nor finances in New York corresponded to Gary, the impact, educationally, was so small as to be imperceptible, at least to me, a pupil. Mainly it was in the political arena that "the school wars" were fought.

In the mayoral campaign of 1917 Mitchell was opposed by a Tammany ward-heeler, "Red Mike" Hylan, who accused the mayor of making the city's public schools "the football of politics." Grist in Hylan's mill was the Gary Plan's link with Rockefeller's Standard Oil and Gary's United States Steel. "I say to you, Mr. Mayor, to the Rockefeller Foundation and to any other private interests who wish to put our children on half-rations of education"—a poke at the platoon system—"hands off our public schools!"

Adding fuel to the flames was World War I. Mitchell urged America's entry on the Allied side which anti-British Irish and Germans resisted. Teachers, turned off by Wirt's refusal to pay them for overtime, were joined by the superintendent of schools who resented Wirt's compensation for one week a month matching his own for four. The last vestiges of educational reform vanished in a vendetta of rich versus poor, masses versus classes, triggering the riot at P.S. 171 in which I cast my first stone against education.

"Red Mike" Hylan routed Mitchell with the largest majority ever accorded a mayoral candidate in the city's history. Pronouncing the Gary Plan dead, he filled public school positions with Tammany toadies. Wirt faded into oblivion in Indiana, an eccentric whose zeal for educational reform was overtaken by aversion to the "Kerensky of the American Revolution," Franklin Roosevelt. And the Rockefeller Foundation, reversing its role, published a paper condemning the Gary Plan as "unsubstantiated, with crude supervision and with students habituated to inferior performance." My mother, I imagine, must be gyrating in her grave.

As for *Horace's Compromise* by Theodore Sizer, I am astonished to learn that since 1985, P.S. 171 is the home of a successor to the Gary Plan—an experimental program based on Sizer's belief that "less is more—it is more important to know some things well than to know many things superficially. Kids need one-on-one attention. Teaching and learning must be personalized to the maximum feasible extent."

Where were you, Ted Sizer, when I needed you?

3

Agonies of Adolescence

DeWitt Clinton High School
New York City, 1920

Though encopresic, pediculous, seditious, apathetic, stupid, and stubborn, at age thirteen I was presented with a diploma testifying that I had successfully completed my elementary education and was eligible to enter the city's secondary system. Appalled at the prospect of another contest with "Red Mike" Hylan's political pedants and unable to afford a private school, my mother took me to Horace Mann High School, a tuition-free institution named after the father of America's public school system, and renowned for the quality of its curriculum. The admissions officer grimaced as he scanned my record. "Madam," he muttered, "if he could see this, Horace Mann would be unhappy." Rebuffed, we applied for admission to Townsend Harris Hall, the city's other haven for exceptional adolescents. "I'm afraid your son is a little *too* exceptional for Townsend Harris Hall," said the registrar. My fate was sealed. In September 1920, I entered DeWitt Clinton High School on Manhattan's west side where, for another four years, my pedagogical pratfalls were doomed to repetition. My mother also enrolled me in the National Academy of Design on upper Amsterdam Avenue to insure that whatever befell me in other areas of my education, my artistic potential was not neglected.

The climate of DeWitt Clinton was distinctively clinical. It smelled like a home for the incontinent aged. Emanations from chemistry and biology labs mingled with the carbolic reek of unflushed toilets. The fumes of formaldehyde in which the viscera of frogs marinated while awaiting dissection compounded the impact of an olfactory bedlam. Arts and humanities which emitted no odors were overwhelmed by the sour smells of science. Clinical too was the surgical approach to our studies. Each subject was laid out on a slab, cold, dead, repulsive. Knives sharpened, cadavers were cut, tissue analyzed, our cognition tested. Prose, poetry, plays, paintings, social studies underwent the same insult. It was like examining Mona Lisa so intently that you never saw her smile.

English literature centered on *Silas Marner*. Doled out daily, in spoonfuls like cod-liver oil, it was just as tasteless. Nevertheless, a ravenous reader, I devoured the novel in a single sitting. Sensing that I had disobeyed the order to focus on pages one to five, the teacher warned me to stick to passages on which I would be tested. "Remember," he scolded, "you're here to *study Silas Marner,* not to *enjoy* him!"

My foreign language was French. *Les Miserables* was our text and, like *Silas Marner,* Victor Hugo's epic was so atomized as to obliterate meaning. Each sentence, miscroscopically scrutinized, slowed the author's flow from a torrent to a trickle. Impatient with the escargot pace at which the plot unfolded, I read the book in English. The final exam required me to write an essay on Jean Valjean's chase through the sewers of Paris. I searched the dictionary for the French word for *sewer* and wrote: *Jean Valjean a couru par les couseuses de Paris.* This translated into "Jean Valjean ran through the seamstresses of Paris," earning me an F for French.

From Bull Run to Appomattox the Civil War was fought in the classroom over almost as much time as it took Grant to take Richmond. Quizzed on the reason why Lee and Meade met at Gettys-

burg in the war's climactic battle, I relied on a novel I had read
rather than quoting the cut-and-dried causes cited in the text.
There were shoe factories in Pennsylvania, I wrote, and Lee's bare-
foot army needed boots. Rigid were the rules. Don't deviate.
Regurgitate. Another F adorned my record.

Only math exceeded the languid pace of literature, history, and
social studies, moving with dizzy speed from cube roots to quadri-
lateral equations, leaving me lost in a maze of triangles, trape-
zoids, and parallelopipeds. Algebraic abstractions and space con-
figurations eluded my understanding. Classmates with steel-trap
minds that anticipated computers relished problems that boggled
my brain. The teacher brushed aside my complaint that coeffi-
cients and cosines had no practical meaning for me. "Practical
meaning isn't the point of math," he insisted. "Like Latin, math is
taught to train your mind. Without discipline your mind remains
unruly."

I looked up the word in Websters. "Discipline . . . training that
corrects, molds or perfects the mental faculties or moral character
. . . control gained by enforcing obedience or order." Discipline
definitely was not my dish. Neither, as defined by Webster, was I a
disciple—"one who accepts or assists in spreading the doctrines of
another."

Discipline was also the doctrine of the National Academy of
Design which I attended evenings. Beginners sat amid a cemetery
of plaster casts of Greek and Roman extraction. As death pre-
ceded the dissection of frogs in DeWitt Clinton's biology lab, so
did death dominate my drawing. Ancient, pale, inanimate statues
lacked the life of the naked ladies who modeled upstairs for adult
artists. Whenever the instructor was absent I peeked through a
door-crack at the pink nipples and dusky pubic patches of flesh-
and-blood females, only to be caught, scolded, and sent below to
do my umpteenth sketch of Julius Caesar. "My boy," mourned the
teacher, shaking his head at my doodle. "What you need is discipline. Lack of discipline will be your undoing."

Sex, alas, was my undoing. Biology delved deeply into lungs,
livers, and all other organs except the reproductive. When wet
dreams, masturbation, and other pubescent outlets demanded recognition, the principal himself addressed the issue. Assured that
the classroom door was shut and everyone under fifteen excluded,
he bellied up to the blackboard, picked up a piece of chalk, and

drew a penis. "Erect," he said, "this is the male tool of reproduction." The class was convulsed. "Silence!" roared the principal. "I grant you I am not an artist. If anyone can draw any better than I you're welcome to try." Egged on by classmates aware of my talent, I tiptoed to the blackboard and sketched a naked lady. "Flat," I said, "this is the female tool of reproduction." Unable to quell the tumult, the principal erased my sketch and shouted "Class dismissed!" So was the subject. And so was I.

In retrospect, little that happened in school mattered much to my maturation. Like other adolescents I learned from life itself, the principal inputs being parents, peers, media, and early experiences in the streets, in sports, and in employment. My first summer job was as a page at the Waldorf Astoria hotel, then located on lower Fifth Avenue. Studded with brass buttons and ringing a bell, I strolled Peacock Alley intoning notables' names and running their errands. Queen Marie of Roumania warmed me with her smile. Calvin Coolidge froze me with his frown. Nothing I did delighted me more than operating the hydraulic elevator which bounced up and down before I could manage a level landing. General Pershing was one of my passengers. "Black Jack" paled at my performance. "Young man," he mumbled, "this is the first time I've ever been scared."

As in school, sex also undid me at the Waldorf. Among my duties was racing items from Trezise the Chemist in the lobby to guests on upper floors. A favorite of mine was Miss Wilson to whose suite I delivered cosmetics, shampoos, and other toiletries essential to beautiful blondes. One day, when the buzzer sounded, I picked up a package from Dr. Trezise, ascended to her floor, knocked on her door, and called out "Good morning, Miss Wilson, here are your sanitary napkins and hope you have a nice picnic!" Instead of the customary quarter, the door slammed in my face. Down below, Dr. Trezise was livid. From him, from all the other bell boys, I learned what DeWitt Clinton had failed to teach —more, indeed, than I really needed to know.

A second summer passed on Wall Street where, garbed in the gray livery of the New York Stock Exchange, I worked as a runner. Data conveyed today by computers was then delivered through underground passages by boys like me who dropped the daily record in brokers' offices throughout the financial district. Numbers suddenly assumed importance. Dow Jones averages, dividends, price-earning ratios dripped off my tongue with the deftness of a Morgan. I invested my pay in a sure-fire high flyer. The market dipped and wiped me out. Tuition in the school of hard knocks was high, but beyond price were its lessons.

Other influences were the local YMCA where, as a Boy Scout, I learned to "be prepared"; the first futile gropings with girls; my adulation of athletes like Benny Leonard, the boxer; the death of my dearest friend from a mastoid infection; the sense of loss as his body was borne away. The ecstacy of love, the fragility of life, the agony of loneliness—lessons absent from the empty realms of acadeeme—I learned from exposure, experience, exploration. In ways difficult to understand or explain—genetic, environmental, accidental, supernaturally pre-ordained—my individuality emerged from the pupa of pubescence, craving option and independence over compulsion and compliance. Incentive over imposition. Realism over abstraction. Self-realization over competition. Originality, experimentation, creativity rather than obedience, acceptance, regurgitation. From such impulses, embryonic and crudely expressed in cartoons and poems in the *Magpie,* Clinton's monthly magazine which I edited, I salvaged a measure of self-esteem from my academic insolvency.

Hovering over all else was a presence, impalpable but ubiquitous, that shadowed my existence. Whereas, at the elementary level, education was regulated by New York City's Board of Education, secondary education was governed by the Regents of the University of the State of New York. Located in Albany, the state capital, hundreds of miles up the Hudson River, the Regents were physically remote, but every high-school boy and girl understood that admission to higher education depended on the passage of Regents exams. Not until many years later, in Japan, did I learn about *Shiken Jigoku* "Examination Hell," an oriental instrument of torture in which information, force-fed into students' minds, was excreted in annual seizures of data-diarrhea. The Regents served the same purpose—to identify those capable of rote-memorization of textbook content and reward them with college admission.

How, by a hair's breadth, I passed the Regents, remains a mystery. So does the question of why, instead of joyous, education was so oppressive.

4

The Teutonic Plague Infects Education

Wist Hall
February 1987

My doctoral studies pay off. A dusty tome written by Dr. James E. Russell, dean of Teachers College, Columbia University, informs me of how the Teutonic Plague infected DeWitt Clinton High School. It also foretells the future of American education. Dean Russell was delegated by the Board of Regents of the State of New York, at its invocation of July 1893, to be the board's special agent for the study of German education. His report, entitled *German Higher Schools, the History, Organization and Methods of Secondary Education in Germany,* reflects overwhelming admiration for almost every aspect of Prussian pedagogy. According to Russell:

> German schools are masterpieces of intelligent design. . . . Two dominant forces in the development of the German school system are state and university. State is authoritative, autocratic, conservative. It compels parents to send children to school from 6 to 14, directs their training, sets standards for promotion and production, exercises central control, insists on high scholarship, provides thorough professional training for all teachers, dignifies teaching as a profession, honors it and supports it even unto death. . . . Prussia has not only created a teaching profession, but she has trained up a body of men to occupy it who are without rivals the world over. This is not mere flattery . . . the Prussian teacher is a man of noble character, high ideals, generous impulses, broad and accurate scholarship and technical skill; he is a gentleman, patriot and educator.

Russell concludes:

> The experience of Germany can teach us much if we will but learn to consider it aright. Indeed, the future of American civilization and the rich blessings of republican institutions will be assured if we can interest the best talent of the country in education and evolve a school system which shall be as nicely adjusted to our national requirements as the German system is to Germany.

A different assessment of German education is contained in *Students, Society and Politics in Imperial Germany* by Konrad H. Jarausch. According to him, the Prussian system was characterized by (1) idealization of culturation *(bildung)* on a classical Greek and Roman model converted to a Prussian paragon. (2) Scholarly specialization, eroding neohumanism and making its moral pretensions meaningless. (3) Widespread elitism setting academics apart from the industrial-commerical bourgeoisie and working masses, and adding education to birth and wealth as a social entitlement. (4) Anti-Semitism, antifeminism, reflex patriotism (chauvinism) evolving toward nationalism, glorification of the Kaiser, support of German power and world dominion. (5) Emphasis on science and technology, increasing specialization of individual disciplines, breaking up the philosophical unity of knowledge, and leading to training as distinct from education. (6) Routinized lecturing, reduced faculty-student contact, increased *Junker* bravado, brusqueness to those below, sycophancy toward those above, arrogance toward non-Germans, a *Deutschland uber alles* mentality, and a will to war.

German education was put in yet another perspective by Adolf Hitler's Minister of Education: "Universal education is the most corroding and disintegrating poison. The intellect is a disease of life. Knowledge is ruin to any young man. The whole function of German education is to create Nazis."

But I am getting ahead of my story. Back to 1924, to New York City where, the Regents overcome and diploma in hand, I was about to be corroded and disintegrated by a college education.

5

Education Begins on New York's Bowery

The College of the City of New York
New York City, 1924–1928

The engines of higher education are stoked by upwardly mobile mothers. Without mine I would have quit school after kindergarten. College might have attracted me if I could have entered Yale. But without money to pay tuition and other costs of Ivy League enlightenment, my only recourse was the College of the City of New York. Established in 1847 to enable boys of immigrant backgrounds to realize the American dream of a classless society, CCNY graduates themselves achieved upper-class status as doctors, lawyers, entrepreneurs. Unlike Europe's universities that profited the privileged, free higher education in America served the poor. I cannot stem tears of gratitude as I pass Ellis Island where my parents had disembarked and entered upon an adventure that cast me at City College's gothic gates. Here too I cried. But the tears I shed in City College were tears of fear, fury, and frustration.

City College offered two degrees, a Bachelor of Arts and a Bachelor of Science. The first required Latin, the second, math. Caught between the Scylla of the classics and the Charybdis of calculus, I opted for the first and came a cropper on Virgil's opening line—*arma virumque cano*—"I sing of arms and the man." Every history textbook sang the same sorry song of men and munitions. The French and Indian War. The Revolutionary War. The War of 1812. The Mexican War. The Civil War. The Spanish-American War. World War I. As though America's wars were not enough, now upon my plate were heaped the wars of Athens, Troy, Sparta, Rome, and Gaul. That Latin rhapsodized pillage, plunder, pyromania signaled something wrong.

So did the old devil "discipline." Latin allegedly trained the mind. Rather than reading modern English, it was deemed more desirable to dissect a corpse as dead as Latin. Once again were my own creative juices quenched by a curriculum arbitrarily designed to discipline my mind. Of the debacle this induced no better evidence exists than the transcript of my freshman record—a B in hygiene; C's in remedial English, public speaking, and military science; F's in math and Latin. I flunked Latin once. I failed Latin twice. To strike out three times meant expulsion, disgrace, and the demise of my mother.

And so a switch—from a Bachelor of Arts to a Bachelor of Science. From the *Iliad* and *Odyssey* to differential and integral calculus, chemistry, physics, statistics, and "arts," meaning mechanical drawing. Foreclosed was admission to philosophy, psychology, sociology, journalism, drama, the visual arts. Locked were the doors to City College's constellation of celebrated lecturers—Morris Raphael Cohen, Harry Overstreet, Bertrand Russell. Never, in all four years of torment, did this weird assortment of uncongenial courses recognize and accommodate my artistic ambitions.

Accenting the anomaly was the contrast between my course work and my capabilities as exhibited in extracurricular activities. Editor of the *Mercury*, the college magazine. Editor of the *Microcosm*, the year book. Contributor to *College Humor*. "Poet laureate" of the class and its most prolific cartoonist. Such potential as could have been cultivated in a collegian so at odds with the curriculum was sacrificed on the altar at which City College worshipped—discipline.

Discipline was enforced every Friday in a course common to both the arts and sciences—ROTC. The Reserve Officers Training Corps was the currency with which we repaid the nation for our free feast of the fruits from the tree of knowlege. Clad in itchy khaki we marched, saluted, executed the manual of arms. However disagreeable, discipline as demanded by the army was honest. The aim of the army was instant, unquestioning obedience to order. The army didn't pretend to educate. It trained. It drilled. It inculcated discipline essential for war and, implicitly, death. Education, contrarily, was discipline in academic drag, explicitly deceitful and detrimental to its proper purpose—love of life.

The ordeal ended with a BS degree and the gold bars of a reserve lieutenant. My achievement was recognized with an award for "the greatest progress against the greatest odds." The dean's praise was extravagant. "You have proved it possible," he declaimed, "for a person without an affinity for mathematics to overcome his handicap, thereby justifying the time-honored truism that no better way exists to discipline the mind than mathematics."

Had I been invited to respond to the dean's panegyric, and had I the courage, I would have said, "This prize pays tribute to the idiocy of American education which has wasted years of my life and taxpayers' money in forcing upon me a discipline for which, in the past, I have had no vocation and for which, in the future, I foresee no use. Had the teachers' time and effort not been wasted on a mathematical moron like me, far more benefit might have accrued to mankind, at far less cost in money and misery." (To which, today, I might add that, in over 80 years, I have never needed to square a root, equalize an algebraic equation, or do anything more than simple arithmetic to earn my bread, balance my budget, and satisfy the Internal Revenue Service.)

Framed, my diploma adorned my mother's parlor until she passed away. To her it evidenced my academic accomplishment. To me it symbolized all I had missed in sixteen years of schooling. I hungered for an antidote to my odious education, something that might fill the empty areas in my studies and substitute reality for the bunk in the books. I was drawn to New York's Bowery as a bum.

Unshaven, arrayed in a soiled sweater, frayed jeans, and battered sneakers, I begged alms on the city's streets, ate swill served by the Salvation Army, lined up at Fulton Market for a job unloading fish, slept in flophouses on cots impacted with the dried vomit of earlier occupants, surrounded by sounds and smells of delirious winos in chicken-wire cubicles rented for a nickel a night. One week on the Bowery taught more about the human condition than the preachments of a thousand pedants. Laundered linen, a decent diet, a bathroom with soap, towels, and toilet paper—everything earlier taken for granted I saw as God-given good fortune, a benchmark by which to measure the remainder of my life.

The literature of autobiography is curiously deficient in the area of education—that is to say, there are few accounts of the lives of educators. Though diligent in propounding whatever principles they espouse, educators remain elusive about those aspects of their existence, from infancy to eminence, that explain where they are and how they got there—as though the conclusions to which they came were without any personal experiences other than those provided by the library and the laboratory.

However, autobiographies of eminent noneducators amply affirm that I was not alone in my academic agony. Evidence abounds that "most boys pregnant with genius have serious problems with school curricula and dull, irrational teachers." This sentence is from *The Last Lion, Winston Spencer Churchill* (Sphere Books, London: William Manchester.) Noting that Churchill found himself in "an Alice in Wonderland world at the portals of which stood Quadratic Equations, followed by the dim chambers inhabited by the Differential Calculus, and then a strange corridor of sines and cosines in a highly square-rooted condition . . . I am glad," Churchill concluded, "that there are quite a number of people born with a gift and a liking for all this." Winston was not one of them.

According to the *Encyclopaedia of World Biography* (London: McGraw Hill), Albert Einstein was unable to speak fluently at age nine. He found life in school intolerable. His teacher expelled him for the negative effects his rebellious attitude was having on the morale of his classmates. Einstein's formal secondary education was abruptly terminated at sixteen. He tried to enter the Federal Institute of Technology in Zurich but failed the entrance examination. For six months, without the restrictions imposed by formal schooling, Einstein taught himself calculus and higher mathematics.

To mention one more account akin to my own experience, *Out of Step* by Sidney Hook (New York: Harper and Row), describes his education in New York City in the same system and time frame as my own. Elementary school was "a terrible bore . . . discipline was exacting but to most of us the boredom was worse than the discipline." Entering Boys High School in 1916: "The pedagogy was execrable. The text book was the only authority . . . instruction was geared to passing the Regents exams . . . teaching was not only authoritarian but conducted in a spirit of hostility." Hook actually studied under Morris Raphael Cohen whose "browbeating, sarcasm and absence of simple courtesy marked his dialectical interrogations."

Although Hook gained far more academic enrichment than did I from City College's curriculum, I would agree with his conclusion: "It was an education [students] could not have afforded elsewhere. . . . This speaks to the perpetual glory of City College."

6

Waves of Reform
Wash Over America . . .

Wist Hall
March 1987

A dozen books on Prof. Ralph Stueber's agenda testify that lock-step education such as mine was being bombarded by many of the best, the brightest, the most mordant minds in America. John Dewey attacked the rigidity and uniformity of the curriculum, the reliance on rote memorization, the suppression of students' interests, urging instead that children learn best from experience. Psychological experimentation proved that Latin and math taught Latin and math rather than precision, concentration, or any other mental discipline transferable to another subject. Harold Rugg and Ann Shumaker denounced conventional schools as "places of fears, restraints and long, weary hours of suppression," based on a bankrupt belief in discipline. William H. Kilpatrick, a Teachers College dean, taught several generations of teacher trainees at Columbia that the best way to educate children was through their own experiences rather than "subject matter fixed in advance." A consensus existed that the essence of education was experience, that the focus of instruction should be the child's motivation, interest, and ability, that newspapers should supplement text-books, and that examinations, grades, and extraneous rewards thwarted learning. Why, with such waves of reform washing over America, did I never get wet?

Although I derive some satisfaction from the knowledge that so solid a phalanx of wisdom stands behind me, it does little to diminish the pain of having been the last victim of an ancient regime that turned classrooms into torture chambers. Indeed, as I delve deeper into the literature of "progressive education," as these crusades came to be called, such gratification as I feel is overcome by embarrassment at the lengths to which the pendulum swung. Movements labelled, "Open," "Free School," "Alternative School," and "Deschooling" espouse everything from total abdication of education to children's whims to severance of schools from society. Little wonder that the pretensions of progressive education, punctured by Sputnik, sent American schools reeling back to basics.

Our doctoral course currently concentrates on *Educational Wastelands, The Retreat From Learning in Our Public Schools* by Arthur Bestor. He rages against the ineptitude of American education, principally its failure to teach "the power to think"—a power provided by training in recognized disciplines such as mathematics, chemistry, and physics as distinct from the arts and humanities. Rather than specialists in such subjects, he claims, Colleges of Education produce generalists concerned with *how* to teach rather than *what* to teach. No longer informed by the rigors of the major disciplines, the nation's schools suffer ever lower standards.

A retrospective by Foster McMurray espouses the absurdity of Bestor's thesis. Rather than producing "the power to think," McMurray argues that organized disciplines are not so much a way of thinking as a way of doing research within a specific field of knowledge. Thus, the teaching of chemistry by a professor from the chemistry faculty is to teach how to think in the manner of a chemist. For a mathematician to teach math is to focus attention upon the nature, vocabulary, and technical concepts peculiar to math.

Deeply divided on Bestor's book are America's most eminent educators. Lawrence Cremin of Columbia's Teachers College praises Bestor's writings as "by far the most serious, searching, and influential criticisms of progressive education." R. Will Burnett, professor of education at the University of Illinois charges that "*Educational Wastelands* is shot through with distortions, half-truths, and pseudo-scholarship." Gordon Chalmers, quondam president of Kenyon College, supports Bestor's belief that "professional educationists have lowered the aims of the American public schools." Fletcher Watson of Harvard's Graduate School of Education writes that "Bestor does not know how to begin to deal with America's educational problems." Dismayed by the differences that divide experts on so basic a question, I hesitate to enter the fray. But this paragraph from McMurray's paper neatly puts my personal position:

> A young man—let us say his name is Arthur—takes a course in analytic geometry with a teacher who usually succeeds in getting his students to understand the subject matter at a more than superficial level and to form a new found respect for it. Some even get to like it. But not Arthur. He finds that even when he manages to do well on tests and to feel that he understands what analytic geometry is about, he is not favorably disposed to learning more. Analytic geometry is not his cup of tea. Does this mean that in his case educational values were not realized? Certainly not. For anyone to discover, after fair and adequate exposure to a facet of school-taught cultural heritage, that it is not for him is an acceptable educational outcome.

How then to deal with the dearth of mathematicians, scientists, and engineers on which America's "competitiveness" depends? By wasting the precious expertise of too-few teachers in these areas on the Arthurs of America, or, relieved of responsibility for mathematical morons like me enabling them to cultivate the country's embryonic Einsteins—to push ahead of the Russians, the Germans, the Japanese, and others who long ago learned this simple lesson: silk purses can't be made from sow's ears?

7

Education Advances on the Battlefields of France

Heidelberg University
Germany, 1928

My father had two favorite expressions. One was "when my ship comes in," a reference to a mythical vessel bearing the fortune that eluded him in the world of work. The other was "it isn't *what* you know but *who* you know." Both proved prophetic. While working as a runner for the New York Stock Exchange I had made a friend in the Standard Oil Company through whose intercession I was signed on as an able-bodied seaman aboard the *Benjamin Brewster,* a tanker sailing from Hoboken, New Jersey, to Hamburg, Germany, to pick up a cargo of fuel.

The bos'n, an enormous Irishman with scant respect for a Bachelor's degree, armed me with a hammer and chisel and sent me below to chip rust from the boilers. It was as inauspicious an introduction to the sea as was my first day at school, the only difference being that this time, instead of encopresis, the problem was emesis. Rhythmically, as the ship heaved, so did I. Unless I could contrive an escape from the bowels of the *Benjamin Brewster,* it seemed certain that a dead or seriously disable-bodied seaman would be borne off the ship when it dropped the hook in Hamburg.

Inspiration struck. Advised that, as an artist, I could refurbish the lettering on the tanker's lifeboats and buoys, the bos'n set me up in a studio abaft the bridge. Dividing the number of boats and buoys by days at sea, I synchronized the last flick of my paint brush with the first sight of land. The *Brewster* and I, both bright with paint, parted in the port. The bos'n shook my hand as I headed for the gangplank and invited me to join him for a drink that evening in a St. Pauli bar. After a long day's rubber-necking in the splendid Hanseatic city I craved the crew's companionship and joined the bos'n at the Alkazar, a bar and bordello where, after several steins of Bavarian beer, I was sent upstairs with my first doxy. A fleshy blonde, young but adept at her art, she removed her slip, stretched out on the bed, and beckoned me to lie down beside her. I stared at her vulva through beer-addled eyes. Round, rosy, freshly shaven as a cheek with a deep depression, it looked like a dimple. I couldn't get it up. I couldn't put it in. I earned another F for fucking.

Half a *wanderjahr* stretched ahead. All that in classrooms and textbooks had been dead as mutton suddenly sprang to life. French turned out to be something people spoke. Dotted lines on maps became borders I couldn't cross without visas, customs' probes, and currency conversions. Dollars changed for francs, marks, and lira taught me the decimal system. From Versailles to the Vatican, from the Louvre to the Prado, from fish and chips in London to pizza in Perugia I imbibed more art, architecture, edibles, and alcohol than in all my earlier existence.

I bought a bicycle in Belgium and pedaled down the Western Front from Brussels to Verdun. The Menin Gate in Ypres honored 50,000 Tommies who had no graves, their flesh blended like fertilizer in the Flemish loam. In Passchendaele 300,000 more had expired in a sea of slime, driven by generals eager to add a few hundred feet of mud on their maps. A long chain of cemeteries linked Tyne Cot and Vimy Ridge where 66,655 Canadians were killed, their bodies buried beside 37,000 Germans—just a few of the 1,800,000 who fell to fulfill the Kaiser's dream of *Deutschland uber Alles*. As I pedaled, a poem echoed in my mind:

> They went with songs to the battle, they were young,
> Straight of limb, true of eye, steady and aglow.
> They were staunch to the end against odds uncounted,
> They fell with their faces to the foe.

How could words so eloquent have, in classrooms, been so empty?

I traveled south, down the valley of the Marne, through villages, each with its time-pocked stone *poilu*. To Belleau Wood where doughboys stopped Ludendorff's last offensive, leaving 12,246 lying in America's largest Golgotha. To Verdun where, as far as my eyes could see, spread myriad markers of Christian, Jewish, Muslim, Buddhist, and unidentified dead.

And so it was here, in France, that the curriculum came together.

Reading: Here rests in honored glory
      A COMRADE IN ARMS
      known but to God.

Writing: In Flanders fields the poppies grow
      Between the crosses, row on row . . .

Arithmetic: Adding just the numbers in my notebook, the dead of World War I came to 1,310,617. Were Russians, Italians, and others added, civilians as well as soldiers, the tally would be tripled, and tripled again, and again.

Geography: Thousands of square miles of tormented terrain strewn with bones, barbed wire, shrapnel, messkits, and other detritus dug up by farmers, heaped high in their barnyards.

History: Hatreds cultivated by kings, kaisers, priests, pedants, Krupps, and Creusots, from one Dark Age to another.

French: *Pour la Patrie!*

German: *Gott mit uns.*

Latin: *Arma virumque cano.*

Wearying of war, I visited Oxford, Cambridge, the Sorbonne, Ulm, Bologna. How, I wondered, did higher education in these ancient institutions compare with America's? In Heidelberg, I met a young German, Kurt Schneider, twenty-five, a lecturer in the university who opened doors to classrooms, dueling chambers, and student cafés.

The lecture hall fell silent as the professor entered. He placed his notes on a pedestal and, in the manner of a hypnotist mesmerizing his subject, proceeded to put the audience to sleep. Long ago a German philosopher, Johann Friedrich Herbart, had devised a "Five Step" formula for elucidation of any subject: preparation, presentation, association, generalization, application. Once embodied in a lecture, it became the basis for endless repetition, ruling out spontaneity, originality, interrogation and student participation.

In the dueling chamber Kurt introduced me to Heidelberg's hidden curriculum through which *bildung, wissenschaft,* and *kultur* —civilization, scientific scholarship, and culture—achieved expression. Dueling separated students into two camps, those who, having fought and been scarred by sabres, had earned entitlement to enter the *Corps* of Germany's student elites. Others, never having defended their honor with blood, comprised the lower classes. Donning masks protective of their eyes and throats but exposing their cheeks to an opponent's razor-edged blade, aristocratic adversaries engaged in a flurry of parries and thrusts until deep cuts drew blood. Wounds were stitched with thick thread to create *schmisse,* vivid scars, Heidelberg's shibboleths—duty, honor, courage—engraved on human skin.

Honor satisfied, duelists saluted, and were swept off to celebrate in the student pubs where, downing beer after beer and pounding the tables with their mugs, they sang "I am a Prussian and you know my colors."

I asked Kurt about his early education. It was much like mine. "The teacher held up cards covered with dots. We had a second to call out the correct number—the *gestalte* idea—an ability to count as many as ninety-five dots in a single second!" Arithmetic by rote. History as glorification of military men—Frederick the Great, Bismarck, Von Hindenburg. Math and Latin to train the mind. Mythology as opposed to reality, and a great deal of romanticism —idealization of the Greeks and Romans as martial models. Walkurian music. German nobility of character apotheosized by Goethe, Herder, Schiller. Teachers? "My first grade teacher had only one arm. The other he lost in Verdun. That added to his authority. Authority! That is the secret of Germany's success. It is only when authority weakens that, as in the war, we suffer defeat."

I asked Kurt why, so ardent a German, no *schmisse* scarred his face. Kurt shook his head. "I am a Jew, and the *Corps* is anti-Semitic. I belonged to the *Burschenschaft,* the liberal students' organization. But the two have something in common—circumcision. We slash the penis. They slash the cheek."

This was the system that James Russell, the New York State Regent sent to Germany to study its higher schools, had so admired and brought back to America.

Kurt and I said *auf wiedersehen.* "Come back to Heidelberg," he urged. I said that some day, somehow, I would. And, one day, I did.

8

"The Main Battlefield Is the School"

Wist Hall
March 1987

Robert Potter, a superb professor with an encyclopaedic brain atop a bicyclist's body, asks for a paper covering in historical depth some aspect of American education that demonstrates ability to research a subject in the scholarly manner a doctoral degree subsumes. Picking up on what has begun to dawn on me as Prussia's pivotal impact upon America's schools, I submit this essay:

Immanuel Kant cast the crucible in which Germany's universities were molded in the nineteenth century. Dealing with the duties of philosophers and kings, Kant considered it indispensable that kings should not permit professors to perish or to become mute, but should allow them to speak openly. Such freedom, he believed, would serve the interests of the state by advancing scientific knowledge. More importantly, concluded Kant, the king could thereby ensure the loyalty of an intellectual elite unlikely ever to band together to upset a system so solicitous of its freedoms to teach and to learn. Thus could the king secure the prosperity and harmony of both state and academe.

Lernfreiheit "freedom of learning" and *Lehrfreiheit* "freedom of teaching" became hallmarks of German higher education. Unshackled from tradition, Germany surged to the forefront of the sciences, humanities, and arts, setting a standard to which scholars and students of every nationality rallied, exerting a greater influence on higher education than any other, most especially in America.

Until Kant's intercession, German education had lagged behind the French. Napoleon had given France's system a sociological, political and military edge. "Of all political questions," Napoleon asserted, "education is perhaps the most important." French armies swept across Europe from Spain to the Urals, defeating weak German forces in the battle of Jena.

A loose confederation of principalities, fiefdoms and feeble statelets, Germany's fate seemed sealed until a philosopher, Johann Gottlieb Fichte, made several "Addresses to the German Nation." "If Germany is to be saved, the nation . . . must realize its character and destiny, and through a conscious control of education, it must liberate all its potentialities—moral, intellectual, physical, vocational—for national service. . . . Nothing but education can rescue us from all the miseries that overwhelm us."

Fichte kindled the passion of the German people. Industrious, disciplined, romantic—lovers of folk lore, fairy tales, myth, music —they recognized education as the avenue to their regeneration and enthusiastically enlisted in the national service Fichte saw as their salvation. In the vanguard of this renaissance were Prussia's philosophers and professors. None better manipulated teutonic traits than Wilhelm von Humboldt who held up before Germany the image of "the ultimate man," the Greek gladiator, the Roman legionnaire—the perfection of body, mind, and spirit that typified the Aryan ideal. Von Humboldt gave voice to his doctrine in a simple slogan, *Kultur Macht Frei* "Culture makes one free"— omen of *arbeit macht frei* in the death camps of another era.

Transition from despair to dauntless chauvinism was swift. In

1808 the Department of Public Instruction was transferred to the Director of Police. In 1809 von Humboldt became Minister of Science and Education. In 1810, under his direction, the University of Berlin was founded, keystone of an arch of ancient German universities—Gottingen, Giessen, Leipzig, Bonn—surpassing Oxford, Cambridge, the Sorbonne, Bologna, and all other institutions of learning in its scientific skills. To feed the universities, von Humboldt built a subsystem of kindergartens, folk schools, and gymnasia superior to any other in existence—the seed bed from which sprang the old-boy network of university alumni that governed the renascent nation.

Prussian innovation astonished the world: knowledge fragmented into different disciplines; in each discipline intensive specialization, with research defined as "the conquest of a subject" and raised above instruction. Publication of research in learned journals a requisite for promotion. Testing, measuring, grading to sort out students. Autonomous departments under the finest professors in their fields. Above all, science—a sentiment variously expressed by kaisers, chancellors, professors, and other devotees of *wissenschaft,* scientific scholarship: "Science is power and a guarantee of the strength of the nation. . . . The idea of science governs every department of human activity. . . . The most scrupulous research and inspired love of Fatherland go hand in hand. . . . The University has the duty of being an intellectual fortress of the Fatherland and of offering it an arsenal of scholarly weapons."

Linked with Fatherland was the royal prerogative: "In the affairs of nations Monarchy is a necessity of nature; the most original, irreplaceable and most beneficial institution of public life. In order to grasp subversion at the root and stifle it in its inception one has to influence young people." Hence, as Fichte ordained, "the main battlefield is the school."

Professors became civil servants, tenured, paid, and pensioned by the state to whose political and social credo they owed allegiance. Evidential of status was the doctoral degree. As Russell had written, "the PhD stood erect and stiff as a statue, buttoned to the chin and in faultless attire, his speech as short, sharp and imperious in the classroom as that on the parade field." The underlying ethos: "We are and we must remain a nation of soldiers. When we cease to be that we are nothing."

The Franco-Prussian feud became, at core, a contest between

two competitive educational ideologies. Chemistry, physics, metallurgy, mathematics as evolved in German university laboratories were hammered by Krupp into howitzers that outmatched the French *mitrailleuse*. Nor could *poilus* overcome German infantry whose disciplined efficiency overwhelmed Gallic *elan*. In 1870 the German army marched into Paris. In 1890 Kaiser Wilhelm admonished a conference of German educators that "Schools must be German. It is your duty to educate boys to become Germans and not Romans and Greeks. Remember, I am looking for soldiers."

Kaiser Wilhelm II got what he wanted. In 1914, achieving the apogee of its power, the German juggernaut unleashed its energies in a single, sacred cause: *"Deutschland uber alles . . ." Germany above all!*

Such was the inspiration of American education—science-based, technologically oriented, autocratic, militant, anti-Semitic, antifeminist. Early in the nineteenth century Everett, Cogswell, Bancroft of Harvard, Ticknor of Dartmouth, Mann of Massachusetts came, saw, and were conquered by the educational colossus that, through scientific scholarship, had lifted a vanquished people from the ashes of defeat to dominance of Europe. Returning home and preaching a gospel more persuasive than the Puritan, they set in train a trans-Atlantic torrent of eager aspirants for postgraduate education unavailable in any American institution. Before World War I stemmed the tide, ten thousand potential American professors became intellectual subjects of Germany, teutonized by what Huxley exalted as "the most intensely cultivated and the most productive corporation the world has ever seen."

A chorus of eminent Americans echoed his enthusiasm. German universities, they believed, constituted a principal bulwark of ideal culture in our age. Abraham Flexner of Rockefeller fame alleged that "in theory and practice Germany has come nearest to giving higher education its true position than any other." G. Stanley Hall of Clark University called Germany, educationally, "the freest spot on earth." Russell of Columbia summed up the accolade: "The greatest service that the German States have done for the cause of education is unquestionably the creation of a teaching profession. The first step taken by Humboldt in 1810 which provided for the examination and certification of teachers was the inauguration of a policy to which Prussia has converted the civilized world."

By late nineteenth century most American professors belonged to the Herbart Society, seduced by an associative psychology of Germanic origin according to which neither the content nor the form of knowledge is furnished by the mind. Charles Eliot, after two years in German schools, assumed the presidency of Harvard in 1868 and transformed it from an American Oxbridge to a shadow of Berlin, introducing an elective system of scientific studies, and erecting a superstructure of professional schools over the undergraduate college. The collegiate life-style adapted from the English gave way to the depersonalization of the German system. Professors no longer lived in close association with students but, pursuing research, writing, and seeking financial assistance from government, foundations, and rich individuals, locked their doors against student intrusion. "Sort them out, sort them out!" was Eliot's attitude toward students who, once placed in their proper pigeonholes, enjoyed unimagined freedoms. German *bierstubes* bordered the campus and class attendance was voluntary. One father learned too late that his son, rather than studying at Harvard, was roistering in Havana.

Daniel Gilman brought the Prussian blueprint to Baltimore and built Johns Hopkins University to German specifications. Capping an assemblage of first-class scholars, almost all with German doctorates, a combined hospital and medical school became the model American medical institution. State universities embraced the scientific spirit as did independent institutions. Horace Mann set up Massachusetts' public schools in the Prussian pattern he admired so that, from kindergarten to college and upward to the graduate schools, American education acquired a Fritzian accent.

That German scientism wrought its wonders throughout the world is undeniable. Meticulous research did away with deadly diseases, accelerated agricultural abundance, conquered time and space. But a price was paid. Something was missing in Prussian pedagogy best revealed, perhaps, in the little poem teachers later taught their pupils to recite:

> Fold your little hands, bow your little head.
> Think of him who gives us each our daily bread.
> Adolph Hitler is his name.
> Him we as our savior claim.

The essay earns an A, but Professor Potter's comment casts a shadow on my doctoral prospects. "Your paper reads very interestingly. . . . It is certainly a different kind of paper than most graduate papers. I am not sure what the conditions of your admission were in regard to a dissertation, but I doubt that the Graduate Division would accept such an informally structured dissertation, regardless of its creativeness."

9

Encounters with Hirohito, Gandhi, Mussolini, Hitler

Around the World
1935–1936

1928. Manhattan's skyline slid past the SS *Hamburg* as it entered the Hudson River and crept upstream to its midtown pier. I stood at the rail wondering where, amid all that massive masonry, would there be a niche for me, twenty-one, returning home after six months abroad. Who would put me on his payroll? How could I carve the first step in a career? Simply stated, career meant a grab for the almighty dollar, cash for clothes, a car, dates with girls, and other gratifications that folding money, the long green, big bucks could buy. At a higher level, opportunity to travel, to extend the European adventure, to learn what lessons Asia,

Africa, South America had in store. Taking inventory of the talents I had to trade for such treasure, two stood out, however modest. One was writing, the other sketching. Words plus pictures plus greed added up to advertising.

A business directory listed the ten most prestigious agencies on Madison Avenue. In nine I encountered receptionists who, after asking who I was, called an executive and said, "there's a young man out here who says he's a good friend of yours, but refuses to give me his name." Ushered into his office and revealed as an impostor, I was summarily dismissed. The tenth was Amos Parrish, a short, enthusiastic dynamo with crew-cut hair, bifocals, and an agonizing stutter. "W-w-what," he wanted to know, "m-m-makes you think you have a-a-anything to offer in a-a-advertising?" I placed before him the journal I had kept in Europe, the latest in a long series dating back to the illuminated manuscripts of medieval monks that had inspired me as a child. Parrish perused page after page of sketches and script, nodding approval of my *mannequi-pis* in Brussels, my impressions of the Place Pigalle, and the melancholy mood induced by Ypres' Menin Gate. "S-s-sensitive," he said, and acquired an office boy.

Parrish proved to be not so much an advertising man as an efficiency expert whose clients included the aces of America's merchandising industry, mainly department stores and manufacturers of products they purveyed. Landing a job with him proved providential. The United States in 1929 verged on a depression in which dime-a-dozen ad men wound up selling apples while efficiency engineers flourished. As clients sought advice on how to survive the economic calamity that befell the country, several in the men's apparel industry—Arrow Shirts, Interwoven Socks, Stetson Hats—formed the nucleus of a group over which, with Amos' guidance, I came to preside.

One personage dominated masculine fashion, the Prince of Wales. The width of his collar, the line of his lapels, the drape of his slacks dictated what was in and what was out. On London's Saville Row I scouted his tailors and cobblers. On the Faubourg St. Honore in Paris I shopped haberdashers who held the Prince's favor. On Rome's Via Condotti I sought out the creators of his cravats. As Hitler's armies redeemed the Rhineland, Mussolini's Black Shirts entered Rome, and Chamberlain brought home peace in our time written on a piece of paper, I was there, a witness to the action.

The *New York Herald Tribune,* seeking advertising revenue in the men's apparel industry, hired Amos Parrish as a consultant. Helen Rogers Reid, the paper's proprietress, appreciated my services in the *Trib*'s behalf and fell an easy victim to my next ambition, a trip around the world. Credentialed as a *Trib* reporter, I set sail from San Francisco on the *Asama Maru* and arrived in Tokyo in time for the Emperor's annual garden party. Wilfred Fleischer, editor of the *Japan Advertiser* to whom I carried a note from Helen Reid, provided me with an invitation and the address of an outfitter who rented the required cutaway coat and striped trousers. Elegantly attired, I bowed before the small myopic monarch and mingled with the diplomatic and military set until a sudden shower drenched the guests. No one could leave until Hirohito himself signaled an end to the ceremony. Bone-dry beneath a canvas canopy, this he seemed loathe to do. Returning my rented raiment, sodden with rain and sadly shrunken, I was refused a refund of my deposit. Like the Prince of Wales, the Sun God left a royal imprint on my life, but not without cost.

In Peking I set out to sample that most succulent of celestial delicacies, Heavenly Duck. Accompanied by two other guests of my pension, our rickshaws headed for a restaurant in an ancient quarter of the city. Seeking shelter from the cold, our rickshaw boys squatted in the corners. The Heavenly Duck arrived in a procession of pancakes, dumplings, gizzards, soups, and skin, none resembling an edible drumstick or recognizable remnant of duck. We passed each dish to the coolies. Two were Muslims, forbidden to eat food contaminated by ingredients not sanctioned by their faith. My boy ate all three Heavenly Ducks, leaving me with nothing but the bill.

Hungry, we remounted our rickshaws. My boy could hardly squeeze between the shafts. Clutching his stomach, he stumbled a few steps and collapsed in the gutter. At an age when such a crisis didn't daunt me, I placed him in the rickshaw, picked up the shafts and started to run. At a busy intersection we were stopped by a policeman and taken to a courtroom populated by pickpockets, prostitutes, and other Peking rabble. A walnut of a magistrate, round, brown, and wrinkled, presided. He listened to the constable's accusation, questioned several witnesses, overruled my attempt to explain my behavior, and ordered me to pay the court clerk five dollars. The clerk filled in a set of forms, stamped each with a chop, and handed me a receipt for the fine.

The rickshaw boy having recovered, we returned to our pension. Angrily I tossed the receipt on the bar and expressed my contempt for a kangaroo court that fined me five dollars without hearing my side of the story. Our hostess studied the piece of paper presented by the clerk and shook her head. "This not receipt for fine. This license to pull rickshaw."

Next lesson, Bangkok. When he came to America for a cataract operation, King Prajadapok of Siam had resided in Helen Reid's home, Opal Hall. She had given me a letter to his brother, Prince Amoradat, whose palace I approached with eager anticipation of the royal hospitality I was about to receive—exotic edibles served by sloe-eyed concubines whose invitations to bejewelled beds I could not refuse. A sentry standing at the gate read Mrs. Reid's note and sounded an alarm. Rushed to an underground cell I was searched, grilled, and released only after convincing my captors that I was not an assassin intent on slaying the sovereign. Too late did I learn that Prince Amoradat had recently led a coup against the king.

Next lesson, India. Among the clients underwriting my wanderlust was a textile manufacturer by whom I was commissioned to comb the world for neckware novelties. In Calcutta my eye was seized by a regiment of Bengal Lancers, led by a British colonel caparisoned in scarlet tunic, chalked breeches, and a magnificent turban, a silken shimmer of silver, gold, and crimson threads on a field of blue. Smitten with the thought that so handsome a design would make a marvelous collection of neckties named "Indian Regimentals," I followed the Lancers to their barracks and begged the colonel for a swatch of his turban. Intrigued that the Prince of Wales might one day wear a cravat fashioned from his regimental colors, the colonel complied and provided me, additionally, with the British-Indian order of battle.

From the Khyber Pass to Cape Comorin, from Bengal to Bombay, I extracted from quartermasters of the Rajputana Rifles, the Mahratta Light Infantry, Hodson's Horse, and other Sikh, Punjab, and Jat regiments snippets of silks destined to set masculine attire ablaze with the beauty of Indian regimentals. In the process I learned how a few thousand Britons held in thrall five hundred million Hindus, Muslims, Buddhists, and members of other Asian sects. I also became aware that British power was contested by a half-naked mummy of a man who, like Hirohito, also hosted a garden party in his ashram in Sevagram. No cutaways, striped pants, or epaulettes on this sun-drenched plot of sand; simply pilgrims who, defying distance, heat, and flies, had come in scores to heed Mahatma Gandhi's words and gain his blessing.

"In the *Bhagavad Gita*," the Mahatma whispered, "the Lord Krishna showed Arjuna that his enemies were self-destroyed by their own evil. Neither by bayonets nor violence can we be freed. Violence overlooks the fact that evil cannot be overcome by evil. It ceases only with good. As the means, so the end."

Gandhi asked what I had seen in India. I told of my travels in search of Indian army regimentals. I described the British Indian army, meticulously trained, magnificently led, formidably armed. "Is spirituality," I asked, "a match for such material power?"

Gandhi's mouth moved as if he were tasting my words. "May it not be that the British are spiritual and we the wielders of material power? May it not be that the goodness within a Christian people will cause their government to give way? May it not be that in the prayers of five hundred million human beings the world will discover a new dimension of power?"

Next lesson, Moscow. I arrived on the seventeenth anniversary of the October revolution. With a newly acquired Leica camera, I snapped pictures as Soviet infantry, artillery, tanks paraded past, saluting Stalin and his henchmen atop Lenin's tomb. At midday a policeman checked credentials and arrested me for photographing Russian weapons without permission.

Across Red Square, in the basement of the GUM department store, officials confiscated my camera and cast me into a cell where I mentally reviewed the chilling evidence that stamped me as a spy. Not until midnight was I released, the camera returned, and a long loop of film tossed into my hand. Outside, holding up the film to lamplight, I learned what had saved me from Siberia. As so often before, I had forgotten to remove the cap from the lens.

Next lesson, Italy. Rome's Piazza Venezia sizzled with excitement. *DUCE! DUCE! DUCE!* roared the crowd. From a balcony hung a banner with the Fascist watchwords: *CREDERE! OBBE-*

DIRE! COMBATTERE! "Believe, obey, fight!" Regiments of Black Shirts cheered as chin upthrust, hands on hips, Mussolini ignited an ecstatic audience.

> The State is the only real being. The individual does not exist unless he is identified with the State. Freedom is an attribute of the State, not of the individual. Everything being of the State, Fascism is totalitarian. Perpetual peace is neither possible nor useful to the human race. War alone brings all our energies to their highest state of tension, and stamps with the seal of nobility the peoples who dare to face it. Let our youth remember: books are only half your lives, the other half is the rifle. Better to live one day as a lion than a hundred years as a sheep.

Last lesson, Berlin. In the *Sportpalast,* Berlin's Madison Square Garden, Adolf Hitler was scheduled to speak. Flashing my *Herald Tribune* press pass I entered the swastika-draped arena and was escorted by a brown-shirted storm trooper to a seat on the stage. Bugles, drums, a thunderous outcry accompanied the *Fuhrer* as he marched down the middle aisle, mounted the dais and, a few feet from where I sat, began in a murmur to mesmerize the mob.

> The folkish State must adjust education toward the breeding of healthy bodies rather than the inculcation of useless knowledge. Girls should give the nation new beauty by resisting seduction by bow-legged repulsive Jewish bastards and maintain the purity of the Aryan race. The whole education of a German boy must be so ordered as to give him the conviction that he is absolutely superior to others, preparing him for future military service. The youthful brain must not be burdened with unnecessary knowledge. History must serve the continued existence of our nationality. Historical instruction is only a means to that end, and must raise the racial question to a dominant position.

From a whisper Hitler's voice rose to a shriek.

> Above all, the crown of the folkish State's entire work of education must be to burn the racial sense into the instinct and intellect, the heart and brain of the youth entrusted to it. No boy, no girl must leave school without having been led to the ultimate realization of the necessity of blood purity. Let us never forget that the Jew is our misfortune. The world is moving toward a great revolution. The question can only be whether it will redound to the benefit of Aryan humanity or to the profit of the eternal Jew!

Before leaving Germany I drove down the new *autobahn* to Heidelberg for a reunion with Kurt Schneider. I begged Kurt to come to America. "Why?" he asked, "because of that Austrian impostor? For the moment he has cast a spell on our people but, educated as we are by the world's best teachers in the world's best schools, you can count on our culture. You Americans have more to worry about with your Father Coughlin, your Ku Klux Klan, your Marxist Wobblies than does a Jew in Germany. This is my country. These are my people. This is where I belong."

10

"I Am a Child"

Wist Hall
March 1987

No professor possesses a greater grasp of education's literature than does Ralph Stueber. The textbook for his course on the history of American education is Clarence J. Karier's *The Individual, Society, and Education,* an admirable account of the twists and turns, the confusions and contradictions, the certitudes and dissonances of the American educational experience. Although the subtitle describes the book as *A History of American Educational Ideas,* the European origins of our system are immediately admitted. St. Augustine's *City of God,* St. Thomas Aquinas' *Summa Theologiae,* Plato's *Republic* weighed heavily on the minds of men like Ralph Waldo Emerson and Thomas Jefferson, presaging the constant quarrels that characterize American education.

Emerson worshipped Plato as "an American genius" prizing

intuition over intellect. "Pure intellect," to Emerson, was "the pure devil when you have got off all the marks of Mephistopheles." Jefferson, contrarily, portrayed Plato as "a sophist whose ideas were a dunghill of metaphysics," at odds with his own faith in the empirical science and social meliorism of Bacon, Newton, and Locke. Condorcet, Voltaire, and Descartes also left their marks on the minds of the men who freed the colonies of British rule and authored a Constitution that, as if foreseeing the foibles to which it is heir, omitted any mention of education.

Other European ideas turned America's schools into the cockpits of controversy they have ever since become. A Frenchman, Jean-Jacques Rousseau (1712–1778) wrote *Emile*, the first sentence of which is "All things are good as they come out of the hands of their Creator, but everything degenerates in the hands of man"—everything, in particular, being the child who, born good and left to nature, would become Godlike were it protected from schools, teachers, and texts. Rousseau did not practice the goodness he preached, siring several bastards whom he neither acknowledged, supported, nor, true to his principle, sent to school.

Johann Heinrich Pestalozzi (1746–1827), of Swiss-German extraction, after failing in every other occupation for fifty years, finally found a footing in education—progenitor of the old saw that "those who can do, do; those who can't, teach." Pestalozzi taught that "the child cannot understand two or three in the abstract; he must see them in reality," much as with my mother's grapes. He introduced the "see, touch, feel" system later developed by John Dewey, to say nothing of my mom who added "eat." Less to Pestalozzi's credit, perhaps, were *Leonard and Gertrude,* earliest of the *Dick and Jane* books later generations suffered.

Karier also cites three philosophers, Hegel, Comte, and Spencer. Hegel is identified with the "Absolute Idea" within which "the individual becomes a pawn of the greater cosmic forces which require discipline to conform to a cultural destiny—a system that could justify the growing materialistic spirit of the German state which required discipline to God, Country and Emperor."

Comte, "father of sociology," predicted that "the scientific method would usher in the Golden Age in which men could create a scientific society based on positive knowledge"—to which Karier adds: "Of course, what Comte could not have known was that the very science on which he placed so much faith would, in the 20th century, cast serious doubt on the certainty of ever gaining such positive knowledge."

Herbert Spencer coined the phrase "survival of the fittest". "The poor, the weak, the downtrodden, the stupid and the lazy," he declared, "must be allowed to die off." The Good Society for Spencer was a highly competitive system from which would evolve the "Superman" so dear to German hearts.

Other Europeans molding the American mind were Friedrich Nietzsche who cried out "God is dead and we have killed him"; Ernst Junger who idealized charismatic leadership as later embodied in *Der Fuhrer;* and Vilfredo Paredo whose belief in scientific sociology underwrote Italy's infatuation with Fascism.

Pondering Karier's pages, it seems to me that something akin to insanity characterizes the creatures holding sway over America's schools. As in a *danse macabre,* one eccentric after another flits across the stage, seizes the spotlight, seduces students with his bizarre beliefs.

William Graham Sumner, professor of political and social science at Yale and a graduate of Gottingen, advised that "life is very much a case of root, hog or die. . . . A drunkard in the gutter is just where he ought to be. Nature is working away at him to get him out of the way."

Lester Frank Ward, dean of American sociologists, took an opposite tack. "I would not consign the drunkard to the gutter to suffer the natural consequences of his vice, but would consider the kind of education and social conditions which made him a drunkard in the first place . . . the inmates of our prisons are but victims of untoward circumstances. The murderer has but acted out his education."

Charles Sanders Peirce and William James, in an optimistic American reaction to Europe's pessimism, produced "Pragmatism," described by no less an authority than Mortimer Adler as "the most indigenous to this soil, the most original and originally American of all the philosophies we have produced." Peirce could never hold a job and died a pauper. James was suicidal. The two engaged in a form of philosophical fornication which produced pragmatism over which they disagreed so violently as to elicit one observer's view that "pragmatism was largely the result of James' misunderstanding of Peirce, and vice versa." So divided were their definitions that Peirce renamed the philosophy "pragmaticism—a word ugly enough to be safe from kidnappers like James." James retorted that "a terrible flavor of humbug masks the work of any psychologist who claims perfect consistency and exactitude in all his statements." James' works impelled an overseas admirer to write:

> The pragmatism of William James was of great use to me in my political career. James taught me that an action should be judged rather by its results than by its doctrinary basis. I learned from James that faith in action, that ardent will to live and fight, to which Fascism owes a great part of its success.
>
> Benito Mussolini

Not even John Dewey, most prolific of American pedagogues, escapes unscathed. This paragraph is drawn from *Anti-intellectualism in American Life* which earned for Richard Hofstadter a Pulitzer Prize:

> Dewey was hard to read and interpret. He wrote a prose of terrible vagueness and plasticity, which William James once characterized as "damnable; you might even say God-damnable." His style is like the cannonading of distant armies; one concludes that something portentous is going on at a remote and inaccessible distance, but one cannot determine just what it is. . . . Far more probable than the thesis that Dewey was perversely distorted by obtuse or over-enthusiastic followers is the idea that the unresolved problems of interpretation to which his work gave rise were tokens of real ambiguities and gaps in thought which themselves express certain difficulties and unresolved problems in educational theory and in our culture.

Further lengths to which America's educators went are revealed by Karier in later chapters. When Prof. Stueber asks for our reactions thus far to Karier's history of American educational ideas, I note that there appear to be no discernible *American* ideas in education. All are offspring of *European* ideas. Weighed in the scales of peace, war, and the enhancement of human happiness, they seem of dubious merit. I entitle my essay "I Am a Child."

I am a child. I was born in the 16th century and taught by priests to worship God.

I am a child. I was born in the 17th century and taught that

there are many Gods, but only my God was good and all other
Gods evil. I was taught that I myself was born evil; that evil children needed to be whipped and even slain; that witches needed to
be burned; and that, to go to heaven, I needed to be prosperous on
earth, because prosperity, to God, was proof of virtue.

I am a child. I was born in the 18th century and so I was not
evil, but good. Unless corrupted by education I would grow up to
be pure, wise, the ideal citizen in a perfect society. I was taught
that although I should not be corrupted by education, Latin and
Greek would train my mind, that discipline would improve my
mind, and that only in a state of nature could I become the creature God had in mind.

I am a child. I was born in the 19th century and learned that
God is dead, that science is God, that my destiny was mine to
command, but that my survival depended on whether I was fittest.
That drunkards should die in the gutter, but that being drunk was
a matter of one's education.

I am a child. I was born in the 20th century. I am a product of
public schools that squeeze the 16th, 17th, 18th and 19th centuries into a 12 year curriculum. I am recapitulated, representing in
my body and mind the total evolution of the human race since
Adam, Eve and Charles Darwin. Latin no longer trains my mind;
ever since Sputnik, my mind is trained by math. With a disciplined
mind I am ruggedly individual and a social being, optimistic and
pessimistic, idealistic and materialistic, pragmatic and pragmatis-
tic, God's creation and the offspring of an ape.

I am a child. I seem to be an American child, but actually I am
German, fathered by Kant, Hegel, Heidegger, Herbart, and
Hitler. I am a graduate of *kindergartens, gymnasia* and *universi-
tats* built to a Kaiser's specifications, brought to America by
Horace Mann, tailored to Yankee tastes. Fighting one war after
another, I pursue a phantom with the features of Plato, Pestalozzi
and Peirce. Of Darwin, Dennis and Dewey. Of Cotton, Comte,
Counts, Cremin and Conant. Of one apodictic oracle after
another, none of whom ever heard of Alfred North Whitehead
who said: "In philosophical discussion, the merest hint of dog-
matic certainty as to finality of statement is an exhibition of folly."

I am not a child. I am a guinea pig. My school is a cage. I am an
object of educational experimentation. Pedants and politicians
manipulate my mind. Not only God is dead. So am I.

11

Betty Grable Teaches Troops to Read a Map

The Pentagon
Washington D.C. 1942

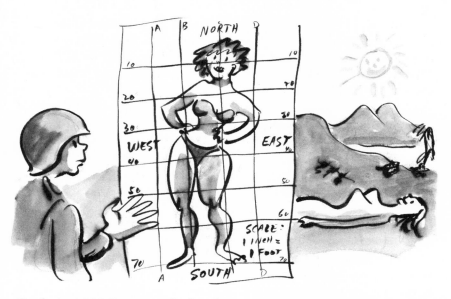

Early in 1939 I approached *Life,* proposing that were men's fashions made an editorial feature of the magazine, advertising revenue might richly reward the effort. Epicenter of Henry Luce's inner circle was C. D. Jackson, handsome, genial, shrewd, who considered the suggestion. In the course of several sessions a relationship was established that would prove crucial in quite a different context. Hitler's invasion of Poland put the proposition on a back burner. With Europe once again at war, *Life*'s pages had other fish to fry than whether men's jackets would be single- or double-breasted.

So did I. A client, manufacturer of Palm Beach suits, depended on dyes produced by a Swiss concern in Basel. Believed by Britain's economic warfare agency to contain chemicals from a German source, the dyes were quarantined and Palm Beach mills in Sanford, Maine, threatened with closure. Given the command of French and German I had gained in my travels overseas, no one seemed better able than I to deal with the problem and in October 1939, I recrossed the Atlantic. My mission was to establish the neutrality of the dyestuffs and to arrange for their shipment from Genoa before Italy entered the war and bottled them up in Basel.

With proof that the dyes were without Nazi blemish, I left for London to win British approval for their passage past the quarantine in Gibraltar. My train arrived in Paris on May 10, 1940, the day the Panzers flanked the Maginot Line. In the ensuing frenzy I was fortunate in reaching the channel and boarding a ferry, jammed with Belgian and Dutch refugees. In London, knocking vainly on the door of David Bowes-Lyon, the queen's brother who headed England's economic warfare, I turned for help to the American ambassador, Joseph Kennedy, a Massachusetts man sensitive to any threat to New England's textile industry. His phone call to Bowes-Lyon paved the way to an appointment. Persuaded by my proof, Bowes-Lyon signaled the fleet to permit the dye's passage, scant weeks before Mussolini pounced on stricken France and cut the sea lanes. The dyes left Genoa on the last vessel to carry cargo across the Atlantic, and arrived in time to keep America cool in Palm Beach clothing.

It was not long before Japanese bombs fell on Pearl Harbor and a telegram arrived ordering me to Camp Lee, Virginia. Nor did it take long for the commanding officer, Brigadier General James Edmonds, to learn that he had a second lieutenant at hand who had stood eyeball to eyeball with Hirohito, Mussolini, and Adolf Hitler. Edmonds asked me to devise a program to teach draftees what the war was all about.

I submitted a memorandum with several suggestions. No GI should be sent abroad without knowledge of his adversaries. Minimally, that meant understanding the background, outlook, training, equipment, and fighting characteristics of the German and Japanese soldier, the Nazi credo as expounded in *Mein Kampf,* the grand strategy of the Axis in political and territorial terms, and the all-embracing nature of total war. Given what the army already knew about the literacy of the average American soldier—it was low—simple language and lots of pictures were essential.

Edmonds endorsed my prospectus. The problem was how to flesh out the bare bones of so ambitious a project. The task seemed hopeless until the image of a tall, shrewd, genial executive flashed into mind. I called C. D. Jackson in New York and said we needed help in educating the American soldier. C. D. said, "*Life* is yours to command."

Orders were cut. In New York C. D. reviewed my proposal. Within three hours—repeat, three hours—he lined up a cast of collaborators that predestined success. *Life*'s military expert, Garrett Underhill, would describe the German soldier. Wilfred Fleischer of the *Japan Advertiser,* now in New York, would do the job on the Japanese. Dorothy Thompson agreed to abstract *Mein Kampf,* and Walter Millis, author of *Road to War,* went to work on the geopolitical menace to America. Total war was assigned to Hanson Baldwin of the *New York Times.* And, for a summary of events leading to America's entry into war, C. D. enlisted Walter Lippmann. Drafts were due within five days. Allowing another five for matching text with photographs, plus three to print and bind pages, I should be back in Camp Lee, project completed, within two weeks. If any ambition could be said to vault, this was it.

Scripts arrived on schedule. *Life*'s picture morgue provided instant translation of text into its graphic equivalents. C. D.'s girl Friday, Ethel Schroeder, masterminded production of six picture portfolios, five feet high, three feet wide, forty pages thick, enclosed in hard covers that folded over to form an easel.

Back at Camp Lee General Edmonds assembled 162 officers and NCOs. The theater was overheated, the lights dim, the audience restless. One after the other, I unveiled the flip charts. Hesitant to anticipate the general's verdict, no one spoke until a sergeant rose. "Excuse me, sir," he said, "but if I had something like that to show my squad I'd really be in business." Everyone agreed. Edmonds turned to me. "Pack up, lieutenant, you're going to Washington in the morning."

In 1942 the War Department was quartered in the Munitions Building, a delapidated World War I edifice on Constitution Avenue. A meeting was set up to preview the project. Twenty field-grade officers wearing the green medallion of the General Staff attended. All agreed the project had value and that I be ordered to thirty days' duty with the War Department to explore its potential. I entrained for an immediate test with troops of Ben Lear's Second Army in Memphis, Tennessee. A big man, impressive in star-studded suntans, Lear leaped from one portfolio to another and turned to his adjutant. "Send this Lieutenant to Fort Jackson and have Eichelberger try it out on the 77th Division."

In a replay of Camp Lee, the portfolios' content and method won approval. General Eichelberger wrote Lear, "Unlike lectures, they keep soldiers awake. We need these very much, *and soon!*" Back in Memphis, Lear tacked his concurrence to Eichelberger's verdict.

My thirty days expired. Despite Lear's validation, the project was disapproved. The reason? "Your method lowers military instruction to standards set by the least educated element of the Army. It is believed better to lift the Army up to the West Point level."

I was packing up the portfolios when a gray-haired colonel put his hand on my shoulder. "Look, lieutenant," he said, his eyes glinting behind steel-rimmed spectacles, "it's too late for you to educate the Army. Schools should have done that long ago and they fell on their faces. What we need now is military training, soldiers who can shoot, read a map, stop a tank. You and your pictures should be working for Clarence Huebner. Old Hueb's in charge of basic training and needs your help. Instead of going back to Lee, you're being transferred to Huebner's outfit across the river."

Buck Lanham, later to gain fame as commander of the 4th Infantry Division and Ernest Hemingway's bosom buddy, drove me over to the newly opened Pentagon and introduced me to "Old Hueb," a stocky, icy-eyed ex-sergeant risen up the ranks to Brigadier. Huebner echoed Lanham's complaint. "If schools had done their job, training troops would be easy. Rookies would know what this war is all about. They could read a field manual. They could figure windage on a rifle and know where they are on a map. Well, the schools didn't and the GIs don't, and now we've got to work with what we've got. Shooting in this Army stinks. I want you to figure out a way to fix it."

Lieutenants don't argue with generals. On the train to the Infantry School at Fort Benning, where the blade of the new American army was being forged, I read the official U.S. Army manual on marksmanship. It began with instructions on how to clean the M1 rifle.

> Grasp the follower rod at the knurled portion and disengage it from the follower arm by pressure toward the muzzle. If necessary remove the compensating spring from the follower rod by grasping the compensating spring with the left hand and exerting a slight pull to the right. Move the operating rod slowly to the rear, pulling the operating rod handle upward and away from the receiver. This will disengage the operating rod from the bolt when the lug on the operating rod slides up into the dismount notch of the operating guide groove . . . etc. etc.

No wonder the Army's shooting was lousy. But who was I to convert city slickers into Davy Crocketts? As an ROTC cadet, lacking size, strength, steadiness of hand and eye, and with a tendency to flinch when pulling the trigger, I had never scored a bull's-eye. That *I* be chosen to teach the U.S. Army how to shoot seemed a travesty touching on tragedy. It was an opinion shared by the chief of the light weapons section at Benning, a weary Lieutenant Colonel named Baughman, who watched my bullets miss the mark and rolled his eyeballs. "Old Hueb must be mad to think I could ever shape you into a sharpshooter!"

Baughman tried. Slipping off his shirt, he lay down on the turf in his skivvies, forced his left forearm into a vertical plane, and rested the rifle in the palm of his hand. "Watch my bones," he ordered. "They build a steady platform beneath the piece. Joe Louis himself couldn't keep nine pounds of tilted rifle steady. Now try it, holding your forearm straight up!" I did. I held the rifle steady, but jerked the trigger, flinched, and missed.

Baughman reached into his pocket and pulled out a tube of toothpaste. Applying sudden pressure, paste gushed out, uncontrolled. Then he squeezed the tube gently and laid a neat inch of paste on an extended finger. I learned to squeeze the trigger and began to score hits. Baughman took away my rifle and handed me another. Forearm upright, body aligned to buffer the recoil's blow, bull's-eye poised on the front sight, trigger squeeze controlled, I missed the target. Baughman smiled. "Got a girl?" he asked. I nodded. "Well, no two girls are alike, and neither are any two rifles. A man must go with a girl for a while, figure her out, squeeze her gently, make allowances for differences in how she reacts before he gets results. Same way with a rifle. A rifle's like a girl. You've got to learn its characteristics, baby it a bit, adjust the way it shoots and zero in."

Each day's shooting done, I drew Baughman's method in a sketchbook. On the bared body of a soldier I superimposed his skeletal structure, revealing the steady platform engineered by an upright forearm. The toothpaste tube, the pretty girl, other home-spun analogies added a hint of humor, and made marksmanship a matter of common sense. On the seventh day I fired for record. Bullet after bullet ripped into the bull's-eye.

Pinning an expert's badge on my dungarees, Baughman said "Don't you dare show your pictures of toothpaste tubes and pretty girls to Old Hueb. He'll have me busted for breaking all the rules." I said, "Colonel, you're the best teacher I've ever known. You deserve to be promoted." Baughman was neither busted nor pro-moted. Flying from Benning to Camp Gordon, his plane crashed and he was killed.

Two sergeants accompanied me to New York where C. D. Jackson turned *Life* into a miniature Benning. Gjon Mili's strobo-scopic cameras, capable of stopping a racehorse's legs, a hum-mingbird's wings, caught every movement of the soldiers' bodies as they shot from all positions, standing, kneeling, prone, and delivering skirmishers' fire. Enlivened with photos of German and Japanese riflemen under combat conditions, the package was delivered to the Government Printing Office in Washington and in August 1942, the first portfolios on rifle marksmanship arrived in training camps across the country.

Others followed. *Scouting and Patrolling. Defense Against Chemical Warfare. First Aid for the Soldier.* Even *How to Keep Fit* for the Wacs whose curves, enhanced by starchy Army chow, stretched the seams of their tunics too tightly. Huebner was pleased. I was promoted. Eager to go overseas, I asked for a trans-fer to an activated division. Huebner refused. "A general," he said, "is a dogface who can read a map. We don't have enough generals to go around. Map reading must be mastered by every soldier. You're going to the Engineering School at Fort Belvoir and work out a way to turn GIs into generals."

Huebner had not exaggerated the problem. Map reading was

the toughest subject in basic training. The difficulty derived from the inability to translate a two-dimensional piece of paper, a map, into three-dimensionsal terrain. Wiggly contour lines failed to signify the height and shape of hills, or the depths of draws, ravines, and rivers. Scale—the compression of miles of land into inches on the map—baffled. So did the designation of targets by numbers marked on the margins of maps. Little wonder that map reading remained a mystery only generals could master.

Hopelessly lost in a loop of the Shenandoah river, I puzzled over a map, seeking somehow to relate the land to a piece of paper. A soldier lying beside me pulled out a girlie magazine and flashed a picture of Betty Grable. "Jeez what a dame!" summed up the squad's reaction. Suddenly, the solution! It was not a dame the men admired. It was a picture of a dame. The picture was flat, yet with one glance a man knew what stood out and what curved in. Therein lay the way to teach contour. Betty's head was north, her feet were south—in map terms, Betty was "oriented." In the picture she was ten inches tall, in real life sixty. In the ratio of ten inches to sixty lay the secret of scale. And by drawing and numbering horizontal and vertical lines over the photo of Betty's body, the dumbest draftee could pinpoint her left bosom at 69–88, her navel at 69–86 and the dimple in her right knee at 68–83. The enigma of grid coordinates suddenly lay at the threshold of solution.

So did map reading, except for the fact that no area of land duplicated Betty Grable's body, with hills, slopes, and valleys corresponding to her configuration. My left hand, in which my sketchbook rested, attracted my eye. The base of the thumb resembled a hill, the thumb a ridge. Palm creases resembled ravines. Fingers became ranges divided by rivers that, flowing downward into the valley of the palm, fed an imaginery lake. In every soldier's hand, in short, lay a key to terrain, a constant to which he could relate a map of "Hand-Land."

To create "Hand-Land," C. D. Jackson called on Norman Bel Geddes, the stage designer who modeled a human hand from a massive piece of plaster. Slicing it into thin horizontal planes, he produced contour lines. Slicing it vertically, he exposed in profile each crease that provided cover. Then he embellished the bare plaster with houses, hedges, telephone lines, to which mine fields, supply dumps, and other military installations were added. As each phase of Bel Geddes' mock-up was readied, photos were taken, enabling a soldier to trace, on his own hand, everything a map could teach about terrain. *Map Reading for the Soldier* didn't turn GIs into generals, but it put Betty Grable on the map.

Clarence Huebner pinned captain's bars on my shoulders and bid me goodbye. He was leaving the Pentagon to command the "Big Red One," the First Infantry Division, in the impending invasion of Europe. I asked him to take me along. "Sorry, son," said Huebner. "You've done more for military training than any man in the Army. It's time you got back to education."

12

Training Versus Education

Wist Hall
April 1987

In *The Naked and the Dead,* Norman Mailer derided the use of Betty Grable's body to teach map reading as an example of military mindlessness. Feminists today would have fits about anything so sexist. Forty-two years after *Map Reading for the Soldier* was published, it may be pointless to revert to the past, but, to a doctoral candidate in education in 1987, World War II seems not without meaning to our times.

Results of the 1940 census revealed that one American in seven was functionally illiterate; he could not read signs, or names on maps, or instructions of a mechanical nature. One third of recruits had not gone beyond grade school. According to the army's general classification tests, three men in ten rated as slow learners, incapable of initiative and original thinking. Altogether, the army estimated that fifteen divisions were lost to service because that many young men were capable of little more than scrawling their signatures.

What of today? According to a recent report of the Census Bureau, sixty million American adults cannot read newspaper editorials, job instructions, or the United States Constitution. At the university level, over half the students cannot locate Chicago on a map; 7 percent cannot find the Atlantic Ocean; too many Texan boys and girls can't name the nation below the border. Other studies note that, since 1969, average credits earned by high school students have dropped by 11 percent in U.S. history, 7 percent in algebra, and 6 percent in chemistry—declines offset by a rise of 75 percent in driver-training enrollments, 16 percent in "cooperative education" (undefined), and 9 percent in general shop courses. John J. Goodlad, in *A Study of Schooling,* based on systematic observation of students and teachers in 1,016 classrooms across the country, concludes that "large numbers of students are leaving school (after a 12-year continuum) ill-prepared for jobs and effective citizenship."

Since World War II, little has been learned from that cataclysmic occurrence. Menaced by Germany and Japan, America conscripted every asset in its educational inventory to instruct millions of men in martial arts and the science of survival. Money was appropriated in large amounts and, by and large, well spent. Enormous advances were made in teaching technique. Films, film strips, graphic portfolios, overhead projectors—hardware rarely seen in schools—flooded the cantonments. Frank Capra's films on *Why We Fight* stirred soldiers' hearts and minds. Whereas pictures in peacetime texts are mainly adornments to relieve the tedium of print, military manuals deployed pictures to illustrate stress points, turning corporals, sergeants, and second lieutenants into competent instructors. Simplified text reflected recognition that the secret of writing was to learn the big words and then not use them. Jargon gave way to GI jive.

In my own role, whatever I needed—from the two soldiers to model marksmanship in Gjon Mili's studio in New York to the Government Printing Office's presses off which rolled the finished product—was instantly provided. *Life's* formidable resources were volunteered. The nation's top talent was tapped. Publicists augmented professors. Visual aids I devised were reproduced as books by *The Infantry Journal* and sold in PXs. More than a million copies were bought by GIs eager for instruction in the arts of war.

Faced by a threat to its existence, the nation responded rapidly to the need to turn civilians into soldiers. It set priorities as to subjects to be taught, determined the most effective ways to teach them, estimated the abilities of teachers and trainees, and adapted instructional aids to such estimates. With all its faults, training had focus, direction, concentration, determination. It turned out troops that won a war in French hedgerows and Pacific atolls which few Americans knew existed until taught by sweat, blood, and tears.

Buck Lanham and Clarence Huebner had it right. In war, the time was past for education. What the army needed was training in specific skills required for effective use of instruments and tactics designed to overcome an enemy. Its definition of training was true to Webster: "to instruct or drill in habits of thought or action. To shape or develop character by discipline or precept. To teach or exercise someone in an art, trade or occupation. To direct in attaining a skill. To teach to obey commands."

By Webster's definition, education intends "the growth or expansion of knowledge, wisdom, desirable qualities of mind or character, physical health, or general competence, by a course of formal study or instruction." Recognition of the difference between training and education is an unlearned lesson of World War II. War demands *training* for lethal purposes. Peace demands *education* for the purposes of life.

In the years since Germany and Japan surrendered, universities seem not only rooted in processes of the past, but more determined than ever to become a system of specialized vocational training at the highest level. The need is not to suppress the provision of fine-tuned surgeons, scientists, industrialists, and engineers, but to balance their brilliance with the wisdom to achieve a society in which not only they but peace can prosper.

13

America's Army Readies for Invasion

European Theater of Operations
1944–1945

Standing seven feet tall in his socks, Major General Frederick Osborn, my new boss, towered over my five feet five. His domain was the army's morale, admittedly a mystery. To solve it, Osborn had assembled an extraordinary team. Francis Keppel, destined to be dean of Harvard's Graduate School of Education and a United States Commissioner of Education was his aide. Munro Leaf, father of *Ferdinand the Bull,* wrote antimalaria pamphlets. The drawing board of Ted Geisel, later famed as Dr. Seuss, added a Noah's Ark of antic animals to the army mule. Writers and artists in khaki serviced camp newspapers across the country. Others, overseas, published *Yank,* the weekly magazine, and daily editions of *The Stars and Stripes.* Back-stopping the media were social scientists and psychologists who tested GIs to establish their IQs, evaluate their gripes, and size up their stand on subjects related to information and education. Together these constituted crucial elements in maintaining what every general from Caesar to Napoleon declared a determinant of defeat or victory—morale.

Nowhere in the United States Army, according to Osborn, was morale lower than in the East Coast Processing Center (ECPC), a stockade in Camp Edwards, Massachusetts, where three thousand deserters, felons, psychopaths, and perverts were imprisoned. "They have no sense of antagonism toward the enemy," Osborn said. "I'd like you to go up there and find out why."

The colonel in command of the clink examined my orders and shook his head. "You're wasting your time, but I'll fish out a few specimens for you to interview if that's what you're after." I said I wanted to enter the stockade as a gangplank jumper. And so, as private Arthur Goodwin of the 445th Quartermaster Battalion, shipping out from Camp Kilmer, New Jersey, to the Port of Embarkation, I was picked up by Military Police on Scollay Square in Boston and, as a deserter, sent to the slammer.

Under a pall of soot belching from hundreds of chimneys, the ECPC bulked grim in the bleak New England winter. For ten days and nights I mingled with human swill seemingly beyond salvage. Some played poker, picked fights, solicited sexual favors, stole cigarettes and soap, practiced petty skills such as tattooing, barbering, and shaping forks and spoons into stilettos. Others swapped grievances, listened to guardhouse lawyers, declared themselves innocent of crimes no greater than balking at uncongenial job assignments, overstaying leaves with girl friends, or going AWOL because pay allotments had been withheld from parents. Amid the din of discord and obscenity, the drivel of the clowns and crackpots, the sobbing of the sad sacks, one heard the heartbeat of the uneducated, unmotivated, alienated by-products of the public schools.

Caked with coal dust, no specimen more loathsome than I ever left the ECPC. General Osborn read my findings and approved my recommendations: separation of salvagable individuals from incorrigibles. Swift investigation of grievances and, where justified, their satisfaction. Compassionate leave for men with family problems, and recognition that when troop trains traveled close to homes and lovers, AWOL merited mercy. For corrigibles, swift release and reassignment. For degenerates, dishonorable discharge. As for the main purpose of my assignment, the matter of morale, nowhere in the army was it higher. Nowhere was antagonism toward the enemy so intense. The only trouble was that the enemy was the army.

Urgently needed, half the ECPC's inmates were salvaged and sent to England. So was I. Four armies comprising more than three million men were gathering for the liberation of Europe. It was the greatest invasion instrument ever assembled, and its psychological preparation prompted a spate of messages from Eisenhower to Osborn. A conference of special service officers responsible for morale was scheduled in Bournemouth, a resort town on England's southern coast and I was ordered overseas to attend.

Wreathed in barbed wire, the Ambassador Hotel overlooked the channel across which the enemy waited. Several hundred officers assembled in the ballroom. A scrawny colonel greeted us. "Lots of people think morale depends on mail, female, and liquor. They're wrong. Morale depends on soldiers having plenty of bats and balls for sports and games, and something to nudge their noggins."

The colonel passed out copies of a pocket-sized pamphlet entitled *Army Talks*. Each issue dealt with a different topic. Titles ranged from "The British Wife in Wartime" and "Jobs After the War," to "Words are Weapons Too." Several minutes passed while officers studied the subject matter; then an infantry lieutenant held up a copy of "Pattern for Air Victory" and said he had no objection to the flyboys winning the war without the infantry's assistance. The ballroom rumbled with laughter. Someone wondered whether half his men would be around to take a job when the war was over. Another asked how he could meet a British wife in wartime. "What words," wondered a weatherbeaten paratrooper, "does the army suggest I use as weapons when I hit the beach?"

The colonel admitted some of the subjects seemed off the mark. "But remember, it's written in the regulations. Every outfit gets an hour a week of training time for discussion of *Army Talks*. What your men need most is something educational to take their minds off the monotony of military training." "Right," an artillery captain agreed. "*Army Talks* sure beats bedding down a British broad!"

A pale captain with merry eyes and an enthusiastic manner took over the meeting. "M," he said, "stands for morale. M also stands for music. Nothing cheers up a soldier like music, and the good Lord knows we all need cheering up at times like these." He passed out ocarinas. "All it takes to play this little sweet potato is patience and practice. Put your thumb in this hole underneath and rest the other fingers on the holes on top of the instrument. Then blow."

The special service officers blew. Barked a pugnacious little Ranger, "If I go back to my outfit and try to peddle that shit on my CO, he'll shoot me on the spot!" Someone added: "You think that ocarina makes music? Well, you wait until you hear old Hubcap sing!" "Old Hubcap" was Clarence Huebner, now commanding the Big Red One, the First Infantry Division. The lieutenant said the Fighting First was training on the western downs of England near a town called Blandford and invited me to visit.

Chief of Special Services in the European Theater of Operations (ETO) was Colonel Oscar Solbert, a tall, trim West Pointer, his tunic ablaze with ribbons, his headquarters in a row of Mayfair mansions on London's Upper Brook Street. Solbert winced at my report. "Eisenhower is unhappy with *Army Talks*. So am I. There's no one on my staff to do it right. While you're here in England, I'd like you to look around, suggest a solution."

General Huebner, headquartered in a Tudor manor hidden in a copse of oaks and yews, quickly fell in with my intention—to join the "Fighting First" as a GI replacement and learn what I could from veterans of the North African campaigns. As Private Goodwin, mustered into Company A, First Battalion of the 26th Infantry Regiment, I unpacked my gear in a Nissan hut embellished with a pin-up of Betty Grable. Pasted on it was the cigarette slogan: "So round, so firm, so fully packed—so quick and easy on the draw." Features of Betty's anatomy pinpointed by grid coordinates were various and rather vulgar.

Although women were central to all soldier talk, veterans had a broader experience on which to draw and gabfests focused on Kasserine, Faid, Bizerte, and other fields on which they had fought. Replacements asked about the German army rifle, machine pistol, burp gun. How could they defend themselves against stick grenades and 88s? How did our tanks compare with theirs, and what did you say to a French broad to get laid? Aside from sex, a single theme dominated every discussion. Survival. How to kill krauts and get back home with intact balls.

Trade-talk of the troops was interrupted by *Army Talks*. On Saturday morning the company assembled to hear the special service lieutenant read the current edition entitled "The Nature of a Free Man": "If England," he intoned, "had fallen in 1940 America would not have been able to face the Axis alone. We were unprepared. Our conduct between the two wars was faulty. We took freedom for granted." The lieutenant singled out a private. "What have you to say about that?" The private said "I don't reckon I have anything to say." Efforts to provoke discussion ended when a sergeant volunteered, "Lieutenant, you're one day too soon. Why don't you save that shit for Sunday morning's sermon?"

Back in London I told Solbert that orientation was miles away from the soldiers' immediate interests and anxieties. On the GI's mind was the impending invasion, the enemy's capabilities as compared with his own, his chances of survival. It was folly to play catch-up with the failures of the schools. Orientation needed to get down in the foxhole with the rifleman and see the world through the sights of his gun.

Solbert requested my transfer to the ETO as chief of orientation. Osborn acquiesced. I inherited a staff consisting of Lieutenant Barrett Parker, a teacher in civilian life, Sergeant Hamilton Whitman, a burly newspaperman, and Gwenda Priddis, an exquisite English woman who typed and brewed tea in our tiny warren atop 37 Upper Brook Street. How was it possible, I asked, for such piffle as *Army Talks* to be published? Parker put his finger on the problem. *Army Talks* was the product of a board of advisors— Herbert Agar, cultural attaché in the American Embassy, Harvey Gibson, director of the Red Cross, and Lieutenant General John C. H. Lee, commanding the Services of Supply. The board nominated subjects, screened text, and took from three to five weeks to clear a typescript for production. No change could be made in *Army Talks* without the board's approval. In Parker's and Whitman's opinion, chances of changing the situation were zilch.

Priddis took down a memo to Eisenhower asking that he issue a directive to make *Army Talks* responsive to the soldier's need to know about the enemy, the causes and objectives of the war, and his role in the impending invasion. Solbert signed off on the memo. Eisenhower approved and on April 24, 1944, General Lee received this letter:

Supreme Headquarters
Allied Expeditionary Forces
Office of the Supreme Commander

Dear Lee,

I feel strongly that as the day of our combined offensive approaches, it is necessary to make absolutely clear to our men the stark and elemental facts as to the character of our Nazi enemy, the absolute need for crushing him, if we are to survive, and finally, to drive home the fact that we have defeated them before and can do it again. It is only necessary to steel ourselves to the task.

The inculcation of this fighting spirit is an essential part of the final training, and a command function. There is authorized an orientation officer for each unit of regimental level and above and current instructions in this theater provide for periodic orientation talks by company officers under his guidance. It is necessary now, to direct these talks as indicated in the preceding paragraph. I desire that you instruct your subordinate commanders to take energetic action to insure the success of this aspect of our training, utilizing all available agencies for putting material at the disposal of company commanders.

Theater Headquarters will furnish commanders with "News Maps" and "Army Talks"; these will be supplemented by material to appear in Yank, Stars and Stripes, and to be broadcast over the American Forces Network.

This is not the time for long discussions on the roots and causes of the war. Our soldiers have heard this before. What is required now is to impress on them that only hard—and successful—fighting will bring victory; and that the way home is via Berlin.

Sincerely,
Dwight D. Eisenhower
General, U.S. Army

Copies went to Bradley, Patton, Spaatz, and every other army and air force commander. Overnight the situation changed. Released from Lee's control, the first issue of the new *Army Talks* reached the troops on May 3, 1944. "The Enemy and You" portrayed the German soldier as a strong, skilled, but vulnerable adversary. On May 10, sixty thousand copies of *Army Talks* entitled "These Guys Fought 'Em" presented lessons learned by the Big Red One. Seasoned soldiers told how they had routed Rommel.

On May 17, *Mein Kampf* as abstracted by Dorothy Thompson revealed Hitler's thoughts on race, religion, education, world domination. "We will destroy France first, then get England, after which we will have the United States cornered without a fight." May 24: "How Russians Kill Germans." Three wounded Russian soldiers, transferred from the eastern front to the Soviet Embassy in London, told how to put panzers out of business and fight from house to house. "There must be two of you to rush a house. You and a grenade. Let the grenade go first. Then you follow. You go forward. Forward. Always forward."

Solbert called me to his office. He sat sphinx-like behind his desk. I read his eyes. I got his message. *"Achtung!"* rolled off the presses on the night of May 31 and was rushed to marshalling areas in the south of England. It condensed information hitherto classified about what waited on the beaches, in the hedgerows, in the air over Normandy.

Soldiers read it as they sailed for France.

14

An Ecological View of Hawaiian Education

Wist Hall
May 1987

Professor Potter asks for a paper evidential of our ability to critique, from an historical viewpoint, a published article on education. Suicidally, I address an article he himself has written on higher education in Hawaii, covering the hundred-odd years from the founding of Oahu College (1853) to the expansion of the University of Hawaii when it had digested the influx of World War II veterans generated by the GI Bill. The university, he stated, following the national pattern, "blossomed as a graduate research institution receiving many millions of Federal dollars for research annually."

Potter's piece makes clear that the University of Hawaii is caught in the turmoil that, ever since Sputnik, has made American education the target of hostile public opinion. This is especially true of Hawaii, where educational inadequacies among elementary and secondary school students, as statistically established by consistently low scores in national surveys, reflect deficiencies at the university level. (A recent study reveals that one in five islanders is illiterate.)

I commend Professor Potter's statement to anyone seeking data on the genesis and development of the University of Hawaii, but fault it for falling short of the opportunities inherent in the subject. Positioned as it is in a mid-point of the Pacific, a cultural, commercial, military pivot around which the future may revolve, and populated by a kaleidoscopic array of Asian, Polynesian, and Caucasian people, Hawaii offers an uncluttered overview of the educational scene from a Pacific perspective which, in my opinion, eludes Dr. Potter's otherwise observant eye. And so I write:

If a history of education in Hawaii is to have meaning in the context of the argument about the quality of American education, it seems essential that it begin with education's origins in America, and their implications for the fiftieth state. Two developments that determined the direction in which American education has moved were one, the establishment in New England of a Puritan tradition. Two, the impact of the Prussian system on American educators who, lacking graduate schools at home, improved their scholarship overseas. From the kindergarten to the highly specialized, research-oriented graduate schools of modern American universities, including that of Hawaii, the shadow of European philosophies and practice fell across America. From Harvard, Yale and other elite institutions of the east, the tide of Puritan-Prussian inspiration swept westward, following the frontier, and leaping fathoms of seawater to position itself in the Pacific.

Ecologically, such a transfer could not possibly succeed. Both Britain and Germany occupy northern latitudes where weather, flora, fauna, natural resources, historical phenomena, cultural and linguistic characteristics produce peoples and societies peculiar and congenial to these climes. The fountainhead of the Puritan faith, Emmanuel College at Cambridge, is shaded by enormous elms that prosper in English soil. Similarly, the harsh winters of

Berlin propitiate trees that grace boulevards called *Unter den Linden.* Neither elms nor lindens, their seeds sown in Hawaii, would likely survive.

Herein lies the rub of Hawaii's education. Though the seeds of northern Europe's vegetation might thrive in Massachusetts, in Hawaii they would die. Nothing in Hawaii corresponds to conditions so disparate. Neither the cotton mills of Manchester nor the steel mills of the Ruhr have Hawaiian counterparts. Napoleonic wars, the mobilization of Prussian schools to produce educated armies, the British need to create an efficient corps of colonial administrators—these seem remote from the local Polynesian, Japanese, Chinese, Filipino milieu and irrelevant to island interests. Nevertheless the seeds of northern European education here have been sown without regard for whether such alien corn can possibly prosper in soil so indigenously different.

Doubtless Hawaii's politicians and pedants deem it essential that the State adhere to the mainland model, and that federal dollars will flow into its schools only if federal standards are followed. Specialization, departmentalization, government subsidization, nationalization and scientization of education are commonalities of the accepted system and Hawaii cannot hold itself aloof from the norms by which other states abide. Hierarchical faculty structures, the tenure system, publishing versus perishing, researching versus teaching, other peculiarities of Prussian inspiration from which America's educational facilities are cloned —to deviate from these would risk disaccreditation.

Yet, since Hawaii's place is in the Pacific, how well does a system that started with Cotton Mather and Frederick the Great accommodate Hawaiian nature, need and aspiration? Given their ethnic and other characteristics, are Hawaii's children best served by textbooks, curricula, teaching techniques originating in circumstances so distant from their own, and applicable to such different situations? Granting that Hawaii cannot escape the modern world, that an accommodation must be made to western standards, and that its economy cannot prosper independently from mainland markets, may this not blind Hawaii to the provenance whence came the majority of its citizens that links them—ethnically, culturally, linguistically—with the peoples of the Pacific perimeter? Might not Hawaii's schools identify more intimately with those of Japan, China, Korea, Taiwan, Hong Kong and Singapore than with systems more habituated to occidental than oriental modes of thought and action?

Specifically, given the desperate need of American industry for bilingual speakers in English, Japanese, Chinese, Korean, Malaysian, Filipino and other Asian tongues; given the fact that many Hawaiian children already have an affinity for Asian languages which are spoken in their homes; given the importance of tourism, largely originating in Asia, to Hawaii's economy; given a multitude of other reasons why Hawaii's schools should have an oriental rather than occidental inclination—what more sensible role might Hawaii's schools fulfill than certification of the state as America's linchpin with Asia?

Ever since the first missionary set foot on island sands, Hawaii has suffered from tunnel vision. Overwhelmed by the mainland presence, it has never designed a school system uniquely its own. It is unlikely to do so unless the harsh glare of history is trained on its schools, and in its failure to do so, I take issue with Dr. Potter's otherwise excellent article.

On the day my paper is passed to Dr. Potter, our class adjourns to attend a session with Hawaii's new Governor, John Waihee, to consider ways and means whereby his administration might improve the state's schools. Waihee states that he has already acted to patch and paint the schools, and to provide teachers with whatever they need in the way of supplies and equipment. What more, he asks, does the university suggest to improve school performance?

Overwhelmingly, answers are to raise the pay of professors, principals, and teachers; accede to union demands for better working conditions; establish master-teacher programs; improve research and other facilities so that Hawaii will attract and retain the cream of the academic crop. In short, what education in Hawaii needs is money.

Rather than making my suggestion in the heat of discussion, I write a letter.

Dear Governor Waihee,

Over the years, rather than facing the fact that the very origin of our school system predetermines its difficulties, successive generations have applied bandaids to a serious disease. I would therefore suggest that you, as the Governor of Hawaii, become the first person in your position ever to examine the profound illness that affects education and to consider the necessity of a radically new approach.

Indicating the need to switch schools from their western orientation to the Pacific posture inherent in Hawaii's location, languages, ethnic interests and instincts, I conclude:

> Were you to signal the need, not for *reform* of a discredited system but for its *replacement,* by a more appropriate mode, not only Hawaii but all of America might be awakened to appropriate action.

From Prof. Potter, my essay earns an A. From the executive chambers I receive a reply, signed by the governor's administrative director, reminding me that "the Governor has stated on numerous occasions that one of his goals is to create a public school system in Hawaii which is second to none."

To inform myself on the governor's concept of a school system second to none, I visit the Waikiki Elementary School which abuts my residence. The governor is living up to his promise. The buildings have been patched and painted, and the parking lot is being scarified, recompacted, and resurfaced at a cost of $31,996.

15

The Power of the Press?

Stars and Stripes
European Theater of Operations, 1945

On D-day plus four, with the editor of *The Stars and Stripes*, Lt. Col. Ensley Llewellyn, I sailed for Normandy on the *Fagerbro,* a Norwegian freighter loaded with a special "liberation issue" of the army's newspaper. Quartermasters on Omaha Beach quickly identified the cargo. From one end of Omaha to the other rose a cry, "It's the *Stripes!*" Llewellyn commandeered a jeep and, racing past blasted pillboxes and tanks, we tossed papers right and left to infantrymen in their foxholes. "D-day!" yelled Llewellyn. "Read all about it!" Gazing incredulously at the headlines, soldiers jigged with joy. "Hey guys, here's how we did it!" "Jesus, it's like mail from home!"

Llewellyn, a sandy-haired man of middle age and height, exuded nervous energy that well served the *Stripes*. It was to him

72

that, on March 4, 1942, an order from the War Department arrived, to establish a newspaper for U.S. forces serving in the British Isles. He had promptly put together a four-page weekly tabloid that soon became a daily. Overcoming problems of policy, personnel, and newsprint, he had produced a paper of which the army could be proud. It came, therefore, as a shock that on August 24, 1944, I received orders to replace Llewellyn as editor-in-chief of *The Stars and Stripes*. I obeyed, with deep reluctance.

The reason for my reluctance was self-evident. The *Stripes* was a military monopoly which, in the circumstances that governed war, demanded obedience to army authority. How could such a newspaper be free? This was the question I faced when, on the premises of *The New York Herald Tribune* on the Rue de Berri in Paris, I took over the helm.

Actually, the question had been answered back in 1942 when a tough-minded lieutenant named Robert Moora had laid down the dictum: "This is a paper for GI Joe. After that it's a tradepaper whose specialized readers are soldiers who want facts, not philosophy or propaganda. After that it isn't anything else no matter what the brass says."

By and large, Llewellyn and Moora had maintained the *Stripes'* integrity, with certain exceptions. Bill Mauldin's cartoon characters, "Willie and Joe" were banned in the ETO due largely to General Patton's aversion to these sloppy, bearded, embittered caricatures of the spit-and-polish types he preferred. Neither did the *Stripes* publish grievances of disgruntled GIs. Editorially, the *Stripes* was always upbeat, avoiding contentious issues that bruised the brass. Adding to such censorship from above were certain taboos of the staff, mainly an abhorrence of anything that made the newspaper seem a house organ of the army. It looked askance at indoctrination, instruction, propaganda. The nature of Nazism, causes and outcomes of the war, reportage of lessons learned in combat—such subjects didn't meet the staff's strict definition of news.

To repair these omissions I made my first moves. Under a feisty sergeant, Lou Rakin, a letter-to-the-editor column, "B-Bag," made its bow. "Blow it out here" was Rakin's invitation to the troops, releasing a barrage of complaints against self-indulgent officers, delayed mail, faulty equipment, liquor rationing, and myriad other examples of military mismanagement. Incensed by "B-Bag,"

General Lee warned that unless the *Stripes* desisted from destroying discipline, he would set matters straight. Mauldin's Willie and Joe shuffled on to the editorial page, grubbier than ever and mouthing "Oh, I likes officers. They make me want to live 'till the war's over." From Headquarters, Third United States Army, Office of the Commanding General, came a stern rebuke.

Editor The Stars and Stripes:

Your cartoons show the dirtiest and most unmilitary soldiers that I have ever seen. Unless you do better I will prohibit any Stars and Stripes reporter in this Army and also the issue of the newspaper. It is definitely an aid to the enemy in that it destroys discipline.

Truly yours.
G. S. Patton, Jr.
Lieut. General, U.S. Army
Commanding

Undeterred, the *Stripes* continued to publish "B-Bag" and "Willie and Joe," balancing their antibrass tilt with a supplement entitled *Warweek,* a gleaning of combat information from the front. And short, illustrated editorials replaced saccharine optimism with a more brutal assessment of the distance to victory, the *Wehrmacht*'s resilience, and other roadblocks to an early journey home.

Prior to my appointment, *Stripes* editorials were wordy, ingenuous, and, frequently, fatuous. As early as August 1944, GIs read: "Germany has lost the war. Allied armies are advancing beyond liberated Paris at a speed which, if maintained, can bring them to the German border within a week." An editorial on the buzzbombs falling in Britain's "Bomb Alley" proclaimed that "every time the enemy attacks a Briton, an American bruises and rises in defiance to fight them all the harder." On August 31, 1944—the date assumes importance in the context of a time when the worst winter of the war still lay ahead—the *Stripes* editorial advised: "Bearded veterans who were over 15 when they traded their jalopies for half-tracks are entitled to a year's post-discharge schooling at Government expense . . . the clanging bell of the Little Red School House is just a faint tinkle beyond the horizon."

None of this accorded with my own experience as an infantry

replacement at the front. Doffing my officer's insignia and, as a rifleman, serving with combat units of the First, the Fourth, the Seventy Seventh and other divisions, I appreciated the GI's devotion to duty, and shared his desire to go home in one piece. But nowhere more than at the front did the *Stripes* editorials seem more silly. The war was not virtually won. Yanks didn't fight harder whenever Hitler bombed a Briton. The Little Red School House's bell could not be heard above the din of battle.

Validating such optimism, news stories published in the *Stripes* fanned a fever of homesickness smouldering in the minds of many soldiers, including me. "Thirteen Separation Camps Opened by Army." "Returned Soldiers Living Like Kings in Miami." "Allied Victories Herald Early End to War." "B-Bag" was swamped with mail asserting the writer's entitlement to early discharge on the basis of a system promulgated by the Pentagon that had GIs calculating their points to the last decimal. If any pipedream played up in the news needed the counterweight of editorial judgment, it was this outpouring of pronouncements touching the innermost aspirations of men committed to combat in Europe, to say nothing of Japan.

To this need I addressed an editorial:

> As long as the Stars and Stripes is a GI journal there will be no stops on letters to the editor. But if you believe all the guff some guys give out on the I want-to-go-home theme, you'd think this was one panty-waist army. It looks like our great big American supermen are all ready to pack up and leave this legalized murder to the nurses, WACS and clubmobile girls.
>
> We wish the homesick boys would lift their heads from their tear-stained pillows and take a look at the wreckage and misery of war around them and thank God their own homes don't look like that.
>
> They're away from home to save themselves a home to go back to. If it takes two or ten years to save it, it's worth it. If it isn't worth it, then why all the hurry to get back?
>
> Maybe all this bitching about going home is just another symptom of good morale. If so, fine. But maybe its the first sign of the let's stay home and let the rest of the world fly a kite spirit that gave Hitler and his gyppy-Jappy pals their big chance.
>
> Sure, Joe, it would be swell to go home and get married and have yourself a son. Then, in 20 years, as he leaves for the wars, you can settle down to read his letters:
>
> "Dear pop," he'll write, "I wanna go home."

Three days later an ashen-faced Rakin entered my office bearing a bundle of mail. "Major," he said, "you've sure as hell overcome apathy in the army, but I think you have a mutiny on your hands."

Rakin was right. Apathy had indeed been overcome, but at what appeared to be an exorbitant price—the integrity of *The Stars and Stripes.* Far into the night I read what soldiers had been moved to write.

> To the chairborn bastard who wrote that stinking editorial: We the members of the 777th Graves Registration Company nominate you "the Cadaver of the Month." (Signed by 172 names.)

> I can't see it possible that you could publish an editorial as the one in your 9/20/44 edition. Is it that terrible for you to suffer a little bitching from a bunch of guys who are saving this mixed up world from disaster? Any psychologist will tell you that bitching is nothing more than a guy getting a load off his chest. You should make a definite apology to those guys at the front. You hit way below the belt bud. Signed, another GI.

> In regard to your "lousy" (and I'll say it again) editorial, there's a few of us "out here" that would like to put in our two cents worth. You're in a helluva position to be giving us the gong. If we could sit back on our haunches and print a newspaper we probably wouldn't mind the war so much either. Now don't get me wrong, we all like the Stars and Stripes, it's just your lousy editorial! Signed, Pvt. Wesley G. Wilson, Inf.

Amid the boos, a rare cheer:

> Having been a working newspaper man for a fair-sized sheet (the San Francisco Chronicle) for ten years, I'm getting one helluva bang out of the gripes against your daily editorials. Looks to me like the beefers have been so blinded by the long-winded tripe that masquerades as editorials in most U.S. papers that they can't take it when the cold facts, unadorned and to the point, are paraded daily before their foggy eyes and numb brains. I don't know who writes em but more power and stripes to him. As far as I'm concerned he's the star of the Stars and Stripes. Signed Herb Caen, 1st Lt., AAF.

Caen has since won fame as a columnist. His hosanna helped, but not nearly enough to overcome my remorse as staffers, returning from the front, reported it was dangerous to wear the *Stripes* shoulder patch linking them with the editorial. Andrew Rooney, today's television star, then an ace writer on the staff, declared the editorial to be "the one completely unethical and immoral thing the Stars and Stripes ever did." I reported to Solbert and requested reassignment. He refused on grounds that such action should await the result of interviews conducted by the Army Research Branch to establish GI reactions to my picture editorials. But even Solbert flinched at my next indiscretion.

It was not my habit to second-guess staffers who readied each day's edition, but on one fateful night I dropped into the bullpen to watch the final stages of the newspaper's make-ready. On page one was a picture, little larger than a postage stamp. I enlarged the photo to full-page size, and substituted it for the regular news which I relegated to inside pages of the paper. Next morning hell broke loose. Page one was pasted upside down throughout the *Tribune* building. Staffers snapped me mock salutes. A petition proclaimed that in the history of journalism no editor had ever displayed his utter incompetence by so amateurish an action. It was signed by a "Firing Squad" eager to expedite my execution.

The picture had been shot by an AP cameraman named Joe Rosenthal, flown to Guam, radioed to San Francisco, wirephotoed to New York, and relayed to Paris. It showed five U.S. Marines raising the flag over Mt. Suribachi in Iwo Jima.

The power of the press! Gathering, writing, editing, illustrating news for readers ranging from Patton to the lowest private. Covering coal strikes in Pennsylvania and air strikes in the Ruhr. Updating infantry on combat intelligence as it flowed in from the front. Contrasting *Mein Kampf* with the Four Freedoms. Putting a global war in perspective. Anticipating peace. Everything—ink, metal, paper, presses, people—coming together. Everything—information, orientation, military instruction, administration, production, distribution—everything except education. And in its absence, armies were fielded, men died, and the press was powerless.

I was at the depth of my despond when, early one morning, the telephone rang. "This is Eisenhower," it said. "And I'm Napoleon," I replied, slamming down the receiver. It *was* Eisenhower. Driving out to his headquarters in Versailles, I felt a sense of relief that the agony would soon be over.

Except for a lamp on his desk, Eisenhower worked in the dark. Kay Sommersby, his gorgeous English assistant, sat behind a screen taking notes of his transactions. Ike had the results of the research branch's inquiry on my editorials. Eighty-six percent liked them. Four percent disliked them. Others had no opinion. As for "So you want to go home," sixty-seven percent said they liked it, seventeen percent disliked it, and sixteen percent had no opinion. Editorials took second place only to "B-Bag" and Mauldin in GI esteem.

Eisenhower said,

> "Your editorials are shaking people up. They belong in the paper. So does B-Bag. So do Willie and Joe. B-Bag is the first thing I turn to every morning. I'm all for B-Bag raising hell about officer privileges. It isn't his insignia that makes an officer. It's how he does his job that counts. I take a hell of a lot of flak from people who don't agree with me. So must you. As editor of *The Stars and Stripes* your job is to call your shots as you see them. Just do the best you can and roll with the punches. If Patton, Lee or anyone else gives you trouble, come see me."

I attended the Nuremburg trials and faced the men who had so faithfully served the Fuhrer. Except for Speer, they showed no contrition. In Berlin, where American and Russian officers met in the *Commandatura* to work out governance of the city, I saw the ugly face of the future. Brothers-in-arms on the battlefield, in peace they confronted each other as foes.

Before leaving for my next assignment, to set up *The Stars and Stripes* in China, I drove down to Heidelberg to look up Kurt Schneider. A clerk in the *Rathaus* consulted his ledger and said Schneider had been rounded up with all the other Jews and sent to some place called Chelmno or Kulmhof, he wasn't sure which. No, he had not returned.

The war went through winter. I was with a patrol that liberated Dachau. Memory flinches as the sight and stench of the camp crowd in. How could any people commit such a crime? No people are more able and industrious than Germans. No laboratories produce better science and technology. Few factories build better cars. No literature is richer, no music sweeter, no churches more Christian, no philosophers more profound.

How could it have happened? How, why, what—other than education?

16

Pols and Pedants
Lose the War

Wist Hall
May 1987

Prof. Potter's appetite for essays activates the enzymes of my mind. He asks for a paper on an educational event that, in our opinion, affected American society so significantly as to deserve special study. My submission deals with the Serviceman's Readjustment Act of 1944, known as the GI Bill, signed into law as American soldiers were consolidating their grip on the Normandy shore:

World War II ended with a revolution in American education. Congress passed the GI Bill. I was in Europe at the time and, as editor of *The Stars and Stripes,* intimately involved in the transformation from war to peace. Academics arrived in the ETO to set up a vast new schooling system to absorb the energies of idle GIs. According to a colonel fresh from Washington, deluxe hotels were being requisitioned in Biarritz, Nice, Shrivenham, and other posh European spas to house a macro-university, accommodating soldier-students in everything they needed to fit them into jobs in a technological economy. After briefing the *Stripes* staff, the colonel invited questions.

Q: Had combat veterans participated in the program's formulation?
A: No, education is a science. It demands disciplines only professionals possess. It cannot brook amateur interference.

Q: Will the curriculum contain courses on international understanding conducive to peace?
A: No area of interest is excluded, but experience teaches that Americans, and especially soldiers, are pragmatic people more interested in arc-welding than in philosophy, the arts, or other esoteric subjects.

Q: Would the veterans' experience of war, their potential for peace, be recognized, utilized, or in any way influence the content of the program?
A: If there are veterans capable of contributing anything to the curriculum, their services will be utilized within the context of the program's basic intent which, of necessity, is largely vocational. Veterans will have a living to make and need to be fitted into the postwar economy. We don't want unemployment and all the social problems it incurs.

Q: In view of your replies, what will education have salvaged from the soldiers' sacrifice? Will the schools of the future be the same as the schools of the past?
A: The schools of the past produced millions of men and women capable of defeating the Nazis and Japs. They will do no less in the future. As for the soldiers' sacrifice, it is recognized and repaid by the GI Bill.

Doctoral studies introduce data of which, engaged as I was in the ETO and China, I have been ignorant. Karier's *The Individual, Society and Education* reveals that

"The Bill's intent was originally to channel veterans back into suitable occupations. Aware that most revolutions in the twentieth century, whether Bolshevist or Fascist, were led by unemployed, disgruntled veterans, there was a very distinct fear that a veteran who returned from the battlefield to the breadline might turn to street fighting in desperation as his counterparts had done in Germany, Italy and Russia after World I. As one congressional committee put it, 'The primary purpose of any educational arrangements should be to meet a national need. We have regarded any benefits which may be extended to individuals in the process as incidental.'

Admission that any benefits to individuals were incidental was a high-water mark in congressional candor. Equally candid were the reactions of leading American educators. As earlier noted, Harvard's president, James B. Conant, feared that "we may find the least capable of the war generation flooding the facilities for advanced education because the Bill failed to distinguish between those who can profit most by advanced education and those who cannot." Robert Hutchins, president of the University of Chicago, declared the Bill "a threat to American education."

Conant and Hutchins earned F's for prophecy. *Fortune* magazine categorized the class of 1949, first of the postwar graduates, as "the soberest, most trained graduating class in U.S. history," that "it looked to big business for security," and that it "turned its back on speculative ventures." This thirst for security, Karier notes, was ultimately reflected in "the suburban life style the veterans adopted and the political and social events they tended to support in the post-war period."

Thus, swords were beaten into corporate plowshares. Fourteen billion dollars were lavished on the greatest of American educational innovations. As the curtain rose on a postwar period of education on such a scale as to change the face of the nation, and even of the world, the old order took over, the ivory tower prevailed, the politicians joined hands with the pedants, and what might have been was not to be.

My paper earns an A. I do not gloat. The war was lost. Rather than a new day dawning, the night of the old descended, foreclosing, perhaps forever, the chance of future generations learning from the past.

17

If You Were Born in Russia

Moscow, Leningrad
1935, 1950, 1983

Discharged from the army in November 1946, I faced a decision on my postwar career. Madison Avenue, money-making, all my prewar motivation, girls excepted, had lost their allure. What mattered now was fending off another foe whose image loomed over the horizon, dwarfing the menace of Hitler's Germany and Tojo's Japan. America's fear, loathing, and ignorance of communism were so obsessive as to rule out any hope of peace unless prejudice was informed by education. Toward that end I joined forces with an army associate, Robert Straus, heir to the R. H. Macy fortune, in an undertaking to comprehend the communist colossus. Straus, a graduate of Harvard and Cambridge, would underwrite the considerable cost of the project and I would create the content. To assist us, we enlisted the dean of correspondents in the USSR, Henry Shapiro, the staff of the America-Russian Institute in New York, and the photographic facilities of *Life*.

It is 1950. Education in the Soviet Union begins with the birth of a boy in the Klara Zetkin Maternity Home in Moscow. Zetkin was a communist member of the last German Reichstag before the Great Patriotic War of 1939–1945. The home is bright with pictures of Lenin. A banner proclaims: "Motherhood is the Social Function of Women!" The new baby, Boris, sleeps as his mother sings:

> There beneath the Kremlin wall
> In a crypt revered by all
> Lies Ilyich within his grave
> He also died our land to save.
> No more dangers now to fear
> For our trusty watchman's near.
> Sleep my baby, rest your head.
> Sleep, my darling, in your bed.

Having had five children, mama is pinned with the Motherhood medal. She is entitled to a government grant of $170 plus $12 a month until Boris is five. This helps the family financially, but the problem is not money. It is nipples. Muscovites joke about the commissar of the rubber industry who is questioned about nipples. He asks, "From what point of view?" "Nipples," the mother replies, "from the philosophical, historical and philological point of view, and also, why it is that we cannot obtain nipples?" "Don't worry," says the commissar, "there will be nipples. The baby must simply wait a little." But, the story concludes, babies are unreasonable. They shamelessly yell "ya!"

Aged twenty-eight days, Boris is brought to the factory nursery, named Krupskaya after Lenin's wife. A streamer says "The Nursery is the Germ Cell of Communist Society." Lenin is also quoted as saying "The Saucepan is the Enemy of the Party Cell," meaning that mothers must be freed of household drudgery so as to fulfill the Five Year Plan. Boris remains in the nursery until he is three. Officially he is an *Oktobriata*, a child of the October Revolution.

When he is eighteen months old he should be toilet-trained. At two and a half he must dress and undress himself. When he is three he should be able to serve food and clean up after eating. If he misbehaves, he is warned "That is not done by a Soviet child!"

Aged three to six, Boris spends his waking hours in kindergarten. Its slogan: "The School Apart from Life, Apart from Politics, is a Lie and a Hypocrisy—Lenin." The children play with "Socialist toys"—tractors, tanks, and guns. Trips are taken to museums, monuments, and Red Square. Teacher points out the inscription on the Iberian Gate: "Religion is the opiate of the People." About the Kremlin she says: "Once the Czars lived here. They were mostly good-for-nothings. When I was a little girl we sang 'Czar's bell does not ring; Czar's cannon does not shoot; Czar Nicholas does not reign.' Well, we got rid of him in the October Revolution. Today we say 'Nothing is above Moscow except the Kremlin, and nothing is above the Kremlin except heaven.' "

Aged seven, Boris begins his elementary education. Teacher reads the twenty rules for Soviet school children printed in the back of the *Tabil* or record book on which his work will be graded. The first rule: "It is the duty of every Soviet schoolchild to strive with tenacity and perseverance to master knowledge in order to become an educated and cultured citizen and to serve most usefully the Soviet motherland."

Boris' arithmetic textbook says "Numbers and measures become weapons for the conquest of knowledge and preparation for the defense of the country." At first, problems are simple. "How much change would you get from ten rubles if you bought a teapot for five rubles?" Gradually, problems become harder. "A detachment had 170 soldiers with rifles and two machine guns. A Red Army man fires eight shots per minute from a rifle and four hundred shots a minute from a machine gun. How many bullets are used if the shooting lasts three hours?" There is a joke about arithmetic. "If a man bought a barrel of apples for thirty rubles and sold it for seventy rubles, what would he get?" The answer: "Three months in jail."

Geography lessons teach Boris that Russia is the world's greatest industrial power, covering one-sixth of the earth's surface. Compared with it the text teaches:

the United States is very small, and in its death agony. Its resources are in the hands of a group of billionaires who stand at the head of

trusts of steel, copper, oil, etc. Especially strong are the two financial concerns of Morgan and Rockefeller in New York, the heart of
capitalism. In New York people are crowded into filthy houses of
stone and wood on the fringes of the city. The cost of living is high.
Negros live in a semi-serflike condition, terrorized by the Ku Klux
Klan. Indians were systematically exterminated. Unemployment is
but one of the factors destined to bring American capitalism to its
knees.

The history text tells that:

> Clans and tribes once held all property in common. Gradually
> tools, land, food became private property. Classes developed, the
> rich and poor. Rich men enslaved the poor, became rulers of their
> tribes, and in this way States were formed. Russia's history is one of
> constant struggle of the enslaved masses against oppressive rulers.
> Rebellions were put down because the peasants, although able to
> kill landlords, didn't know what new order to introduce. This
> knowledge was supplied by the Bolsheviks. The secret of successful
> revolution is first, discredit the government in the eyes of the work-
> ers and peasants. Second, forge an alliance of workers, peasants,
> soldiers and sailors. Third, build a strong Bolshevik Party to rally
> and lead the people. Fourth, wait for the moment when the govern-
> ment is weak and launch the revolution.

Boris' textbook teaches him "irreconcilable hatred toward the enemies of Socialist Society . . . to struggle with him, in time to
unmask him and finally if he does not surrender, to destroy him."

Boris is among the top third of his class who qualify for the final
three years of the ten-year school, corresponding to high school.
Courses include Russian language, literature, the constitution of
the USSR, geography, and a foreign language. Science receives
greatest stress. "Unlike America," the textbook teaches, "with its
monopolies and private interests to safeguard, with patents locked
up in corporation vaults, Soviet science is planned, free and self-
supportive. The results are the wonders of the world, from
Lysenko's discovery that environment—not heredity as the capitalists claim—determines the nature of man, to Soviet supremacy
in space."

Source of Soviet scientific supremacy is Karl Marx who discov-
ered that history itself is a science dictated by laws of production.
No Soviet citizen is educated unless he understands the irrefutable
logic of Dialectical Materialism. Nature, Marx taught, is in a state
of continuous change, with something old, capitalism, dying, and

something new, communism, rising. Change is violent. It is a battle between opposing forces that arise from contradictions within a state. Capitalism abounds with such contradictions. By producing ever larger quantities of goods, capitalism intensifies competition, ruins small entrepreneurs, converts them into proletarians, reduces their purchasing power, and makes it impossible to dispose of the commodities produced. Having the means of production in private hands is clearly incompatible with the social character of the production process. These irreconcilable contradictions create periodical crises of overproduction, compelling capitalists to destroy the commodities they have produced, suspend production, and put millions of people out of work. Capitalism, in short, is commiting suicide because educated workers will no longer stand for these abuses. Inevitably, socialist ownership of the means of production, as practiced and perfected in the USSR, must prevail throughout the world.

Be it in high school, trade school, the Pioneers, the Soviet boy scout system, or the Communist Youth League, no Soviet child can escape this thesis. Every organ of education and information —schools, newspapers, films, radio, television—repeats it. Be grateful, Boris is told, to be born a Marxist. Unlike American children blinded by propaganda to their system's faults and ultimate fate, Soviet citizens are told the truth.

Underlying and permeating Soviet schooling is Lenin's decree: "A revolution is worthwhile only if it can be defended." From age seven when, as Little Octobrists, children play war games, and assemble the Kalashnikov submachine gun, to age eighteen, when *voyenkomats,* draft boards, induct able-bodied males into military service, instruction in close-order drill, marksmanship, battlefield tactics is obligatory. Girls prepare for civil defense, medical, and administrative duties. Two million men are called up every spring and autumn, and serve two years in the army or airforce, or three years in the navy. The cream of the crop will advance to the Supreme Soviet Military Academy where one rule prevails: "The only way to achieve victory is through battle."

Entitled *If You Were Born in Russia,* the Soviet system as of 1950 was published in a book, (Farrar Straus, New York) widely syndicated in the West. Thirty-three years after its publication, I return to Russia with a team from the University of London's

Institute of Education. Stalin has been wiped off the pages of history by a single stroke of the party's pen. But the thrust of Soviet education has not changed.

Bella, our attractive blonde guide, conducts the forty-four people in our group through a tightly scheduled week of visits to Soviet schools. "Brain trust" of Soviet education is the Academy of Pedagogical Science. From it flow directives, curricula, methodology, and texts to three million teachers and thirty-eight million children in elementary, vocational, technical, and finishing schools throughout the land.

Our mentors, Prof. Gafanova from the Institute of Content and Methods, and Prof. Lubovsky, head of the Institute of Defectology, deal frankly with the system's strengths and faults. Whereas the previous Five Year Plan had stressed content, the current plan features methods. Lower grades employ memorization, rote learning, and retention skills. Teaching is formal, didactic, transmissional. Once a child's talent is detected, he or she may be sent to special schools featuring math, science, language, or the arts, such as ballet. The aim is excellence, achieved by intensive training in subjects to which the chosen children are attuned.

Soviet schools, the professors admit, suffer from several problems. One, a tendency to theoretical excesses, "high flying," rather than to tried and true older methods based on tight discipline and lots of homework. Two, an unacceptable increase in divorce rates demands corrective action through courses on ethics. Women have become too emancipated and need to learn tolerance, modesty, and obedience to their husbands. Three, the great majority of teachers are women, with negative impact on the education of boys who are increasingly delinquent. Positive discrimination in favor of male teachers is under consideration.

Asked about computers, the professors reply that development of mental abilities has priority over machines, and therefore computer skills are not taught at elementary and secondary levels. Polytechnical training is stressed: "All children are taught sound labor habits and knowledge of production processes. Those who show aptitude enter trade, computer, language or other schools to which their abilities are suited."

Visits to various institutions have been arranged for our instruction. Specialized English School No. 4 in a bleak suburb is embellished by banners exhorting students to become productive Socialist citizens prepared to defend the motherland against its enemies. Seven hundred pupils—boys in blue uniforms, girls in brown dresses with white aprons—undergo eight years of intensive English language training. The principal explains. "Our purpose is to identify innate ability and to cultivate it without wasting a teacher's time on poor or unmotivated pupils."

A pretty sixth grader escorts us through the school's John Reed Museum and rapidly recites a litany of his exploits. "John Reed dug persistently for the roots of American evil in order to pull them out." The roots of evil are evidenced by photos of strikers in Detroit being beaten by Henry Ford's thugs. Climaxing an impressive afternoon are two plays, *Huckleberry Finn* and *The Prince and the Pauper,* faultlessly enacted by children whose dialects and demeanor capture every nuance of life along the Mississippi. Nowhere in America could children put on such a performance in Russian.

We visit trade schools, vocational schools and Pioneer Palaces, a unique Soviet institution in which children pursue their interests in cooking, sewing, automotive repair, metallurgy, wood working, or whatever other activity strikes their fancy. "It was here," a teacher tells us, "that Karpov developed his chess skills and Pavlova her ballet. Whatever a child's desire, be it baking a cake or repairing a tractor, we seek to gratify it with the understanding that it will be repaid by service to the Party." Disciplinary problems are rare. Two systems keep unruly children in control: *Zvenovoi,* in which older students are elected as commissioners to punish misdemeanors and persuade lazy children to work; and *Sheftsvo,* which obligates better students to tutor weaker ones after hours. The system may not be altogether effective; Soviet kids trail our group offering black market rubles in exchange for cigarettes, lipstick, and nylon stockings.

Highlight of our tour is the University of Leningrad, oldest in the USSR, founded by Peter I in 1724. With twenty-five thousand students and a staff of two thousand, it is organized into sixteen faculties, half specialists in natural science, half in social sciences. Admission is restricted to students with a full secondary school diploma, certifying ten years of study, who succeed in passing entrance examinations which disqualify three applicants out of four. Five years are needed for a first degree, plus three more for postgraduate studies by thesis. Almost all university students are Youth party members.

Rector of the university is Prof. Zelenev, a handsome man of middle age who, speaking perfect English, fields our questions with authority and candor. All students, we learn, have major and minor fields of study. Math majors must also study philosophy, political economy, a foreign language, and the history of the Communist party. "Without knowedge of communism a scientist is like a boat without a rudder." Curricula are set by the Ministry of Higher Education, and successive Five Year Plans adapt courses to job requirements as set by the party. Like 850 other institutions of higher education in the USSR, Leningrad is obligated by law either to place graduates in jobs, or to extend their periods of study until jobs are found. Overall, Zelenev states, excellence of the Soviet system is attested by seven Nobel prizes awarded members of Leningrad's faculty.

I raise my hand. "Impressed as I am with your description of Soviet higher education, could you cite any flaws in the system as you see it?" Zelenev replies,

> Three matters urge attention. One, neither staff nor students are trained to use computers. Two, teaching methods are obsolete. It is difficult to teach old dogs new tricks and too many of our teachers stick to old methods out of habit. Three, students become expert in one subject and are ignorant of everything else. Despite our efforts to balance specialization in industry, trade or agriculture with history, philosophy and the arts, too many fail to see life in a larger focus.

Satiated by Soviet hospitality, we return to reality. A few in our group credit communist education with all of its claims. Others perceive that the party's purpose is paramount, that indoctrination masquerades as education, and that paranoia—fear of the capitalist foe—sickens the system. From birth to death, Soviet citizens march to the beat of a sinister drummer.

And yet there is something to be said for the Soviet system. It seeks out and develops the inborn aptitudes and natural preferences of children. It does not panic when America puts a man on the moon. It does not squander the energies of its qualified teachers in math, science, and other strenuous subjects; it concentrates their precious expertise on pupils best able to profit from difficult disciplines. However dire and didactic, the party line is consistent, relatively immune to the cyclic insanities of educational oracles. The Soviet Union does not saddle its schools with driver education, sex education, drug education, or education in any other area in which society fails to function. It assigns such tasks to Pioneer Palaces, Parks of Culture and Rest, the media, and other instruments of public instruction. Having achieved literacy, citizens are expected to read the papers and keep themselves informed on issues that, in America, are dumped on schools. While communist indoctrination disgraces any definition of decent education, Soviet schools are safeguarded from excessive overload, burned-out teachers, unrealistic expectations, and public contempt.

An acid test of a nation's intention is what it teaches its youth. By that measure, advantages of Soviet schooling are outweighed by its evils. It imposes on the world a Gresham's Law by which bad education drives out the good. Other systems, contaminated by the need to compete with communism, educate, not for peace, but war.

18

Horse Manure
Fertilizes Education

Wist Hall
May 1987

Clarence Karier's excellent text carries an unintended message, at least to me. It takes me back to the origins of education.

God only knows in what primeval wilderness education began, but let's begin with Plato whose *Republic* reserved education for aristocratic boys, denied it to girls, lower classes, and serfs, and sowed the seed of the nation-state, leading to the Greco-Roman wars. In some respects, a sorry start.

Christianity succeeded paganism, pitting Protestants against Catholics, and setting up schools to teach the truths of contesting credos. Superstition, religious rivalry, inquisitions, crusades, and holy wars ensued for several centuries, casting little credit on education's purposes, promises, and prayers.

Nation-states emerged. Vernaculars vied with Latin. Borders became defined. Cultural, economic, military competition took off. Kings called for educated soldiers armed with more lethal weapons. Education enlisted, or was co-opted, to serve the nation-state.

The lens was invented. Equipped with telescope and microscope Copernicus, Galileo, Bacon ushered in a Golden Age of Science. Education assumed a new intention—based on positive knowledge, to tame nature in man's behalf. Taming nature, science reduced much of it to rubble. What remains is threatened by the bomb.

Descartes, Newton, Mill, Locke lit the candle of "The Enlightenment," meaning that educated men could achieve happiness by exercise of their intelligence. However pursued, happiness remains elusive.

Science sired technology. Technology produced the printing press. Text books proliferated. Comenius created the first comics. Across the Western world interest quickened in education. Universities emerged from the ooze of ignorance. Bologna, Freiburg, Ulm, Oxford churned out knowledge that, applied by nation-states to their needs and appetites, enabled educated nations to overcome others that lacked intelligence, industry, and arms essential to survival.

As education enhanced national strength, so did it fire national ambition. Germany goose-stepped to the swan songs of Goethe, Hegel, Lessing, Herder, Schiller who extolled *Kultur* as a realm of the spirit, soul, and mind inaccessible to English empiricists and French rationalists. Education enshrined romantic myth and music, admired masculinity on the Greco-Roman model, celebrated martyrdom for King and Country, sanctified a bloodline of such purity as to exalt the teuton *Volk* above all others. Endowed with what Goethe called "a Fritzian way of thinking," Germany became "a land of thinkers and poets," of jingos and generals.

Prussia's impact on education needs no repetition. Let us skip to John Dewey who Karier describes as "at once both the hero and the villain of the twentieth century educational frontier"—a frontier I perceive as populated by pedagogic gunslingers, quick on the draw, in whose crossfire millions of innocent children were mentally murdered. To the cast of characters earlier introduced are added several other remarkable performers whose educational antics defy understanding.

Granville Stanley Hall (1844–1924), the first American to receive a PhD in psychology, founder of the American Psychological Association and a Gottingen graduate, propagated a faith compounded of Fichte's romanticism, Schopenhauer's voluntarism, Nietzsche's nihilism, all anchored in a set of primitivistic beliefs based on the German concept of the *Volk*. In the human fetus Hall saw the evolution of life's stages leading to the original man. The preadolescent child was a savage with whom reasoning was useless. As with a horse, he advised *dressur* "animal training," with ample use of the whip. To burn out the child's primitive past, myths and superstitions must be taught until, upon adolescence, the teacher appeals, not to reason, but to his emotions. The high school's goals are patriotism, body culture, military discipline, love of authority, and devotion to state. Through selective breeding, genetic psychology, and an educational system under tight state control, "the Kingdom of Superman" would be at hand. "The best education," wrote Hall, "is that which makes us the best and most obedient servants."

George H. Mead (1863–1931) returned from a stint of German study, joined John Dewey at the University of Chicago, and took issue with Hall. "Any psychological or philosophical treatment of human nature," Mead taught, "involves the assumption that the human individual belongs to an organized social community, and derives his human nature from his social interactions and relations with that community as a whole and with the other individual members of it." Seeing his interests as intimately tied to the interests of others, the child becomes a socialized human being, an "organization man," but with a novel, creative, impulsive side that is unpredictable. "Progress," Mead believed, "rests in the application of social-science knowledge to the social melioration process of a planned society."

Edward L. Thorndike (1874–1949) taught thousands of teachers at Columbia University that intelligence could be tested and measured. It was on his work in World War I that the army determined soldiers' occupational assignments in World War II. Statistical techniques established that black children were inferior to whites, that superior intellect produces superior character, and that a positive correlation exists between intelligence, moral character, and making money. "Society," Thorndike taught, "should introduce scientific eugenics to breed the mental and moral best. The able and good should acquire power. The abler persons in the world in the long run are the more clean, decent, just and kind."

John B. Watson (1878–1958) earned his PhD in animal behavior at the University of Chicago where he studied under Dewey. Watson believed that human behavior consists of motor and glandular responses to sensory stimuli.

> There is no such thing as our inheritance of capacity, talent, temperament, mental constitution and characteristics. These things depend on training that goes on mainly in the cradle. Give me a dozen healthy infants, well-formed, and my own specified world to bring them up in and I'll guarantee to take any one at random and train him to become any type of specialist I might select—doctor, lawyer, artist, merchant-chief and yes, even beggar-man and thief, regardless of his talents, penchants, tendencies, abilities, vocations and race of his ancestors.

All that is needed to perform these wonders, Watson alleged, is to pull the right wires which make the human puppet move.

B. F. Skinner (1904–) found the right wires by studying the behavior of rats. Through certain stimuli he could control their responses. If rats' behavior could be controlled, so, he taught, could children's through the application of reinforcement theory to programmed instruction. Man is neither free nor responsible, according to Skinner. He does not have "consciousness" or "mind." Only through behavioral science freed from traditional philosophies, illusions of freedom, and bad historical and cultural habits can he achieve collective happiness.

Infinite, apparently, is the ability of theorists to concoct cure-alls for every affliction that besets society. From progressivism to life adjustment to open education and all the way back to basics, millions of children fall under the influence of experts, each obsessed with the rightness of the nostrum he prescribes. Once administered and briefly endured, the prescription perishes in peristaltic waves that seize the schools, expelling what is taught in one decade as the excrement of the next, emitting nasty smells that make schools unpleasant places. Little wonder that classroom teachers long ago gave up on what descends from the ivory tower, and do what experience necessitates their doing—endure.

It is unlikely that Clarence Karier intended his text to be read as an indictment of education's origins. Nor does my increasing irreverence reflect Prof. Stueber's more balanced belief that schooling is benign. Only my personal intransigence persuades me that the pedigree of pedagogy is not proud. And I, as readers by now know, am a congenital fly in the ointment, a vexatious burr beneath the saddle, a persistent pain in the ass.

Scribbled in a margin of my notebook is a sequel to "I Am a Child":

I am a child, an American child, a twentieth century child. I go to the Big Comprehensive School House to learn my lessons. The Big Comprehensive School House has many rooms and many teachers.

In room number one is John Dewey who teaches instrumental-ism. What instrumentalism is nobody knows. Nobody under-stands Dr. Dewey. Neither do I.

In room number two is G. Stanley Hall who teaches primitiv-ism. Primitivism means a child is like a horse. You don't reason with a horse, says Dr. Hall. You put a bit between his teeth, hit him with a whip, and off you go.

In room number three is Herbert Mead who teaches social behaviorism which means that while a child may be a horse, he's a *social* horse who lives in a stable with other horses, and who behaves more like a Budweiser Clydesdale than a bucking bronco.

In room number four is Edward Thorndike who teaches con-nectionism which means that since humans and horses are ani-mals, a child's mind and a horse's mind are connected. Thus, the way to train a child is to treat him like a horse, preferably a white horse, because white horses are cleaner, kinder and smarter than black horses.

In room number five is Dr. Watson. He teaches that if you lay out the hay, the horse's mouth will water, at which point you pull the right wires to steer him any way you want. It makes no differ-ence to Dr. Watson whether the horse is a hatrack or a hunter; just give him a pony, any pony, and he'll turn him into Man O'War.

In room number six is B. F. Skinner who teaches behavioral

engineering which means the same thing as what Dr. Dewey, Dr. Mead, Dr. Thorndike, and Dr. Watson teach except, instead of horses, children are like rats.

This is the only thing in the curriculum of the Big Comprehensive School House on which everyone agrees.

In the Augean Stables of American education there are heaps of horse manure.

19

A Chinese Picture Is Worth a Thousand Words . . .

Canton, China
1948–1949

Mao's communists controlled northern China. Chiang Kai-shek's armies were in flight. President Truman sought some way whereby America's ancient ally, on which so much money and missionary effort had been spent, might escape the Bolshevik embrace. To that end, in 1948, a Joint Commission on Rural Reconstruction (JCRR) was established. Consisting of five Chinese and five American experts in agriculture, communication, and administration, its mandate was to improve the lot of Chinese farmers so as to create a stake they would defend against the red threat. An invitation to join the commission took me to Canton where my task was to produce training aids for the Chinese farmer comparable to those I had created for the American army.

As the plane crossed the Pacific, I recalled the China I knew as a child. The Chinese laundry where pigtailed men called "chinks" washed and ironed shirts, sheets, and assorted soiled linen. For a cheap meal I was taken to Chinatown, a seedy slum teeming with inscrutable men who belonged to secret societies called "Tongs" where they smoked opium and indulged in other obscene orgies. Chop suey was followed by a fortune cookie containing a slip of paper encoded with "Confucius Say." At the movies we hissed Fu Man Chu and snickered at Charlie Chan, caricatures that depicted Chinese as either sinister, sly, or too clever. Newspapers warned of coolie labor that worked for wages no self-respecting American would accept, and of the need for exclusion laws to protect America from population pollution. Of all immigrants, Chinese were the least assimilable.

So addicted was "the heathen Chinee" to opium that the British army invaded China to break the people of their vicious habit. The Opium War was followed by the Boxer Rebellion when, once again, mobs of unruly Chinese were chastised by upright Western armies, including Americans. The minions of corrupt war lords proved no match for Western rectitude and modern weapons. Such outbreaks of violence exposed Chinese as ingrates, unappreciative of the benevolence of American missionaries and millionaires who strove to imbue evil barbarians with Christian goodness. Indeed, it was only through American universities that Chinese were led out of the dark ages of their feudal past and dragged into the present. In my mind China was an ocean of impoverished humanity deserving of the condescension that accompanied our assistance.

In 1935 I experienced China firsthand, traveling from Tientsin to Shanghai on a British-built railroad, patrolled by Japanese troops, and depositing me in a city sliced into British, French, American, and other foreign concessions. These islands of Western law and order in a sea of Oriental confusion provided privileges that confirmed the white man's sense of superiority, including mine. Coolies pulled my rickshaw, and emptied my "thunder box" or chamber pot. Slit-skirted bar girls shared my bed. Bearded Sikhs kept the Chinese hordes in order, clubbing anyone who disobeyed signs advising that dogs and Chinese were not allowed in public places. None of this disturbed a young American brought up, as was I, to regard Orientals as a subhuman species.

In 1945, I went back to China with the United States Army. Chiang Kai-shek was our ally. His beauteous wife, educated in America, forged a sentimental link between our peoples. Somehow, the war effort against the Japanese was enfeebled by communists whose opposition to Chiang equated, in our minds, with antagonism against America. On a patrol in the Gobi Desert I was ambushed by a communist route army and, though released without harm, Chinese communists replaced the Japanese as our enemy. Before I left Shanghai in 1946, we Americans staged a "Rickshaw Derby" on Bubbling Well Road. A floral horseshoe was draped around the winning coolie's neck to the cheers and jeers of GIs and Seventh Fleet sailors.

Encumbered with this excess baggage, I now landed in Canton and joined the commission in its offices on the island of Shamin. My work did not go well. When rinderpest struck, killing cattle, I drew diagrams to show the causes and cure. Posters went up on village walls, in marketplaces and town halls, teaching farmers that neither poultices nor prayers could cure a sick buffalo. It had to be destroyed, stalls cleaned, and surviving animals injected with serum from the spleen of infected rabbits. Farmers squinted at the pictures, walked away, applied quack cure-alls to their dying cattle. I redrew my sketches, making them so simple the least literate farmer could not possibly miss their meaning. Their meaning remained missed.

In despair I turned to Chiang Mon-lin, one of the Chinese commissioners. He peered at my pictures through rimless glasses. "Don't worry, Ho Pong-yo," he said, using the Chinese equivalent of my name. "You are on the right track. Here in China we invented the saying that one picture is worth a thousand words. But," he added, "perhaps the picture must be Chinese."

Chiang Mon-lin was right. Adapted by a Chinese artist, the message came across. But his counsel came too late. In September

1949 Canton fell to the communists. Humbled, humiliated, fright-
ened, I was the last American to fly from White Cloud airport to
Taipei, Formosa. Reflecting on our failure, I set down an account
of our errors in China. Back home, with C. D. Jackson still on my
team, once again *Life*'s morgue provided photographs to illustrate
my text. Entitled *Through Chinese Eyes,** and bound into an
easeled portfolio for desk-top presentation, it made its debut in the
office of Chester Bowles, a former Madison Avenue mogul and
ambassador to India. Bowles flipped through the pages and
thought they deserved an hour of Truman's time. With Secretary
of State Dean Acheson and other cabinet members, the president
of the United States learned how Chinese perceptions differed
from our own.

We saw supplies sent to feed, clothe, and cure them. They saw
American goods in black markets at prices only the rich could pay.

We saw guns to defend them. They saw guns in the hands of
oppressive soldiers and police.

We saw money to lay economic foundations under progress.
They saw our dollars disappear in the pockets of corrupt politicians.

We saw output raised by tractors, trawlers, other modern
machines. They saw complicated contraptions they could neither
manage, repair, nor afford to fuel.

We saw American experts as their saviors. They saw rich, white
strangers who occupied islands of privilege in an ocean of their
poverty.

We saw America as a model to be copied, our automobiles,
appliances, and high living standards emblematic of a superior civilization. They saw our wealth as something they paid for with
their poverty.

---

*Entitled *The Only War We Seek, Through Chinese Eyes* was published by Farrar Straus
and widely distributed by Americans For Democratic Action.

Communism's tactics accented America's errors. We had worked exclusively with the wealthy, educated elites. They had infiltrated unions, barracks, schools. We had concentrated on the cities. They had gone into the villages. We dispensed charity, they political indoctrination. We had appealed to greed, prestige, power. They had exploited the human craving for work, joy, hope, dignity. We had aimed our message at the classes, they, the masses. We worked from the top down, they from the bottom up. They won. We lost.

The reasons for our failure? Ignorance. Ethnocentricity. Contempt. Condescension. Reliance on money. Blindness to the determination of a proud people to rid themselves of colonial oppression and regain their land, their pride, their spirit.

China taught several lessons. To see our actions through the eyes of others. To relate our goals and actions to the spiritual beliefs and intellectual insights of other cultures. To know and use their communication methods and not only our own. To send abroad Americans willing to soil their hands in helping others to help themselves—Americans as eager to learn as to teach. Last but not least—that power resides in the people, the political base, the constituency without which no politician can long prevail.

When I finished, Bowles pointed out that the key to peace in Asia and elsewhere lay not with bankers, brokers, soldiers, and pseudo-statesmen, on whom we expended our efforts, but on those with whom we had worked the least, the people. The president agreed and asked that, as his envoy, I convey the lessons of China to every American embassy in Asia, from Manila to Teheran. I complied and embarked on yet another journey through a troubled world.

In Vietnam the French were fighting to retain control of a rebellious colony. The American Mission—there was no embassy at the time—was torn between two courses of action. One was to affirm our support of France on the premise that it made no sense to pour Marshall Plan money into Paris and have it hemorrhage in Saigon. The other was to recognize the unpopularity of a white, Western regime among a people to whom nationalism, independence, self-government were entitlements the French withheld.

Contrary to the lessons of China, the decision was to reinforce the French, and, eventually, to replace them, with consequences few at the time foresaw. In Teheran, too, the lessons of China remained unlearned. The American Embassy wooed the Shah without an inkling that his throne was threatened by an unknown Ayatollah.

China still had much to teach.

20

Second Thoughts
on Chinese Education

Wist Hall
July 1987

THE MORE KNOWLEDGE, THE MORE EVIL

Two professors from Beijing Normal University arrive in Honolulu to offer a summer seminar on "Education in China." Dr. Yang
Zhi-ling, director of the Institute of Educational Research, is a
plump, personable man of middle age, actually an overseas Chinese from Malang, Indonesia, who returned to China to share in
its modernization. Dr. Lin Bing, a graduate of St. Mary's College
in Shanghai, is a handsome woman, a mother of two, whose experience before, during, and after the Cultural Revolution enriches
our course. Our group, small and congenial, consists of a retired
air force officer working toward a doctoral degree in education; a

lovely lady of Chinese descent with a doctoral degree in sociology; an intriguing Hawaiian woman whose background spans Alaska and China; and a young woman from Shanghai improving her English in a year of study abroad, her beauty so delicate, her demeanor so quiet, she might have stepped out of a Mandarin scroll. We meet early each morning for three weeks, studying the origins and evolution of education in a country encompassing one-fourth of the planet's population.

Centuries before Rousseau, Cotton Mather, and John Dewey, Emperors Mozi (468–376 BC) and Xunzi (313–238 BC) advanced rival theories about the nature of the child, one elevating it as an innocent creature deserving all-embracing love, the other debasing it as an inherently evil being best taught with a whip. As elsewhere, China's earliest educational institutions were religious and elitist. Sons of farmers, merchants, brothel-keepers, and daughters of whatever social or economic stamp were excluded. With the advent of St. Thomas the Apostle and eventual assistance of Western warships, modern education arrived in the eighteenth century. Missionaries, mainly American, imbued Chinese children with faith in Christ, chemistry, industry, and democracy. Borne by E. P. Cubberly, W. H. Kilpatrick, John Dewey, and other educational evangelists, Western pedagogical practice evicted Confucius and Mencius, replacing all the old verities of the Chinese past with the Dalton Plan, the Gary Plan, the Winnetka Plan, the Batavia System, the Project Method and other variants of Pestalozzi, Montessori, and McGuffey. Social studies supplanted morals. Vocational guidance, psychological screening, standardized tests, other American enthusiasms reigned, waxed, and waned. Nowhere in all the world, perhaps, could the eccentricities of American educational theory be better observed than in twentieth-century China.

With Chiang Kai-shek's assumption of power in 1928, education was employed to promote the political policies of the Kuomintang party. Based largely on the writings of Sun Yat-sen who, in 1892, in Honolulu, had established the Regenerate China Society, "Three People's Principles" stressed nationalism, democracy, and peoples' livelihood—purposes ill-served by American progressivism. American educational practice was replaced by Prussian pedagogy, pointing up national purpose, work skills, scientific excellence, and military training.

Worsened by Kuomintang incompetence, warlords' depredations, and Japanese intervention, conditions in China invited revolution. Chiang's regime collapsed. Veterans of the Long March, trained in Soviet schools or indigenous Marxist-Leninist institutes, introduced Stalinist approaches to government, economics, and education.

My comely classmate from Shanghai confides her experience in communist schools. Both her parents were physicians who, as professional people, survived the stringencies of the revolution. Living in what had hitherto been a British concession, her kindergarten and elementary schools had inherited good buildings and equipment from their earlier occupants. English somehow survived in a curriculum otherwise given more to Mandarin, math, and history. Beginning with the "Peking Man," the planet's original human being, history covered early slavery systems, feudalism, capitalism, communism's conflict with warlords, the Kuomintang, the Japanese and, in 1949, ultimate victory.

In primary school she learned "The Five Loves": "Love our great Socialist motherland. Love our great Chinese people. Love our great Chinese Communist Party. Love our great People's Liberation Army. Love our great leader Chairman Mao." Aged nine, she donned the red kerchief of the Young Pioneers; at fifteen, in high school, she joined the Young Communist League, the normal course youngsters pursued, persuaded as they were of the evils of capitalism, the rectitude of communism, the leadership of Mao, and the need, through education, to make the most of opportunities offered by a Marxist society.

A pleasant adolescence came on hard times in 1961 with the onset of three years of drought, flood, and other natural disasters, capped by a falling out with the Soviet Union. Food was short. As doctors, her parents received fewer coupons than did laborers needing higher caloric intake. However, her family managed and she, aged 13, as a student excelling in English, sciences, and maths, advanced with sixteen of the forty children in her junior high school to senior high, studying calculus, Chinese composition, chemistry, physics, and politics from a Marxist-Leninist perspective. Teachers organized children according to talents, encouraging areas in which each excelled. "Key" schools evolved, with superior teachers, textbooks, equipment, in which exceptional children received specialized instruction in preparation for university admission—duplicating the Soviet system which, despite the rupture in Sino-Soviet relations, remained the model within which almost all Chinese administrators had been trained.

Suddenly, in early June of 1966, everything changed. Students in High School No. 4 in Beijing published a paper advocating abolition of exams for university admission. The *Peoples Daily* picked it up, denounced formal education as feudalistic, revisionist, capitalist. A youth movement sprang up; Red Guards rampaged through schools, drove out teachers, replaced textbooks with the *Selected Works of Mao Zedong*. "Criticize yourself!" they commanded. "Criticize your teachers! Criticize your school! The more knowledge, the more evil!" Targeted were key schools like hers because, possessed of more knowledge, students needed more to be ideologically reformed.

Within one week all classes ended. Teachers turned against teachers. Children impeached their parents. Intellectuals faced exile, torture, death. Students were ordered out into "the real world" to labor in factories and fields. "I was lucky," my classmate recalls.

> I spent three years helping with harvests in a little Mongolian mountain village. The people were illiterate but treated us well. All around us raged the Cultural Revolution. Red Guards rode the railways free of charge, took over homes and hotels, destroyed property, brought the country to the verge of collapse. Mao lost control of the monster he had created. It was Jou Enlai who held China together until the Chairman passed away, and Deng Xiaoping returned us to sanity. English was needed, so I taught it in high school for seven years before passing a provincial exam for the Peking Foreign Language Institute, and in 1986 was sent to Hawaii to study American education.

What, I ask, do you think of American education? My Chinese classmate hesitates, overcomes her qualms and answers.

> It is crazy. I used to think Americans were the most pragmatic people in the world. I've learned you are totally bewildered, with every few years a new psychologist, a new philosopher, or new educator with a new theory that excites you, only to be dropped as the pendulum swings from one insanity to another. No wonder your nation

is at risk. No wonder your best graduate schools have become Chinatowns, filled with Asians who outscore Americans. Under the Communist Party our schools produce experts while yours turn out jacks-of-all-trades, masters of none. Don't you agree that our system is better?

I shrug. "Better, I believe, for a hundred madmen to disagree, than to have one who prevails over all of the others."

My classmate returned to China. We correspond. "I miss America," she wrote, "but it is good to be home. The cultural revolution, the gang of four, all the evils of Mao are behind us. A fresh breeze blows across the land. Students who like myself have tasted democracy are joined together to fulfill the ancient Chinese proverb: Under a mandate from heaven, the people rule."

Ever since, silence . . .

21

"Education" in Our Foreign Service

New Delhi, India
1957–1959

My pictorial essay on China, *Through Chinese Eyes,* had come to the attention of John D. Rockefeller III, founder of the Council on Cultural and Economic Affairs to extend American knowledge of Asia. As the council's first fellow, I was sent with my family to Indonesia to live among its people, the most numerous in Southeast Asia, and lay a foundation for the council's further activities in that area. It was quite a promotion from able-bodied seaman on a Rockefeller oil tanker to amateur anthropologist, but it almost proved fatal.* Devastated by malaria, my family and I returned

---

*An account of the experience can be found in *Rice Roots: An American in Asia,* published by Simon and Schuster, 1958.

home where, recovered, I accepted President Truman's invitation to join our foreign service.

I was posted to India as public affairs officer of Delhi District, serving the northern states of Rajasthan, the Punjab, and Uttar Pradesh, populated by a fourth of India's 480 million souls. Our ambassador, Ellsworth Bunker, headed a staff of upright Americans collectively dedicated to the "Country Plan," insuring that India remained resistant to communism. To this end massive infusions of money, expertise, and information flooded the country. My own role was to fuse two very different democracies by disseminating news, fostering cultural exchange, and, generally, affixing in Indian minds a favorable image of America.

Delhi District was one of four—the others, Bombay, Calcutta, Madras—presided over by a country public affairs officer (CPAO) who set policy and directed programs across all of India. Lodged in headquarters known because of its proximity to a playing field as "Golf Links," his staff comprised senior foreign service officers who had risen in the ranks by virtue of efficiency reports testifying to their superior performance in previous postings.

Our first encounter was not auspicious. A conference of all PAOs* was called to meet with an emissary from the Information Agency's headquarters in Washington. His arrival could not have been better timed. The year was 1957. From Lebanon, keystone in an arch of Levantine states fringing the eastern Mediterranean, had come the first inkling of events destined to engage America, from that day to this, in a series of catastrophic crises. The pro-Western policies of President Camille Chamoun were under attack from Druse tribesmen and Syrian subversives. The Egyptian fleet, beefed up by Soviet submarines, seemed ready to strike. How Washington responded to this threat to Lebanese independence was of crucial importance in India which, despite two billion dollars of American aid, regarded Russia as India's real best friend. A tenderfoot like myself badly needed guidance on how the crisis might be controlled.

The country public affairs officer, my boss, was a large man of benign manner, with a PhD in education. As an officer in General

---

*Public affairs officers (PAOs) are members of the country team headed in each country by our ambassador. They staff the United States Information Service (USIS) operations overseas. Parent organization of USIS is the United States Information Agency (USIA) in Washington, an autonomous activity directly under the president.

MacArthur's Civil Information and Education Section, he had been instrumental in putting Japan's school system on its postwar path. His experience as an education officer in Japan and foreign service officer in India intrigued me. From him, I felt sure, I had much to learn. I was not to be disappointed.

The meeting began with a reminder of our mission in India—to present the policies and objectives of the United States to government officials, educators, managers of communications media, and other "gatekeepers" through whom we gained access to the public. Praise was bestowed on Golf Links' press officer for a record number of column inches of newspaper space gained by his handouts. Cited was an item captioned "Bananas Have Nerves," revealing results of America's scientific inquiry into the anatomy of a banana. The popularity of American jazz, movies, and other evidence of our cultural impact on India was also applauded, at which point the conference was turned over to the Washington emissary whose arrival coincided with the Lebanese crisis.

He brought, he said, splendid news. A career legislation bill before Congress requested the same rights guaranteed State Department personnel—tenure, pensions, and other perquisites—for agency employees. Next, a new policy promised that officers would sandwich two years of domestic duty between every four years of service overseas. Third, recognizing India's crucial importance to America's interests in Asia, agency budgeteers were prepared to give sympathetic attention to our needs. Suggestions were requested as to how additional funding could be expended.

Branch PAOs swiftly responded. One asked for money to erect an animated electric "ticker tape" around his building in downtown Calcutta. It would flash news about America, "like the revolving sign in New York's Times Square." Bombay required hi-fi equipment that, installed in Indian schools, would capitalize on the craze for American jazz. "The syllogism," he said, "is obvious. Indians like jazz. Jazz is American. Therefore Indians like America." Madras urged calendars advertising the United States Information Service. It was agreed that Golf Links request funds for one hundred thousand calendars illustrated with scenes of Americans at work and play.

As the greenest of the conferees, I was confused. Lebanon had somehow gotten lost in all that good news from Washington. Electric signs and jazz didn't seem adequate answers to India's poverty.

Granting that calendars were fine for advertising hair tonic or Coca-Cola, they didn't seem likely to convince many Hindus that America was concerned with shortages of rice and other indices of their economic plight. Since American aid was intended to galvanize the villages where most Indians lived, I asked whether it might not be best to support the Community Development Program on which Prime Minister Nehru placed such stress. Golf Links scoffed. To waste time, money, and effort on illiterate peasants would distract us from our main targets, the educated elites who influenced all that mattered in India. On that note the meeting ended.

One week later, on July 15, 1958, United States forces hit the beaches off Beirut. Indian anger erupted. Mobs marched on the American embassy. Our offices and libraries were cordoned by police. The Press Trust of India bombarded readers with evidence of America's iniquity. I awaited Golf Links' response. None was forthcoming, and Delhi District took independent action. An article placing our Lebanese position in the perspective of time was circulated to Indian press and radio organizations.

For 400 years, I argued, Arabs endured alien rule. Not until an American university was established in Beirut in 1866 did the ideals of the American Revolution ignite an intellectual and political renaissance that swept the Mediterranean from Alexandria to Aleppo. Three out of four of today's Arab leaders had attended its classes. Here Arab nationalism found a father and a friend. An American President, Woodrow Wilson, espoused the Arab cause after World War I, liberating Lebanon, Syria, and Egypt from French and British rule. In November 1956, the time of the Suez crisis, American intervention preserved Egyptian integrity at the risk of alienating our closest allies, England and Israel. Eisenhower's action in Lebanon committed America once again to the preservation of peace and freedom in the middle east.

Delhi District's statement was published and aired across the length and breadth of India. Editorials in *The Statesman, The Times of India,* and other leading dailies, including the vernacular, reconsidered the American move. Our recitation of America's role in the Middle East reduced hysteria and invited reflection.

Rather than cementing Delhi District's relationship with Golf Links, publication of the Lebanese piece widened a wedge between the Country PAO and myself. My policy was to lower the Ameri-

can profile, to embargo such trivia as "bananas have nerves," and
to bid for news space and air time only when we had something to
say of importance to India. I refused to exhibit films from Washington that flaunted our wealth before indigent Indians. In forays
afield, I preferred peasants, workers, and students to affluent
audiences. None of this accorded with Golf Links' desire for max-
imizing column inches in the Indian press, influencing elites, and
awing India with the magnitude and magnificence of the American
presence.

A pile of crates languished in an empty lot outside the embassy.
They contained an exhibit produced by the Advertising Council of
America. Captioned "Peoples' Capitalism," its purpose was to
address the source of India's antagonism to America: capitalism.
Golf Links believed that if anything could arouse greater wrath in
India than Americans landing in Lebanon, it would be to display
the economic mechanism that made America tick. Bolstering its
position was the current copy of *Foreign Affairs,* the American
quarterly of political commentary. It contained an article criticiz-
ing Peoples' Capitalism as "a pure distillate of boisterous enterprise and undiluted laissez-faire that made little or no contact with
the realities of Indian economic life." Its author, destined to
become our next ambassador to India, was John Kenneth Galbraith.

Galbraith's article vindicated Golf Links' decision to leave the
"People's Capitalism" exhibit to the mercy of the impending mon-
soon. Capitalism's reputation further supported its stand. Since
World War II, multinational corporations, mostly American, were
seen as a sinister means whereby capitalism exploited the natural
and human resources of Asia and Africa. The boom-and-bust
swings of America's economy, coupled with persistent unemployment, persuaded Congress party politicians that capitalism was
inefficient and corrupt. Influenced during his Cambridge days by
British socialists like Harold Laski and Stafford Cripps, Jawa-
harlal Nehru deemed the profit motive "vulgar." During a visit to
Moscow in 1927 he had been impressed with Marxism-Leninism,
dialectical materialism, and five-year planning. Deeply embedded
in the Indian psyche was a prejudice against the private sector. As
far back as 300 BC, an Indian emperor, Kautilya, had ruled that
profits be regulated, and that the nation's economy be controlled

by the state. In the Indian mind, two evils, capitalism and colonialism, were inseparably connected.

Opposed to this evidence justifying India's antipathy to capitalism was the simple fact that the socialist path for which it opted proved disastrous to India's economy. Decision making, concentrated in New Delhi, was time-consuming, labored, inefficient. Refusal to license private sector industry curbed competition, discouraged innovation, stifled growth, encouraged graft. To maintain their monopolies, corporations already in existence applauded the government's parsimony toward wider privatization and bribed officials for the licenses, permits, and dispensations they needed. Socialism induced inertia in agriculture and industry and doomed cottage industries to remain a zero factor in India's growth potential. Thus, India's socialism since independence had steered a crash course with American capitalism. Without a buffer between the two opposing systems, Indo-American amity was a facade masking a deep and dangerous division.

My mind retreated to the day in 1935 when, searching for Indian regimentals, I happened upon the father of Indian independence. Might understanding of Gandhi's Vedic faith contain a key to so stubborn a stalemate? Between man and God, Gandhi taught, was unity. The gulf between the two was *avidya* "ignorance." Ignorance could be overcome by self-realization. Only the individual could bring about the inner change needed to regenerate society. The state could not make man moral. Enforced morality denied morality. Individual freedom and initiative formed the bases of moral life—recognition of an individual's responsibility toward others, advancing the good of all.

Capital, Gandhi reasoned, was good. In some form, capital would always be needed. The man who created capital was worthy of respect. Evil consisted of the wrong use to which capital was put. To concentrate capital in any single source, be it an individual, a corporation, a monopoly, a cartel, or the state was evil. The more widely capital was dispersed and used as a trust serving the welfare of all, the better for society. *Sarvodaya* "the welfare of all" could best be achieved by self-help, voluntarism, individual initiative, decentralization of power, and a parallel emphasis on social responsibility.

The spinning wheel served as Gandhi's signature. It was a simple machine. Gandhi was not averse to machinery. Nothing prohibited its use so long as it served the welfare of all. *Sarvodaya,* an Indian principle centuries old, rather than dividing the two democracies, was a bond that, understood and employed, could provide the prosperity, freedom, and peace both peoples desired.

The crates of "Peoples' Capitalism" contained labor-saving devices that multiplied output, lowered costs, broadened markets, enhanced income. We exhibited these machines in a spectacle entitled *Sarvodaya*. Multitudes of Indians packed the aisles, examined the exhibits, pondered their meaning. Many recognized that two peoples bound together by an abiding belief in democratic government were riven by opposing systems, not so much of economics as of education. Mind-sets established by ideologies and cemented by teachers and texts in contesting schools of economic theory had placed the two greatest democracies on earth in diametrically different capitalist and socialist camps. Here, at long last, was reconciliation.

As had the piece on the Lebanese crisis, so did *Sarvodaya* soften Indian prejudice against America. "Is mechanization of production consistent with the Gandhian ideal of decentralized economy?" asked *The Times of India*. "The U.S. Exhibition answers in the affirmative." *The Statesman* noted "how Mahatma Gandhi's ideas have been put into practice in America. Mahatma Gandhi believed, the Exhibit points out, that machinery lightens the burdens of the poor man and that it has come to stay. Also it stresses his belief that only in a free society can the poor prosper. *Sarvodaya* is proof of the understanding that serious study and genuine respect can bring about. Having come to a meeting of the minds about Capitalism, there is no problem Indians and Americans cannot resolve in a similar spirit."

Sarvodaya was small potatoes compared with a multimillion dollar agricultural extravaganza that the United States was about to stage in New Delhi. Requested by Washington to submit a theme, Golf Links came up with "The American Farmer Salutes the Farmers of India," a slogan illustrated by an American plowman standing stiffly at attention, chin up, stomach in, right hand arched above the eyebrow. Washington rejected the submission and asked that Delhi District devise a more suitable solution. Working with Minoru Yamasaki, architect of the building, and Jack Masey who had made his mark in Moscow as designer of the exhibit that pitted Nixon and Khruschev in the kitchen confrontation, we billed the agricultural exhibition as *Ameriki Mela* "American Country Fair," preserving the American farmers' civilian status and harmonizing American and Indian outlooks on agriculture.

I was ordered back to Washington with Golf Links' ultimate accolade, the lowest rating a foreign service officer could earn short of dishonorable discharge. It did not really rate my inefficiency so much as my insubordination. Oddly, the distance separating me from Hindus and Muslims was no wider than a ditch, while between me and the country PAO and his staff yawned a gulf broader than an ocean. Why?

The answer lay, at least in part, in education. With few exceptions, our foreign service recruited intelligent, well-educated individuals, the cream of the collegiate crop. The country PAO held a doctorate degree, as did many other men and women who Washington sent overseas. What did this signify? What did the discipline demanded by the degree do to the academic mind? As I understood it, the PhD process was deeply committed to epistemology, the theory of knowledge. What of its corollary, agnoiology, the theory of ignorance? Did the deeper a PhD dig himself into the subject of his thesis result in ignorance of, or indifference to, all that existed outside his hole?

What, I wondered, had the country PAO accomplished in Japan in setting that country's school system on its postwar path? One day I would go to Japan and seek the answer to so provocative a question.

22

The Dean's December

Spring semester is over. I pause to examine the paperchase to date. Mainly it has been reading, seminars, and writing papers, by and large with profit and an accumulation of A's. Without Karier I would not know how capricious has been the course of American education, how un-American are the educational ideas that under-lay our schools, or that, had I been born a decade later, my Latin and math debacles might have been averted. Without Diane Ra-vitch's account of the New York City "school wars," of which I was a victim, I would be blind to political pressures on the city's system when I was a pupil in P.S. 171. Without James Russell's paean of praise for German higher schools, the rationale of the Board of Regents would remain a riddle, as would be the impact of Prussian pedagogy on scientific excellence and military aggression. For the first time I appreciate how "scholarship," even so superficial and inept as mine, illumines experience, opens vistas, and invites exploration into territory hitherto hidden from my eyes and mind.

On the other hand, never have I felt so imprisoned within a space so circumscribed, the larger world outside the classroom excluded, all other interests sacrificed to an overriding obligation —mastery of that most elusive of mysteries, the human mind. The literature of higher education is often dogma, buttressed by borrowings to the point of professionally validated plagiarism, enveloped in ambiguous prose, composed in jarring jargon. Knowledge is "epistemology." Learning is "cognition." Kids are "cohorts." Digging ever deeper into the subsoil of theory, daylight dims, darkness descends, vision is obscured by the slag heaps of data surrounding the excavation in which I burrow. Creativity, imagery, freedom of thought and expression are buried beneath the pedagogic paydirt piled up by the doctoral shovel.

The great panjandrums of pedagogy ask more questions than either they or I can answer. "Dare the school build a new social order?" asks George Counts. "American education: has the pendulum swung too far?" asks Diane Ravitch. "Are we left only to envy the innocent confidence of a bygone age?" asks Lawrence Cremin. "Why was false vocationalism ever introduced into our schools?" asks Mortimer Adler. Something dubious, querulous, delirious, infects education. As the surgeon general says about cigarettes, addiction to education can be hazardous to health.

As I write, the *Chronicle of Higher Education* for May 1987 circulates into my office. This is the trade paper that feeds university presidents, professors, administrators with what they want and need to know. I list the page-one headlines:

2 Year Colleges Lobbying Aggressively for
Added State Money and Programs.

Administration Bars Science-Agency Aid to Vienna Institute.

Scholars Conducting Research Abroad Are Hit Hard by
High Costs Resulting from the Dollars' Decline.

Surge in Gifts by Individuals Pushes Private Aid to
Colleges to $7.4 Billion.

Benefits and Outside Income Boost College Presidents'
Compensation, but in Some States, the Perks Sometimes
Produce a Political Backlash.

I rub my eyes in disbelief. If such is the stuff on which educators feed, no wonder classrooms stink of their excreta.

Since it is summer, and I have earned respite from the semester's stress and strain, I turn to lighter morsels with which to amuse my mind, and come upon a paperback of Saul Bellow's, *The Dean's December.* In it I read:

> I see poison thought or poison theory. The view we hold of the material world may put us into a case as heavy as lead, a sarcophagus which nobody will even have the art to paint becomingly. The end of philosophy and art will do to "advanced" thought what flakes of lead paint or leaded exhaust fumes do to infants. Which of these do you think will bring us to the end of everything? . . . Real philosophy, not the groveling stuff the universities mainly do. Otherwise: I remember how I used to stare at Mendeleev's chart in the science class. There it all was—Fe, Cu, Na, He. That's what we were made of. I was so impressed! That's what everything was made of . . . and if pure scientists had really understood science they would have realized the morality and poetry implicit in its laws. They didn't. So it's all going to run down the drain, like blood in a Hitchcock movie. The Humanists have also flunked the course. They have no strength because they're ignorant of science. They're bound to be weak because they have no conception of what the main effort of the human mind has been for three centuries and what it has found. . . . I must go back to the classroom and learn what it's all about—*really.* When I've understood the beauty and morality contained in the laws of science, I can take in the decisive struggle—begin to restore the strength of Humanism.

Has any educator ever said it better?

23

Fish Cry, but You Can't See the Tears . . .

West Africa
1960

Another president, Jack Kennedy. Another director of the United States Information Agency, Ed Murrow. Murrow and I had undergone the blitz in Britain. After a few minutes of reminiscence, he said he appreciated my efforts in India. "Maybe we should try your approach in Africa. The only Africans we know are the Bintu." Murrow smiled at my puzzlement and explained. "The Bintu tribe are Africans who have been to London, been to Paris, been to New York—Western-educated elites who eat with knives and forks, and talk better English than you and I. About Africans who live in the bush, we know nothing. Would you be willing to go to Africa, mix with the masses, and learn how we and they can connect?"

I would. The area of my assignment embraced all of West Africa, from Senegal to Zaire. Riding buses from village to village, eating foofoo, a vegetable stew, with my fingers, picked up by fellow travelers who took me to their homes, living with their families and friends, I came to know a people who opened their hearts and minds to a curious stranger. Excerpts from my African journal:

Sierra Leone: Circles of men squat within earshot of a transistor radio, listening to the national news in Krio, the singsong pidgin patois spoken by descendants of repatriated English slaves. A bouncy high life tune sets the theme of my African adventure:

> Come know me at home
> Come see me at home
> You don't reach my home
> You don't know me.
> Friend, come and see me
> You don't reach my home
> You can't know me.

Buses are called "mammy wagons." Each is inscribed with a motto. "Remember your six feet" means man is mortal. "One man no chop" means a lonely man has no appetite. "Abomination has no remedy" means hatred is a sickness of the soul and cannot be cured. A driver asks whether American buses also have slogans. I nod. "If you can read this you're too damned close." Everyone laughs. A market-woman says, "The coops are different but the chickens all have fleas."

We stop beneath a peepul tree, relieve ourselves in the underbrush, and buy foofoo from local vendors. Gossip is swapped. I learn about Big Mammy Berry, a wealthy business woman whose shiftless husband beats her with a stick. She runs off with her lover, leaving her husband without a farthing. An argument ensues about Big Mammy Berry's behavior. Men agree that a wife owes everything to her husband. "A marriage vow may get moldy but it never decays." A woman replies, "Don't tell a wife who is carrying you across the river that she stinks unless you want to get wet."

A mother unbuttons her bodice and presses a nipple between her baby's lips. He pushes it away and emits a lusty cry. The mother soothes him with a song:

> Hush little baby
> Don't cry
> An evil one will hear your voice
> And you will die.

I tell the woman that when I was a baby, my own mother sang much the same song to me. She smiles. "All the earth is a mother. Mother Earth is God's wife."

I visit a village school underneath an enormous cotton tree. Twenty boys and girls, ages six to twelve, recite the names of the months in Mende. January is *pele gbaa,* skeleton of the house, because January is when people build new homes. February is *vui,* sound of the wind. During March women must cook in the morning because danger from cookfires is greatest in the afternoon breeze, so March is called *nya woi,* meaning that women who disobey the law against afternoon cooking are fined. April is *bunui,* time to sow rice. And so on, to September, *saa,* a warning not to cross rivers in spate. November is mist moon, a month of heavy dew. December is called *pondo* or "footprint," because the wind dries the mud, leaving footprints in the land.

The children ask what our months mean in America. I shrug. "I haven't a clue." "How strange," says the teacher. "None of us can read or write, but every child knows the meaning of the months."

The teacher turns to history. An eight year old recites:

The Mende have had many lady chiefs—the Fangowa of Wando, Caulkey of Shengeh, Madame Yoko, paramount chieftainess of the Mende Confederacy. Yoko was born to a poor family near Tiama. As a child she danced more gracefully than any other girl in the province. The local chief, an old man, took her in marriage but died before she could conceive a son. After the funeral, Gbanya, chief of Senahun, took Yoko with him as his wife. Yoko started a *Sande* society and taught girls to dance, weave, cook and to become midwives. They were in great demand as wives and concubines. When Gbanya died, Yoko was elected paramount chief. She made the Mende the most powerful tribe in the territory. Then, having drunk deep of power, she took poison and died.

"No one," the child concludes, "rules forever on the throne of time." The children then recite together: "But even when the cotton tree falls, it is higher than the jungle around it."

There are no arithmetic texts, but the children have coins to count while singing a song of sixpence:

> He who doesn't have sixpence is not honored.
> Everyone who doesn't have sixpence is called a fool.
> Without sixpence, a man can't open his mouth.
> Without sixpence, women can't stand your smell.
> But if you have sixpence you get respect.
> He who has sixpence cannot tell a lie.
> Everyone believes him. No one contradicts him.
> Because you have sixpence, people point you out as a great man.

I ask the teacher where she studied education. She laughs. "My only school is my tribe, the Mende." "But you have no books, no pencils, no paper. How can you teach?" "I do not teach," she answers. "The children learn because they love our songs and stories. Do you have 'learning songs' in America?" "Oh yes," I chant, "one and one are two. Two and two are four."

The teacher tells a story about the birds getting ready for a big feast in the sky. The tortoise begs to go along, so the birds give him enough feathers for a pair of wings and he flies with them to the feast. On the way the tortoise tells the birds that it is customary for God's guests to assume special names before partaking of food. The birds believe the tortoise and change their names. The tortoise calls himself "All-of-you." God greets them in heaven, pours palm wine and serves foofoo. The tortoise asks God, "For whom has this foofoo been cooked?" God replies "For all of you." And so the tortoise eats all the food. The angry birds take away his wings and the tortoise tumbles back to earth. "And that is why," the teacher says, "the tortoise's shell is cracked."

Not far from the cotton tree stands a hut larger than any other in the village. It is the *Porro* where, at puberty, every Mende boy lives for several weeks mastering tribal ritual, martial arts, the secrets of sex. Riddles sharpen the boys' minds.

"The old man is inside the hut but his beard is outside"—smoke from a cookfire inside a house. "The same boiled yam journeys around the world"—the moon. "A fat wife lives within a hedge of thorns"—tongue and teeth. "The chief eats with his asshole, farts with his mouth"—a gun. Asked whether we have riddles in America, I recall the old newspaper wheeze: "What is black and white and read all over?" The village voodoo man answers. "It is America. Black men, white men and blood all over."

I explain that since slavery was ended by the Civil War, progress has been made in civil rights. The voodoo man replies that "A pig shouldn't brag that he's fat." I insist that I do not brag; what I say is truth I can prove with facts and figures. The voodoo man senses my anger. "Don't get so angry in your head that you wear your hat on your behind." Realizing that facts and figures make matters worse, I fall silent.

The chief invites me to his hut, lights a cheroot, and offers advice. "Mende," he says, "don't believe the white man's facts and figures. They are tortoise-talk, lies that you tell to gain an advantage over others who cannot read books and memorize information. To Mende, proverbs are the cavalry of discussion. In a palaver, he who can outflank his adversary with the right proverb wins the fight. A palaver without proverbs is like trying to spear a lion with a straw. If you want to win an argument in Africa, you must master our proverbs."

I follow the chief's advice and, in time, I learn to parry the voodoo man's barbs. "America," he charges, "wants war, otherwise it would lay down its weapons." I reply that only a foolish man sells his sword and wears the sheath to battle. "Why," he asks, "so many swords?" I say, "You don't bridle a bear with thread." "America," he counters, "is a cracked tortoise. It eats all the world's food and leaves others to starve. Better for Africa to seek help from Russia." "Beware the naked man," I warn, "who promises to clothe you."

The voodoo man and I become friends. "Look," I say, "it is better to trade proverbs than blows, but this will not save us from another war. How can the world be rid of all the hatred that threatens to destroy it?" The voodoo man tells about a woman who went to a witch doctor to complain about her husband's neglect. "What can I do," she asked, "to regain his love?" The witch doctor told her to bring him three hairs from a lion's mane. "When I have the lion's hairs in my hand, I will answer your question."

A ferocious lion lived in the bush behind the woman's hut. Each night she staked a lamb outside her door on which the lion feasted. In time he was tamed, allowing the woman to rub his stomach and stroke his head. Thus it was easy, having earned the lion's love, to pluck three hairs and bring them to the witch doctor. "How did you get these hairs?" he asked. The woman explained. "Each night I fed the lion a tender lamb, rubbed his belly, and stroked his head. It was easy, once I won his trust, to pluck the hairs. And now," she demanded, "how can I regain my husband's love?" "The same way," said the witch doctor, "as you plucked the three hairs from the lion's head."

Senegal, Gambia, Guinea, Liberia, Ivory Coast, Mali, Upper Volta, Ghana, Niger, Cameroon, Gabon, Nigeria—I visited thirty-two villages. The coops were different but the chickens all had fleas. Songs, stories, proverbs varied, but all had wit, warmth, and wisdom.

In each capital I met with American Embassy officers, cadged a bath, a drink, and dinner. Eyeing my rags and tatters and learning of my mission, they could hardly hide their horror.

One PAO neatly summed up the conventional wisdom of the foreign service. "Suppose," he said, "I had a budget of just $50 to influence opinion in this country. What better way to spend it than to treat the minister of education to the best lunch $50 could buy and induce him to install a course on American civilization in the local college? Or to present the president with a transistor radio tuned to the Voice of America? Or to offer school children a $50 prize for the best essay on Abraham Lincoln? What alternative is there to making our pitch to the big shots?"

I answered that I'd invest $5 in a bus ticket to the boondocks, live off the land, talk with the locals, and learn what they had on their minds. The remaining $45 I'd turn back to the taxpayers. Why? Because our Constitution begins with "We the People"—not we the bankers, the brokers, the gatekeepers. No politician can survive a crisis without a constituency on which he can count to sustain his position of power. What reputable president or minister of education could be bought for $50? Tribal people might seem backward and, by our standards, bizarre, but they are the political base, the legitimization of power. Unless American policy is true to American principle, we would consistently be snookered by tyrants and dictators.

The year was 1960. Vietnam, Angola, Iran, Nicaragua, Panama hadn't yet happened.

As in India, so in Africa; our foreign service officers were educated individuals who had passed rigid examinations to qualify as representatives of our country overseas. Compared with their degrees, my competence was questionable. Regarded as a weirdo "gone native," I scored no points. My only hope was that Ed Murrow would understand, and help to shift American policy from what seemed to be its fatal course. But when I returned to Washington, Ed Murrow was dead of the Big C, and everyone else cared more about the Bintus than the barbarians in the bush. Without a future in the foreign service, I quit.

Fish cry, but you can't see the tears because of the river.

24

The Life and Death of New College

University of Hawaii
Honolulu, 1970

As earlier noted, my family and I had been smitten with malaria in Indonesia. We were salvaged by the American ambassador, Howard Jones and his wife Marylou. They took us into their home in Djakarta, restored our strength, and sent us off to Switzerland to recover. Upon retirement from the foreign service, Jones became chancellor of the East-West Center in Honolulu. Established in 1960 by the United States Congress, the center brought together "the wise men of east and west" to mingle their expertise in such areas as demography, resource development, and cross-cultural communication. At Jones' invitation I became his assistant, a position in which I served as the center's link with the

126

University of Hawaii on whose campus it was situated. By coincidence, president of the university was Harlan Cleveland, a former State Department official who had been favorably impressed by my work in China with the Joint Commission on Rural Reconstruction, and by my publications on China, India, and Indonesia. Thus, through blind chance and a chain of empathetic chums, I leaped from the depths of diplomacy to the heights of academe—a transfer from the frying pan of the foreign service into the fire of the schoolhouse.

The fire burned brightly as a fledgling experiment in humanistic education was born in Honolulu. Conception had occurred a few years before my arrival when a Council of Humanities had been created at the University of Hawaii to counter the exaggerated impetus given scientific and technological studies by Russia's Sputnik. A brilliant young professor, Richard Rapson, was appointed to formulate a theme whereby the roles of history, biography, philosophy, religion, and the arts could be dramatized in a year-long festival of concerts, exhibits, seminars centering on humanistic subjects. Rapson came up with a very different solution to the plight of the humanities than the council intended. Rather than a festival with a lifetime of a single year, he recommended the creation of a small college, humanistically oriented, with an interdisciplinary curriculum stressing independent study, self-governed by faculty and students who lived and learned together in a residential setting. Named "New College," Rapson put the proposition to Cleveland in 1969.

Cleveland seized on the proposal. Student opposition to the Vietnam War enhanced a pervasive sense of dissatisfaction with higher education in Hawaii. New College, he felt, opened vistas that might quell unrest, deal with irrelevancy, replace strictly structured curricula and habits of governance with fresh outlooks and opportunities. The concept of an interstice of smallness within the enormous campus that UH had become went farther than the festival the council had envisioned. Cleveland provided $50,000 from his discretionary funds to finance the first year, plus a hidden subvention from the regular academic departments in the form of part-time participation of professors.

Such were the circumstances of New College's birth. Rapson, idealistic, imaginative, optimistic. Cleveland, a president with wide experience in world affairs, hospitable to fresh thinking, courageous enough to take calculated risks. A faculty enlisted of enthusiastic volunteers, eager to prove the importance of a humanistic ingredient in an educational system running wild into science. It was a concept, in short, promising release from habits by which higher education was shackled, freeing faculty to teach with less administrative intercession, allowing hearts and minds of students to soar in a collegial environment of their own creation. The euphoria that attended New College's inauguration was easy to understand. When again might a modern university have such a chance to balance the hard sciences' sexy allure with the weight of the humanities' wisdom?

On September 8, 1970, New College was born with suitable ceremony. Rapson's inaugural address identified the ills of higher education that New College hoped to heal. It deemed examinations, grades, credits "a pathetic numbers game" played by standard institutions. At the same time, it was not a do-it-yourself refuge from rigorous learning, a pulpit for political dogmatists, a hippie-haven. In the openness of its options, in its challenge to accepted academic practice, in its democratic procedures rested the fledgling institution's claim to being new. In them lay its potential for uniqueness, for excellence, and, as it proved, for infinite trouble.

Hardly had the introductory remarks ended than a counterculture advocate rose to warn students to avoid "head trips" offered by Cleveland, Rapson, and other speakers. Stressing "sensitivity sessions" and other approaches to "self-realization," he invited the audience to join him on a "blind walk" in which "the heart would take over from the head." Tenured faculty struck back, arguing for intellectual content, critical evaluation, solid structure. Another altercation erupted over the granting of degrees. Authorization of degrees by the director of liberal studies in the conventional College of Arts and Sciences, some contended, compromised the integrity of the infant institution.

Thus, from its first breath, were presaged problems that resisted resolution. Chagrined by the substitution of New College for the festival they preferred, the defunct Humanities Council harbored hard feelings. That New College had come into being without consent of the State Legislature, the Faculty Senate, and the Board of Regents invited their rancor. Rapson's resort to a student group to flesh out the curricular bones of the newborn academy upset a long tradition of faculty authority. Established departments viewed the upstart as competition for pinchpenny funds. That urbane educators have long memories and sharp knives became evident as New College crept through its infancy.

According to one participant,

> We learned things about the academic mind that are concealed in conventional classrooms. In one social science course four campus personalities met in mortal combat, attacking each other with personal ferocity, dealing low blows, the "how can you be so stupid" approach. Professors among whom little prior contact had occurred could not cope with each other except at a level of insult—a sad example of how specialization fractures any sense of unity in education.

At the onset of New College's second year I joined it as chairperson of a second culture course, the object of which was to relate American actions overseas to the nature of other, mainly Asian, societies. The content of the course evolved from several questions: How had Vietnam happened? What did Americans know about the Vietnamese? What was missing in our education about ourselves and others? How could theory and reality be reconciled? My own role was the provision of episodic information that brought issues down from the theoretical stratosphere to actual experience. It said something about New College that I, despite a catastrophic academic record, could chair a course on other cultures, and assume a role conventionally played by a credentialed professor.

As the second year progressed, the worst seemed over. Counterculture personalities phased out. A tightening of academic and administrative control increased tutorial responsibility for student performance, established greater equivalency with University requirements. Critics of the first year's chaos changed their tune. "It was a hell of a year in a positive sense. Much work. Real content. We blew each others' minds. Nothing like a normal classroom. The level of discussion high and tense but never insulting." Challenging students to "creative frustration," in one professor's opinion, enabled them "to learn more in New College in one year than many graduate students learned in five." While such a sentiment seemed extreme, it suggested that New College had hit its stride and was fulfilling its promise.

So successful was New College's performance that Rapson believed it best for him to leave before, as he put it, "the founder became more important than the idea." Recalling the fate of other experimental institutions and their architects—Tussman at Berkeley, Wofford at Westbury, Albers at Bennington—he sought a successor. Consistent with its self-image as an innovative institution democratically directed by faculty and students, a committee was set up to select Rapson's replacement. Rather than a single individual, the committee recommended a "troika" of two faculty persons and one student. This was rejected by Cleveland who desired a fully tenured faculty member with the academic respectability and administrative responsibility Rapson had so admirably personified. The New College committee met Cleveland's requirement by openly appointing a tenured social science professor to succeed Rapson, and secretly adding a student and second faculty person as covert codirectors of the college.

As it happened, the second faculty person secretly to serve in the clandestine troika was a woman who, denied tenure by the English department, had filed a class action lawsuit against the university for sexist discrimination, followed by a second suit claiming equal pay for equal work. A separate action brought her into open contention with the dean of Arts and Sciences who charged that, after her contract had been signed by herself and the dean, she had illegally added stipulations without his consent, leading him to invalidate her employment. She was officially ordered to leave Vancouver House, New College's home, and to desist from any further participation in its affairs.

Within New College it was decided openly to conform to the dean's proscription, but secretly to defy it. The litigious lady continued to participate "invisibly" in New College's direction while a petition was filed for her reinstatment. Faced with what he regarded as devious behavior bordering on insubordination, Cleveland's response was to terminate New College and integrate its activities with ongoing arts and sciences programs—a decision the effect of which was postponed until an independent investigation could be completed of New College's overall performance.

In a New College meeting, the nominal director announced the situation was beyond his control and turned the matter of survival over to the students. By a vote of 66 to 10 the students chose as director-designee the litigious lady. Cleveland quoted his favorite

French phrase: *Il faut vouloir les conséquences de ce qu'en veut* "You've got to not only want what you want; you've got to want what it leads to."

What it led to was a sentence of death ratified by independent investigators who condemned New College on several counts:

> There is no sense of the specific goals of courses . . . no sense of outcomes by which it can be judged . . . impossible to get a clear picture of students' achievement . . . class discussions degenerate into free-wheeling exercises in unexamined self-expression without leadership from an instructor . . . faculty members are often mere amateurs not always familiar with the subject matter of their courses . . . difficulty in development of a coherent, well-directed curriculum.

The list was long and lethal.

At which point there occurred something akin to a miracle. New College students decided themselves to address the decision to guillotine their school and, on their own, without faculty participation, to present their case for its preservation. Respectfully, with none of the mental confusion and brazen indiscretion that characterized their earlier behavior, they appealed the death sentence. New College, they affirmed, was being judged on the basis of the self-same conventional assumptions it had been established to challenge. Their case was restated by Henry Kariel, a political science professor: "Educational institutions should be designed to invite the charge that they squander their assets and talents. They must risk being called wasteful. Their courses of inquiry, experiments, trips and explorations are properly experienced as disorganized, unplanned and deranged—in a word, messy. We learn only in educational structures that are continuously redesigned in the very process of living. Learning takes place on the run."

The investigating committee listened, wavered, and withdrew to reconsider. It concluded that New College should be given three more years of life to correct its faults and demonstrate its merits. The decision was approved by the Arts and Sciences Senate, endorsed by the dean, ratified by the chancellor of Manoa Campus, and passed upward to the central administration. Magically, the agonizing fanfaronade of the students' meetings ended. Doubts about participatory democracy were dispelled. The superiority of experiential over didactic education was demonstrated. If this was what a college could accomplish in three short years, there was hope for humanity.

The die, however, was cast. After due consideration of the students' plea, the Board of Regents subcommittee on academic planning declared New College's name a misnomer. It was neither new nor a college. Its birth, illegitimate. Its objectives, unclear and everchanging. Its method, essentially tutorial, expensive, and unfair to all but 400 of the university's 23,000 students. Its quality, either substandard in terms of arts and sciences equivalency, or, where high, not replicable in the larger university except at enormous expense.

At eleven-thirty on the morning of August 9, 1973, New College expired. It was my task to gather the facts, interview the participants, and write the final record.* What killed New College? Suicide? Political fatuity? Treachery? Was Harlan Cleveland a Brutus faithless at the end to all he had earlier professed? Ego—the determination of a litigious lady to hold New College hostage to the satisfaction of her grievances and ambitions? Murder—a knife plunged into New College's heart by vengeful regents outraged by New College's illegitimacy?

It was anybody's guess and beyond my ability to render judgment. All I knew was that a university, believed by many to be a haven of accumulated wisdom, distilled by ages into disciplines designed to ameliorate error, seemed more like a jungle in which— in the name of the humanities—academic animals snarled, struggled, and salivated over the mangled entrails of education.

---

*The record, entitled *The Life and Death of New College,* exists in a limited edition in University of Hawaii libraries.

25

"Education" at Sea . . .

Semester at Sea
1977

Did any doubt exist that there is life after death, it vanished as, on February 15, 1977, amid flights of frisbees, tooting of horns, clouds of confetti, the SS *Universe* edged from its dock in the Port of Los Angeles and plowed into the Pacific. Packed into the 13,950 tons of gleaming white vessel were 473 students whose education, under the aegis of the University of Colorado and the Institute for Shipboard Education, would derive less from lectures, textbooks, and tests than from actual experience overseas. Among the faculty were Richard Rapson and me. Sorrow over New College's demise gave way to joy as we joined the students' song:

> Gazing out beyond sight's reach
> We hold fast to the railing

Fantasizing the world we will meet
When we get to where we're sailing.
From behind the boundaries of desire
It seems illusory
That the shaping of our future dreams
Lay within this world we soon would see.

The world we soon would see comprised Korea, Taiwan, Hong Kong, Singapore, India, Sri Lanka, Egypt, Greece, Tunis, and Morocco, a voyage of one hundred days. Legions of young men and women had already enjoyed earlier trips operated by Chapman College in California. The pedagogical purpose of Chapman's tours had become obscured by rumors of revelry aboard "the Good Ship Lollipop," as the craft came to be called. That mostly wealthy youngsters could afford the high cost of the cruise did little to dispel its reputation as a "love boat" camouflaged by academic paint. Now, however, the University of Colorado's rigorous standards lifted learning to a level at which credits earned at sea were acceptable to other institutions. A faculty of thirty-seven professors, all PhDs except for me, underwrote the serious side of an educational adventure of exceptional promise.

Boundless were the horizons surrounding Semester at Sea. Here was a city on a ship, a totally integrated community catering to every need, intellectual, physical, emotional, sensual. No phones, no families, no distractions but the swell of the sea and the gabble of the gulls between interludes of educational audacity. A curriculum geared to global reality. Team-teaching ordained by an encompassing ocean that put professors, pupils, and disciplines in one boat, inextricably intermingled—all in all, a collegial setting that provided hands-on contact with peoples who came closer with every pulse-beat of the turbines pushing us across the Pacific.

Faculty, staff, and students gathered in the lounge for a shake-down session. Academic dean, Dr. Alex Anders (in this instance, a pseudonym), announced that "The Good Ship Lollipop" had gone down with the *Titanic*. His T-shirt, emblazoned with the ship's shibboleth—"This is NOT a cruise"—made clear that obedience to Colorado standards would be strict. Professors then introduced themselves and their courses, enabling students to choose those attuned to their tastes. Rapson, a historian, led off with an account of his seminar on U.S. foreign policy, examining assumptions which underlay American actions, and inviting students to assess the nation's performance through perspectives acquired on the voyage. Other professors similarly portrayed the provinces of their expertise—anthropology, psychology, philosophy, geology, literature, political science, the visual arts.

In my own introduction, I suggested that, having circumnavigated the globe several times since 1935, I might be able to contrast conditions in Asia and Africa under colonial rule with developments since independence, and to counsel students on practical problems such as diet, drink, drugs, tripping, tipping, and the temptations of romance. Since there was no studio artist aboard, I would also function as amateur artist-in-residence, helping students in devising diaries, sketch books, photographic and written reportage commemorative of their journey. To that end journals I had illustrated in China, India, Africa, and Europe would be displayed. Sensitive to students' anxieties and interests as they faced the great unknown ahead, two courses were quickly oversubscribed, human sexuality and my own.

Hardly had we settled into a routine when a radio message advised that an oil tanker of Singapore registry en route from Borneo to Seattle had a Filipino cook aboard with a ruptured appendix requiring immediate surgery. Altering course, the *Universe* steamed within a few miles of the *Diana Prosperity* and, at 5:30 next morning, launched a lifeboat in stormy seas. Watched by hundreds of anxious eyes, the perilous passage ended with the cook in stable condition in our infirmary. Captains of the two vessels, theirs a Yugoslav, ours Chinese, swapped salutes and proceeded to their different destinations.

What rules, students asked, governed rescues at sea? According to our Captain Yen, the action took the *Universe* 125 miles off course, placing us eight hours behind schedule and costing several hundred dollars for fuel. How come people who didn't hesitate to massacre each other on *terra firma* were so solicitous at sea? By what agencies were such emergencies regulated, and how could costs be recovered? In the tightness of time binding the curriculum, no leeway existed to consider answers to such questions. Since I was less committed to the predetermined content of catalogued courses, the episode drew students from other classes to mine, and the *Diana Prosperity* became the ad hoc basis for an unscheduled seminar from which there emerged an unanimous conclusion: if compassion at sea were matched on land, most of mankind's knots could be peacefully untangled.

The incident kindled a negative consequence. An unanticipated exigency had interrupted the canned curriculum. Reluctant to mutilate carefully prepared lectures, and to yield precious time to a matter outside areas for which each was responsible, professors were placed in a difficult position. As we approached Pusan, other distractions diminished appetite for standard academic fare. How, students asked, did Koreans react to a repressive regime? Why were American soldiers stationed in so volatile a situation? As with the *Diana Prosperity*, Rapson and I coped with questions that fell outside the academic fold.

There opened a gap between the prescribed curriculum and the impromptu discussions that raged in my class. It was widened by another development that separated teachers from the taught. At first, as the *Universe* put to sea, faculty and students shared all amenities, eating at the same cafeteria tables and elbowing each other at the bar; now a few professors objected to excessive fraternization and demanded a facility where they could confer on academic matters without student intervention. A lounge was set aside for faculty use, leading, in turn, to a faculty table where dining by students was discouraged.

In Pusan, our first port, faculty-student community further frayed. Once ashore, students were picked up by their peers, taken into Korean homes, introduced to local bars, rock concerts, sports, and other diversions. Spontaneity and propinquity were reflected in the vivacity of their journals:

> Pusan. Went to a park and ate snails and watched old ladies selling eels. Bathrooms bisexual or behind a rock. Walked through red light district to Mrs. Kim's house. Met some of the family. Sang some Korean and American songs. Tremendous 10 course dinner on fish wharf—ate crab, clams, etc. for first time—fun, good way to make Korean friends. Koreans really into education. Miss Kim (18) studies 18 hours a day 6 days a week. Speaks 4 languages, plays 3 instruments, etc. When we first got here I thought Koreans were so friendly toward Americans for mainly $ reasons but not now. Mrs. Kim was crying when we left and there was no $ in our relationship at all. Just good people as room mate would say.

With some exceptions, older professors and their wives were fearful of strangers, easily fatigued and overly reliant on organized tours. Of the rich fare set out, from exotic food to erotic adventure, they tasted far less than students. The educational process, turned around, conferred greater value on empirical experience than on texts, lectures, and other pedagogical impedimenta on which instruction so largely relied, placing professors at a disadvantage vis-à-vis pupils.

To these divergencies were added yet another, more deep-seated and less susceptible to being bridged. Shipboard courses were, by the university's rules of engagement, geared more to Colorado than to Korea. Equivalency with land-based curricula allowed few exceptions from learning what was taught on campus. It was as if the *Universe*'s turbines propelled the vessel in opposite directions. One impulse was toward Asia, Africa, Europe. The other was back to Boulder.

By mid-voyage, student polls and journals condemned the academic program as irrelevant to the reality of their daily lives at sea and in port, and contrary to their expectation of experiential education in an observed world, as opposed to textbooks. The journals to which I had access put the problem less politely:

> What is this garbage they are putting us through around here? I sat through anthropology class and I sat through communication class and without any reservations whatsoever I must say these were the worst three hours, most boring, worst planned classes that I have ever sat through . . .

> What is the main priority here? Boulder, Colorado or India? I'm walking blind in these countries. Hey, they said in the catalogue we'd have six days at sea to study a curriculum directly related to the itinerary. What we're getting is a curriculum geared to Colorado!

> Skipped art class today third day in a row. Takes all the joy out of the places. Instead of bearing down on what we're going to see, it covers so much crap about stuff only museum curators give a shit about. Hell, we ought to love art in these places, it's so terrific, nothing like it in the USA. But it isn't the pleasure and the beauty that's stressed. It's all that goddam data, data and still more data.

In the absence of any better source, I strove to string together memories of India, my meeting with the Mahatma, the day I first witnessed the dances of the Devadasis, the half-moons of their bosoms bursting from their bodices as in the erotic frescoes of

Khajorhao. The marvels of the *Mahabharata* and *Ramayana*, well-springs from which Gandhi drew the power of *moksa* and *ahimsa* to snap the British scepter. Caste, cow worship, curry, endless were the students' questions and inadequate were my answers, but, drawn from experience rather than from books, they sufficed until an in-port expert came aboard and did the right thing by India.

Geddes MacGregor was most eminent of our professors, a scholar whose disciplines spanned anthropology and theology. An ordained minister, he presided over the ship's Sunday services and, with an authority emanating from an impressive physical presence, the moral power of his Protestant ethos, and the sheer intellectual attainment of his disciplined mind, he epitomized the quintessential academician.

Geddes objected to my effort. To an anthropologist trained in psychological theory and ethnographic analysis, my ad hoc approach to India was anathema. Hinduism's innumerable deities demanded explication only accredited pundits could provide. Nor could Arjuna, Garuda, Hanuman, and other characters of Hindu mythology be entrusted to a teller of raunchy tales about nautch girls and Indian regimentals. That I was filling in a void until justice could be accorded a subject so profound did not wash with academic authority. Geddes and I were shipmates traveling with different tickets, his first class, mine steerage.

At a faculty meeting to evaluate performance, I put before the group a precis of how things shaped up from students' points of view, stressing their preference for experiential rather than didactic education. It prompted the following memorandum to Dr. Anders:

Postscript to Faculty discussion, May 20:
The purpose of all academic education is to teach people the methodologies that are most effective and economic in the advancement of human knowledge. By training in these methodologies students learn how to think critically and constructively.

There is no place and never can be any place in an academic community *of any kind* for those who, ignorant of what scholarship is, dogmatically oppose that central purpose of academic training in the name of that most ambiguous of concepts "experience." One goes to a university in order to learn how to cope with and handle what is "given" in "experience." There is really no time in the life of an academic community for listening to tedious and uninformed (not to say arrogant) attacks on the work of universities to which the advancement of human knowledge owes virtually all.

What would General Motors do with a disquisition against the profit motive in business, which is as central to the practice of business as are scholarship and intellectual training in the life of the university?

Geddes MacGregor

Geddes' memo aimed at the heart of a dilemma faced by education. I felt impelled to answer:

Geddes, someone has passed to me a copy of your postscript to the faculty discussion of May 20. Herewith my thoughts after reading your remarks:

What are the "methodologies" you cite that, given the wars and other disasters to which man is heir, are proved to be "effective and economic in the advancement of human knowledge"?

Is it correct to say that the purpose of *all* academic education is to teach these rather bankrupt methodologies—or might academic education entertain certain other purposes beyond your own?

Might it not be possible or beneficial to enfold into the broader framework of academic education such a concept as experiential education—or is academic education as you define it as exclusive as you allege?

How, for example, does your definition of scholarship accord with that of the Confucian, or of the Hindu, or of the Islamic, or any of the other cultures we have encountered on this voyage?

And what is the true tradition of western scholarship as evidenced in ancient universities like Bologna, the Sorbonne, Cambridge and the like? Exclusivity or openness? Search or rigidity? Acceptance of heresy, or allegiance to any single, narrow dogma?

Is not the university the sanctuary in which a man's right to demur, defy and innovate is sacred—where, for example, he who might argue for an experiential component in the educational process would be protected from those who, in anger, would accuse him of "dogmatism, ambiguity, tedium, ignorance, arrogance" and whatever other un-Christian epithets enrich the vocabularies of those he offends?

Faculty divided on the issue. Along with Richard Rapson and myself, many urged relaxation of Colorado's rigid rules, and accommodation to the students' wishes for more pragmatism, less pedantry. To this an Old Guard was opposed, warning that credits for shipboard courses would be withheld unless academic authority was respected. Dean Anders said he would give the matter careful consideration and, after discussion with the faculty and communication with Boulder, take appropriate action. This would be deferred until after our passage through Suez and our departure from Alexandria, Egypt.

After India, no port held so much fascination as Egypt. The *Universe* anchored off Safaga on the eastern end of the Suez Canal. Here we boarded a fleet of buses for the trip to Luxor, Karnak, and the upper reaches of the Nile. In the briefing before debarkation, Anders warned that we would be traveling through a military zone and no photographs should be taken until we reached Luxor. Preferring a paint box to a camera, I was not as perturbed by the restriction as were faculty and students whose Kodaks were forbidden.

After a long, lively day we reboarded buses for the return to Safaga. Darkness fell as we sped across the desert. Suddenly, the column screeched to a halt. Egyptian soldiers held us at gunpoint. An officer announced that someone aboard our bus had snapped a picture of a secret military installation. "The flash of your camera has been seen. Someone on this bus is a spy. Not until we confiscate his film will you be permitted to pass. You have ten minutes to comply before the convoy is arrested."

At Anders' command, all cameras were opened, film removed and handed over to the officer. Our journey resumed amid hilarity that followed fright. What an entry in our journals! What a story for the folks back home that espionage was added to our other accomplishments!

As we sailed from Alexandria, Anders called me to his office. "Arthur," he said, "the Safaga affair placed the *Universe* in jeopardy. Despite my warning, a photo was taken, and had I not complied with the Egyptian's request, we all would have landed in jail. It is essential that the spy be identified, and the evidence points to you."

Anders put his finger on a page in *Who's Who in America*. It contained my biodata. "No one else aboard that bus can match your record. Lieutenant Colonel in the army. Legion of Merit. Bronze Star, Croix de Guerre, Combat Infantry badge. Foreign service officer in China, India, Africa. The East-West Center, a federal institution eager for information about overseas academics. It leads to only one conclusion. You are a CIA agent smuggled aboard the *Universe* to cloak espionage under academic respectability."

I bowed my head in shame. "Alex," I said, "denying that I'm a CIA agent is like saying I've stopped beating my wife. All I can add is that I don't own a camera."

Anders shrugged. "You spooks have ways and means we academics can't begin to understand."

For students, faculty, and staff, the voyage of the *Universe* was a treasured experience. In principle, no finer form of education can be imagined. To go beyond texts, lectures, and tests, into the world itself, seems the pinnacle of the teaching-learning process, limited only by its cost.

True, the high hopes many held for semester at sea were not fully realized. Disciplines did not mix. Neither did some of the professors, either with each other, or with students, or with "natives" overseas. Team-teaching didn't happen. Teachers jealously guarded their turf, yielding little to the unexpected, the undefined, the accidents demanding improvisation rather than preparation. The PhD process cultivated competence within specialized fields, but seemingly invited ignorance, indifference, antagonism toward anything beyond their boundaries.

Differences between Geddes and me did not discredit the purpose of the voyage. What the friction did suggest was a certain mind-set of many men and women possessed of a doctoral degree. Like MDs defending medicine against quacks, they stood firmly against invasion of pedagogical principle by uncredentialed interlopers like me.

None of which conceals that I had a mind-set of my own, cemented by a succession of sophistic mishaps making me dubious about the sanctity of the status quo, and prompting several questions: What kind of people aspire to doctoral degrees? What happens to them in graduate schools of education? What is their influence on America's schools, teachers, and children, to say nothing of society as a whole?

An intention dimly discerned in Dachau took on urgency—to seek answers to these questions. To undergo the ordeal of the doctoral degree. To ferret out the fatal flaw in education—its implications for war and peace.

26

The Chicken-shit Principle at Harvard . . .

Graduate School of Education
Harvard University, 1978–1979

Seeking answers to my questions, I studied the catalogue of Harvard's Graduate School of Education.

> The Doctor of Education degree prepares students for a wide range of positions in administration, research and teaching. Graduates traditionally have taken positions as educational administrators and policy makers (superintendents, university and foundation officers, state and federal education officers) educational researchers and analysts, department heads and curricula supervisors, and university professors of education or education-related subjects.

Applicants were advised to submit college records, an MAT score, and a personal statement of purpose in undergoing graduate study. I replied:

On the basis of my experience as a student, teacher and father of three children exposed to American education, I am increasingly disillusioned with its intentions, practices and performance. My efforts to understand and improve it, however, are subjective, intuitive, experimental and undisciplined. On the premise that Ed.D.s control, manage or influence the system, I desire to approximate the Ed.D. experience so as to gain understanding of the forces that mould the Ed.D. mind, and through it, the educational process. My intention is to describe for a lay audience my exposure to the "system" as it exists in a preeminent graduate school of education. Were such a statement to emerge from my work at Harvard it would be reflective of my independent conclusions and not necessarily complimentary to your institution.

To which I received this reply:

I am happy to tell you that by vote of the Committee on Admissions you have been admitted to graduate study for the academic year 1978–79. In this status you may take up to eight half courses for credit. At least half of these must be taken under the Faculty of Education, but up to half of your courses may be other Faculties of the University. Dr. Francis Keppel will co-advise you with Prof. Israel Scheffler.

Francis Keppel was a former comrade-in-arms who had recently returned to Harvard after serving as United States Commissioner of Education under Presidents Kennedy and Johnson. It comforted me to know that at the awesome altitude to which I was ascending, there would be a friendly face. Scheffler soon became, like Keppel, a co-adviser beyond compare. Immediately after inducting me into the Faculty Club, where horsemeat is the *piece de resistance,* they turned me loose on a "Crimson Key" tour of the campus.

Our guide was Steve, a sophomore, class of '81, whose tongue was firmly in his cheek. "We're in Harvard Old Yard," he began.

Once a cow pasture, it's here that all frosh graze for their first year. Built in 1720, Mass Hall is the oldest building on the campus, wrecked by Washington's troops when it was used as a barracks. Frosh have been wrecking it ever since. Harvard Hall was John Harvard's library. Gutted by a fire, one book was saved by a student who returned it to the president. He was expelled for taking a book without permission. Here's John Harvard's statue. The pedestal says he founded the college in 1638. Not true. Harvard was chartered by the Massachusetts Bay Colony in 1636. Harvard's seal shows three books as the source of learning. That's another lie. Learning comes from life, not books. That's three lies on one statue dedicated to *Veritas,* Truth!

Steve pointed out the Science Center.

Paid for by Land, the Polaroid inventor. It resembles a Polaroid camera. Push a button. Out comes an instant Ph.D. Over there is the Carpenter Center for the Visual Arts, the only building in the United States designed by Le Corbusier. "Migod," he said when the building was finished, "they've built it upside down!" Widener Memorial Library is one of the world's biggest. Widener went down with the *Titanic.* He returned to his cabin to get a book and missed the lifeboat. Moral: never go back for a book! Widener drowned which is why, to earn a Harvard diploma, you must be able to swim fifty yards.

The tour wound up at dorms, "named," said Steve, "after great men like Ralph Waldo Emerson."

Emerson said "Our system of education is a system of despair." William James said "No man is educated who has never dallied with the thought of suicide." Thoreau said "Education makes a ditch out of a meandering brook." Oscar Wilde said "Education is an admirable thing but it is well to remember that nothing worth knowing can be taught in school." George Bernard Shaw summed it up. "Education is always driving tacks where the carpet used to be." Harvard is full of famous professors who say something important for five minutes and make no sense for the next fifty-five. Don't dare interrupt them while they're writing papers for publication. Big on research, but teachers? Terrible! Anyway, you don't come to Harvard to be taught. You come to join the old boy network that runs Wall Street, Washington and the world.

I asked Steve why the Faculty Club served horsemeat. Steve shook his head. "All I know is Harvard faculty never eats crow."

Classes began September 10. Dean Paul Ylvisaker, plump and paternal, welcomed us in Longfellow Hall and advised us to avoid the fatal educators' errors. "Don't think that if you read one more book until 3 AM you'll be a better teacher. Or that by using words like salient, disaggregate, reconceptualize and holistic in a single sentence, you're making sense." Derek Bok, Harvard's president, added, "Cultivate curiosity, open mindedness, tolerance for ambiguity. Overcome cultural parochialism. The critical problem

today is adapting education to the international community."
Ghosts of Golf Links and Geddes MacGregor haunted Longfellow
Hall.

Harvard attracted more doctoral candidates than the classrooms could contain. We squatted on floors and crowded into corners as professors peddled their wares prior to our election of
courses. Those I chose opened opportunities to know some of
Harvard's stellar performers. Roland Barth dealt with elementary
education.

> After eight years in public schools I feel a doctorate degree doesn't
> make a teacher great. Good people come out good, jerks come out
> jerks. Often there is an adversary relationship between Ed.D.s and
> teachers who dislike being bossed by academic types. More often
> than not, the Ed.D. operates outside the areas of reality where
> things really happen—the interaction among principals, teachers,
> parents and pupils. My chief concern about Harvard is its preoccu-
> pation with the job market. We let the market become the indepen-
> dent variable, Harvard the dependent. It's an admission that we do
> not have a clear commitment to good education.

Sara Lawrence-Lightfoot's course focused on school reform.

> The Graduate School of Education is incorrectly named. It should
> be called the School of Applied Social Sciences. We have phased out
> training of teachers, superintendents and line administrators, and
> have become an umbrella for research-ship and administrative
> career programs. Few students come to pursue an intellectual pas-
> sion for teaching. What they want are old boy contacts that will
> serve them well in the job market. For those with poor back-
> grounds, Harvard is a place to undo their past. They come for the
> status Harvard confers. They want their money's worth—a humor-
> less realism whereby their financial lives, their social lives, their love
> lives are put together for the best personal payoff.

Joseph Featherstone concentrated on progressive education.

> We have much to learn from others. Our doctoral program should
> be global, to see ourselves in the larger perspectives of the world,
> and our place within it. Education should bridge the chasm between
> nations, recognize the foot soldiers and peasants, and not just the
> generals and elites. For reasons that emerged in the 1880s, Ameri-
> can priorities are administrative. So are Harvard's. Our whole sys-
> tem has a problematic relationship between practitioners and

administrative cadres that rule the roost. Theorists are cut off from
schools, teachers, kids, parents, peers—the connection is non-exist-
ent or pathological. Harvard does little to deal with this.

Israel Scheffler's course related philosophy, cognitive concepts,
and moral education. "The function of a university is to relate
education to human problems. It is not fulfilled by Harvard which
centers its resources on economics, business administration, hard
science with military and industrial application. Harvard's tradition is to be close to government. Its obsessions are specialization,
on research, narrowing inquiry to a cutting edge, overlooking the
essential ethos, and blurring any sense of the whole."

Charles Super had spent several years in Africa living among
tribal peoples. Unlike my personal perceptions, Super's were statistical. As he explained,

> I'm trained as a psychologist whose orientation is toward analysis of
> phenomena in different components and classifications. To under-
> stand phenomena you need a non-humanistic, data-loaded ap-
> proach. You can't separate ethnographic or clinical positions from
> plain bias unless you have data, otherwise you're in a circular argu-
> ment with someone who disagrees. The danger in my position is
> that I may be getting too far from reality, and the theories I teach
> may be wrong. The picture you paint of an attractive, intelligent
> people is certainly more interesting than mine, but as an academi-
> cian I have no choice but to stress psychological theory, cross-cul-
> tural testing, ethnographic analysis.

Frank Keppel cochaired a seminar on ethical aspects of professional practice in education.

> When I left the army, Conant tapped me to set the Graduate School
> of Education on its post-war path. I brought to the job the realiza-
> tion that America had been exposed to the world, and bore respon-
> sibilities earlier unknown. How could we educate new generations
> about Asia, Africa, the middle east, Europe, the USSR so as to
> avoid another war? How could humanity survive unless develop-
> ments in technology are matched by history, philosophy, ethics? I
> saw the role of schools as engines of democracy, producing citizens
> able to make intelligent decisions about national and world affairs.
> Well, I'm sorry to say that Harvard spends its energies on manage-
> ment, pushing the levers of power, gaining control, making more
> money. That's bad news for Harvard, for America, and for all of
> humanity.

I asked Frank how he had earned his PhD. "I never did," he said, "which may explain why I feel as I do about education."

William Graves Perry spanned Harvard regimes from Nathan Pusey to Derek Bok.

Pusey and I were standing at adjacent urinals after a faculty meeting. "Bill," he asked, "what's the matter with these Ph.D.s, always squabbling with each other?" I said, "Nate, it's the chicken-shit principle, the result of budget contraction. When faculty types are pushing chicken-shit, they call it principle, which leads to Perry's Law. $Q_E \propto 1/p^2 g_m$. Q_E, the quality of ethics at Harvard, varies inversely with the pretensions to g_m good motives. P, pretensions, is squared because professors always pretend they have the highest motives, and cut the throats of all who disagree. Only priests are more motivated than professors, which is why religion is even more demonic than education.

Having taken the faculty's pulse, I turned to doctoral candidates. The first several interviewees were chosen by chance—individuals encountered in classrooms, cafeterias, the library who agreed to give me time. News spread that the interviews were "cheap therapy," putting lives into hitherto hidden perspectives. Volunteers brought the total up to thirty-seven—female, twenty-one; male, sixteen; white, twenty-six; black, seven; Hispanic, two; Asian, two. The average interview lasted one hour. Interviewees were informed about the purpose of the study and invited to tell the stories of their lives—family influences, schooling, socialization, motivation, career decisions, financial burdens, future plans, the Harvard experience—whatever came into their minds that might explain who they were, where they were, and to what they aspired. What I wrote down was the product of each person's self-perception.

The profile that emerged was of a person born and brought up in a poor or moderately well-off family in which parents had little education themselves. Whatever their educational background, parents were supportive of education, believing it to be the way whereby the child could rise above such disabilities as the family suffered.

Quite common was a sense of social inferiority induced by sex, race, economic status. Learning early that smart girls were unpopular with boys, and, often, with teachers, female interviewees cited tendencies to remain intellectually low key and sexually inconspicuous, asking no questions in class and avoiding evidence of scholastic achievement.

Most respondents disliked elementary school. They recalled antagonistic teachers, dull classes, unrewarding studies. Many suffered a poor self-image, a sense of unworthiness, of being plain, or in other respects physically or mentally inferior to their peers. Discontent with elementary school usually increased in high school as did their poor self-image. Teachers were perceived as intellectually inferior, indifferent to students' nature and needs, inept in establishing model roles.

Most excelled in their studies and had little difficulty getting admission to colleges of their choice. Few entertained education as a career. In college, most majored in subjects akin to their interests and abilities as they saw them at the time, be it science, math, art, literature, history, and so on. Such choices often turned out to be averse to other, deeper, more abiding interests.

As graduation approached, realization of the need to make a career choice induced a sense of panic. For the first time, self-assessments were made of their desires, qualifications, disabilities —often with the painful knowledge that they were ill-prepared. To the degree that a teaching career seemed attractive, it was often for such reasons as a desire to mingle with interesting people, attend conferences, achieve a higher status hitherto denied to their race, sex, or economic position.

Respondents underwent what might be called "crisis situations" —indecision about themselves, their careers, marital failures, moral and societal conflicts induced by the Vietnam War, the idealism and violence of the 60s, hidden or overt guilt feelings deepened by the realization that they were ill-prepared to pay off their families' sacrifices.

For whatever reason—the climate of the times, Kennedy idealism, increased federal aid to education as a means of redressing social and economic inequities—many slipped or stumbled into teaching as a career. Entrance into education seemed inadvertent.

Under conditions established by such organizations as the Peace Corps, Vista, Upward Bound, and other federally sponsored educational improvisations, teaching credentials were lax or unnecessary, easing access into education.

Early on, the classroom was perceived as an intellectual and financial cul-de-sac from which higher credentials provided the only escape. The reasons: for many, the realization that teaching was a dead end; that to bring about change, one had to have power; that power rested on possession of an advanced degree; that in the given situation faced within education, the most promising area for rewarding employment was in administration, planning, and social policy. The consequence: matriculation in masters and doctoral programs, mainly management rather than hands-on teaching.

A common reason for choosing Harvard was its credentials—the international recognition accorded its degree, its "old boy network," the prestige it bestows upon its graduates, the promise of status, power, high-paying employment.

Careers were variously described—service to society; improving the lot of minorities, the poor, the disadvantaged; exercising power to upgrade the quality of education at federal, state, local levels. The denominator of career intentions, however, was self-interest—the achievement of power and position, ascent to an executive role, pay and perquisites justifying so heavy an investment in time, anxiety, energy, and money. Here are some of the more candid expressions of this attitude:

> The simple truth is that I don't like children, and the thought of having to spend my days coping with their dumbness, indifference, bad behavior and refusal to learn was intolerable. It was either opting out of education altogether, or maneuvering out of the classroom and into administration, policy, research—anything that would take me away from those kids.

> Christmas, Easter and summer vacations drew me into teaching, but once I realized the price I paid in headaches, depression, exhaustion, there was nowhere to go but out of the classroom into higher education.

> I'm here at Harvard because I want more money for less work, and that is spelled Ed.D.

> In a nutshell, it's the five Ps—promotion, power, prestige, pay and perks—plus self-preservation—that makes the Ed.D. rat-race pay off.

> I slid into teaching through a side door and decided I'm not the chalk-dust type. I like to rub elbows with high-class people, attend

seminars, travel, enjoy life on a college campus, and maybe earn fame and fortune by writing a textbook that catches on.

> For a country boy like me who no one ever thought was worth a good goddam, to be called doctor—well, that's all I need to make this hogwash worth my while.

Transcripts were supplied to all interviewees, with no limits imposed on any changes to make them accurately reflect what he or she had said. Of the thirty-seven transcripts, ten were returned without substantial alteration. Five were so laundered as to repudiate their original content. One charged that "by emphasis, omission and considerable inaccuracy, your account of our interview seriously distorts my perceptions and misrepresents my interests here at Harvard." Twenty-one respondents had second thoughts about their statements and withdrew them from the study. Several threats were received that, were their revelations published, legal action would be taken. It was deemed wise to destroy the statements and to publish only the profile.

Such self-protective anxiety about the consequences of their candor was probably prudent. It may say more about the motivation of doctoral candidates, the nature of the process, and the ills of education than anything else in the study.

In *The Education of Henry Adams* appears this paragraph: "Harvard was probably less hurtful than any other university then in existence. It taught little, and that little ill, but it left the mind open, free from bias, ignorant of facts but docile. The graduate had few strong prejudices. He knew little, but his mind remained supple, ready to receive knowledge." I would agree.

Adams, an undergraduate, had not attended Harvard's Graduate School of Education. I did, for one eye-opening year. It put me on a path I had unconsciously entered at Dachau, in an everexpanding investigation of education's ills. And onward to this struggle for a doctoral degree, in the belief that the only way to understand it is to undergo it. And that the only way to change the educational hierarchy is to join it.

More involved in research than course work, I sought and earned no credits at Harvard. The doctoral degree was deferred to a later time, another locus.

27

"The Kitten that Ought to be Drowned"

Wist Hall
July 1987

Just received is *Harvard Magazine* for May–June 1987. Amid advertisements by bankers, brokers, merchants of automobiles, and other caterers to ostentatious wealth, is an article by Derek Bok, Harvard's president, entitled "The Challenge to Schools of Education":

> In contrast to our schools of law, business and medicine, the Faculty of Education has experienced repeated shifts from one set of programs to the next in response to the changing desires of presidents, foundations and government agencies. The progress of the school has resembled nothing so much as the path of a ball in an arcade machine, bouncing hither and yon, from one bumper to the

next and back again in a constant quest to make the lights flash on
to signal that the big prize has finally been won. . . .

Several reasons help explain this erratic behavior. To begin with,
education has lacked a firm core of professional knowledge on
which to build a stable curriculum. Unlike medicine, with its base of
scientific knowledge, or law, with its analytic methods that contrib-
ute to "thinking like a lawyer," education is more noted for transi-
tory fads and theories such as the open classroom, the child-cen-
tered school, and the "new" math. . . . Because they have neither a
strong profession nor a distinctive body of knowledge to impart,
education faculties have no firm anchor for their programs and curricula. Instead, external forces push them first in one direction and
then in another . . .

Education schools are continually pressed to alter their teaching
and research activities to the constantly changing priorities of foundations and government agencies. Unable to find enough able students interested in public school teaching, professors tend to shift
their interest from teacher training to specialized programs that will
attract more talented applicants. Uncertain about their status in the
university and anxious to win the respect of their arts and science
colleagues, education faculties often appoint professors with strong
scholarly reputations who have little interest in public schools and
carry on research only tenuously related to education. In the opinion of one Harvard president (Abbott Lawrence Lowell), the Graduate School of Education reminded him of "a kitten that ought to be
drowned . . ."

Hence, schools of education that aspire to excellence face a fun-
damental challenge, for they have yet to prove that they can fashion
a stable marriage of teaching and research at a level of quality
appropriate to a major university. . . . Part of the problem un-
doubtedly has to do with the difficulty of the enterprise. Few phenomena are more complicated than the human brain, and few
under-takings more baffling than the effort to isolate the influence
of formal education from the myriad of factors that shape the development of a human being. . . . The prevailing view is that scholars
have contributed little to improve practice in the schools.

Overwhelmed by the odds, I frequently falter. Is my thesis insane,
my method profane, my intention so quixotic as to hold out no
hope for change? Derek Bok's is a voice in the wilderness. Echoing
in my mind is his invocation: "Cultivate curiosity, open mindedness, tolerance for ambiguity. Overcome cultural parochialism.
The critical problem today is adapting education to the international community."

28

"Education" in the Peace Corps

The Peace Corps
The Philippines, 1979–1980

In July 1901 a converted cattle ship, the *Thomas,* brought six hundred American teachers to the Philippines. Called "Thomasites," they spread across the islands, laying the groundwork for self-government toward which the people slowly moved. Ordinary folk who, under Spanish friars, could recite little but the catechism, learned English, algebra, science. Education enabled farmers' children to become doctors, lawyers, bankers, merchants, statesmen ranging in repute from Manual Quezon to Ferdinand Marcos.

World War II took a heavy toll. Under Japanese occupation, development withered. Not until victory was its momentum regained. Millions in Marshall Plan money rebuilt the newly independent nation's roads, bridges, hospitals, schools, factories, farms. Through US/AID, the World Bank, UNICEF, and other agencies, more dollars undergirded Filipino development. Then, to financial assistance, was added a human dimension—126 Peace Corps volunteers arrived in Manila in October 1961. Like the Thomasites, they were teachers who flowed into the educational system until 40 percent of high school instructors were volunteers. Unlike other agencies whose medium was money, the Peace Corps offered sweat, skills, and a spirit of service. In 1979 I became a Peace Corps volunteer.

Our group, the 148th sent to the Philippines, assembled in Seattle. It consisted of eighteen men, sixteen women, most in their twenties, the rest ranging from middle age to me. Our specialty was health. A few had some health-related expertise; most did not but expected to acquire some useful skill in training. As diverse in appearance, accent, temperament, and ethnic origin as only Americans can be, we were bonded by common innocence and curiosity about our impending experience. Staffers from Washington infused us with regulations, innoculations, and esprit, but not until our arrival in the island nation of forty-nine million people did we face our fate.

In Dagupan on the Lingayan Gulf where MacArthur had landed, we embarked on a twelve-week training cycle. I entered it with keen anticipation. Years before, the University of Hawaii had held a Peace Corps contract to provide Asia-bound volunteers with the cultural, linguistic, and vocational tools essential to their endeavor. A synthetic Asian village had been built on the Big Island, complete with carabaos, nipa huts, and pit privies. My experience in China, Indonesia, Africa, and India was tapped, and I made many visits to the Waipio Valley encampment. Academic and artificial, the method failed and Washington wisely decided to train volunteers in the countries of their service where acculturation could occur through contact, where language learning could be spontaneous, and where lectures, texts, and classroom exercises could be subordinated to empirical experience. Hundreds of volunteers had lived among these people for two long years, mapped the mine fields of their minds, learning where not to tread and what avenues led to trust, friendship, and understanding. Their experience, gained at such expense, could ease our entrance into the *terra incognita* that stretched ahead.

It was not to be. Acculturation consisted of tired tracts authored by academicians whose scholarship, however impressive on a college campus, had little relevance to reality. One expert catalogued as uniquely Filipino such evils as nepotism, influence peddling, bribery, and a tendency to cover up iniquitous behavior. Filipinos were lauded by another authority as differing from Americans in their belief in God, respect for family, love for children, and sexual prowess. An anthropologist advised us to ingratiate ourselves with Filipinos by disguising our true characters and intentions behind a mask of artificial manners. Yet another instructor, a devotee of "transactional analysis," stressed that Filipinos and Americans differed in their needs for "stroking," which he described as the basic unit of human interaction. "But even bad strokes," he professed, "are less destructive than stroke-deprivation." Credulity was stretched beyond its limits by an adolescent pair afflicted with acne who divided our adult group into men and women, warning each of the evils of unbridled sexual misbehavior.

Our first task as health specialists was to conduct a survey. "Draw a map," we were told. "Mark down every house. Then talk to the residents and collect everything you can about the family. Births, education, income, illness, deaths. How many have toilets, and do they use them? What do they do after dark, like family planning? What contraceptives do they use, and do they work?"

Clipboards in one hand, ballpoints in the other, volunteers paired with Tagalog-speaking staff, entered homes, asked questions, noted replies, and tallied statistics. Not until the damage was done did its significance sink in. As one volunteer put it, "What would happen in my home town if thirty-four Filipinos walked in and asked about our toilet habits?" Obedience to the training regimen began to change from docility to doubt.

It was on language that training mainly dwelt. In setting up the Peace Corps, Congress had legislated that "No person shall be assigned to duty as a volunteer in any foreign country or area unless at the time of such assignment he possesses such reasonable proficiency as his assignment requires in speaking the language of the country or area to which he is assigned." In fulfillment of this condition, Peace Corps Headquarters in Manila—PC/P in local parlance—had settled on a method developed by a psycholinguist named Caleb Gattegno. Entitled "The Silent Way," the method demanded that teachers conform to two principles. One, remain silent. Two, substitute for speech a series of hand signals, tapping tables with colored rods and mutely waving at wall charts with wooden pointers. As explained in Gattegno's book, *Teaching Foreign Language in Schools,* "The requirement of active vocalization presentation interferes with effective coding operations . . . The nonvoiced items in a serial recall task are processed to a deeper level than the voiced items"—an explanation that begged for elucidation.

Among the volunteers was an expert in deaf rehabilitation. According to her, no system could possibly insure failure in language-learning as did The Silent Way. "It has long been realized that the major barrier hindering a deaf person's ability to master speech is that he cannot hear the language he is to imitate. By incorporating this acknowledged barrier into its language training, PC/P artificially creates the condition of silence impairing speech and sets itself up for failure."

None of our instructors, to whom the system was force-fed one week before classes began, could lead us out of the graveyard in which our linguistic ambitions were buried. Hour after hour, day after day, we sat in silence while they gestured with rods toward little wooden blocks arranged on tables to simulate a marketplace. (Gattegno described these rods as "austere" and "mesmerizing.") Tapping charts with pointers, they sought silent answers to unspoken questions. Should a volunteer whisper so much as a word, a monitor appeared, finger to lips, sternly enforcing quiet. Never to hear a syllable spoken, never to utter aloud a single sentence, never to articulate a want or ask a direction—all amid the din of Filipinos infatuated with sound who waited outside the classroom to engage us in conversation—such pantomime was punishment, inhumane and unproductive. Our complaints that the Silent Way actually impeded our efforts to learn Cebuano, the idiom of the Visayas, were dismissed by PC/P as lacking any scientific basis.

Inevitably, volunteers acquired Cebuano in *sari-sari* stores vending beer, groceries, and gossip. Much that we learned was in the local dialect, salted with slang, obscene, and as distant from the Silent Way as the Tower of Babel. When examiners arrived from Manila to test our competence, they found our vocabularies vulgar, our accents uncouth, our loquacity a "slur on the Peace Corps."

Experts arrived heavily weighted with hogwash. Nutrition, one stressed, was extremely important. Every Filipino child needed food to "grow, glow and go." Milk, meat, salads contained proteins, vitamins, and carbohydrates essential to health. How, we asked, did "grow, glow and go" translate into Cebuano? And how was a Filipino family barely able to buy a bag of rice to pay for bread, butter, milk, and meat? A demure little female volunteer put the problem perfectly if somewhat profanely. "Hundreds of Volunteers laid their lives on the line to acquire experience we need for our work. Instead of the lessons they learned, these academic assholes feed us shit!"

Training finally ended. For the third time—once in the army in the shadow of Hitler, once in the Foreign Service in the illusion of American omnipotence, and now in the Peace Corps amid the Islamic imprecations of the Ayatollah Khomeini—I pledged allegiance to the Constitution and promised "to well and faithfully serve the people of the Philippines as we discharge our duties in the Peace Corps."

Before leaving for our sites volunteers were asked to rate our training. I replied:

How well our training has prepared us for the hazards ahead cannot be known until it is tested under field conditions. At the moment, it seems to err in five areas. One, though the Peace Corps has existed for 18 years no doctrine drawn from experience underlies and structures a plausible program. Instead, training is a patchwork of improvisation, exaggeration, contradiction and confusion, much of it exalting the very ideas that colonial experience should teach us to avoid. Two, though our trainers insist that to catalyze change at the lowest level is our aim, texts, lectures, visual aids and other educational input are almost entirely elitist, with little to instruct or energize the common people. Three, PC/P dogma is culturally divisive. Stressing differences between Filipinos and ourselves, and neglecting the common qualities, anxieties and aspirations that bind all human beings, it heightens the sense of strangeness, fosters fear, induces doubts and otherwise widens the gulf we seek to bridge. Four, the Silent Way of teaching language, substituting gestures, grimaces and grotesque pantomime for speech, confounds communication and hinders understanding. Five, training lasts too long, is excessively expensive and, as patience ebbs, becomes self-defeating.

My site was Bohol, a small island in the Visayas with a population of about 100 thousand people, mainly farmers and fishermen. I was assigned to a maternal health care and family planning clinic. Visits to local schools revealed an absence of texts on all subjects, including health. Evident too was the popularity of comics; twenty-two million copies were bought, borrowed, and rented every month throughout the Philippines. I produced thirty comics on diseases to which Filipinos are prey, and added information on family planning. Entitled *The Adventures of Superboy Lito and Supergirl Lita,* they were tested in barrio schools and sent to the Ministry of Health, the Ministry of Education, and the Commission on Population in Manila as an indigenous solution to national problems of illiteracy, disease, and overpopulation.

A second assignment was to the University of Bohol which lacked someone to teach French to its graduate students. My confession to the Dean of Arts and Sciences that no one could possibly be less qualified than I to conduct such a course was unavailing. "In a community of the blind," she said, "a man with one eye is all-seeing." My method was "The Noisy Way." The decibels with which students shouted French more than made up for any defects in their accent.

After four months in the field volunteers met again at Silliman University in Dumaguete City. Uppermost in our minds was the urgency of exchanging experiences, learning from each other's failures and successes, and gaining from Silliman's faculty the technical data we lacked. Having measured our strengths and weaknesses against the needs of our sites, our purpose was to plug the gaps in our earlier training and professionalize our skills. From PC/P we expected treatment, not as wet-eared neophytes, but as the blooded combat veterans we had become.

Familiar faces seemed altered, the younger more mature, the older somehow younger, the ebullient subdued, the introverts extroverted, everyone exhilarated by the sheer fact of survival and high in anticipation of our time together. But a surprise was in store. PC/P had hired an outfit called Community Organization for People Effectiveness—COPE for short—to shape us up. Introduced were Micky, Vicki, and Sophie, smarmy salespersons of pseudo-psychiatric hype. Peddling a far-out panacea guaranteed to save us from ourselves, COPE monopolized every minute of the meeting, leaving little time for volunteer interaction.

Between ivory tower and nipa hut yawned a gulf. Why, once again, theory, lectures and game-playing instead of realism? What could these manicured eggheads from Manila tell thirty-three veterans fresh from four months at the front? The front! A survivor of World War II, I penned a parable:

The troops left the training camp and entered the trenches. After four months in combat without relief, they were returning to the rear. What they had so eagerly anticipated throughout their lonely service at the front was finally about to happen. Sitting over beers they would exchange experiences, tell it like it was, each take his turn to talk about success and failure. Among themselves, without the constant classroom kindergarten jive that had fucked their training, they would build their own systems of self-support. This would be their show. Veterans, never again would they be talked down to, coddled and kicked around like raw recruits.

The Brass was there to lay down the law. No beer in the barracks. And a strict schedule would account for every hour of every man from dawn to dusk. Officers, expert in a new tactic guaranteed by the high command to win the war, were introduced. Upper class, enthusiastic, beautifully barbered, they had never been in combat. But, in elegant accents, they promised that if only the troops would do as they were told, they would learn how to cope when they went back into battle.

And so, day after day, the troops struggled to analyze "environmental factors," "resource levels" and "community values," matching these with "conflicting and supporting forces," and integrating "personal and task levels" "proposed strategies" and "support requirements" into a "6 month work program."

Staunch soldiers, the troops sat through session after session with vacant eyes and minds, matching obtuse questions with opaque answers and endless silences. Not until nightfall, in bistros outside the barracks, did they agonize over the ignominious obliteration of their expectations.

The week ended in maudlin remarks by the immaculate officers. Bravely they avowed that despite all they had suffered throughout a grueling week, pounding brilliant doctrine into unreceptive brains, they would once again, if summoned, return to teach the troops the tricks of their trade. This self-sacrificial offer was accepted by the Brass. Adorned with medals, the experts marched off to an antiseptic future. The troops went back to the shit.

Whatever one's bias, the week was proclaimed a success. The Brass was ecstatic. As for the grunts, rarely were soldiers on R and R so eager to return to the trenches.

Like Dagupan, Dumaguete was a disaster. But it shed light on the bureaucratic minds that wrought such havoc. PC/P's mental processes assumed a discernible pattern. Mystified by how to manage volunteers, it sought solutions in psychodynamics, the Silent Way, Transactional Analysis, COPE—the more pseudo-scientific, the more popular and pretentious, the more attuned to whatever the American fad of the I'm Okay/You're Okay order, the more likely were "experts" to wind up with a contract.

Two years of service passed swiftly and profitably. My students learned French, if not to relish *Les Miserables,* at least to order bed and breakfast. The Lito and Lita comics, approved by the ministries in Manila, were translated into several tongues and distributed to children in Filipino schools, and to their mothers in maternal health-care clinics. Twenty-seven survivors gathered at a close-of-service celebration. Unlike anthropologists who, with clinical precision, studied Filipinos as though they were butterflies impaled on pins, we had gathered friends rather than statistics.

Asked to sum up our experience, I answered:

A veteran of many careers, I can recall none so fulfilling in friendship, so rich in adventure, so satisfying in service as the Peace Corps. As a former Foreign Service Officer I wish that every President, every Secretary of State, and every Ambassador would undergo its rigors and learn its lessons. As an educator I know no classroom, no text book, no lecture or laboratory that teaches so much about the human condition as does hands-on involvement. As a soldier who fought in World War II and dreads the drift to yet another conflict, I envisage no better instrument for peace than service overseas, shoulder to shoulder with the impoverished multitudes who inhabit our planet. After 20 years, the Peace Corps ideal beams brighter than ever. Nothing says more about its vitality than its ability to overcome the academic imbeciles who strive so hard to drag down so superb a concept to the pits of their pedantry.

29

The Puritan Past of American Education

Cambridge University
England, 1982

Spring was inching into England when I arrived in March of 1982. Daffodils bloomed beside the Cam, and Cambridge glowed with a green incandescence. Burly, benign, impressively British, Sir Peter Swinnerton-Dyer, vice-chancellor of the university, greeted me in his study at St. Catherine's College and considered my request to attend Cambridge in pursuit of my research on education's ills. My purposes, I explained, were to examine the roots of American education—the Puritan influence on the origins of America's schools—and to examine the PhD process as it affected English education: who chose to undergo the ordeal, what were their motives, and how might English education be affected by their elevation into positions of power?

Sir Peter described certain differences between American and British universities.

> Derek Bok runs Harvard, but I don't run Cambridge. Cambridge consists of several autonomous colleges, admission to which lies totally within each institution's discretion. Your interest in the origins of the American system suggests Emmanuel College because of its close identification with the Puritan past. But since your concern is with the Ph.D. phenomenon, I'd propose Hughes Hall, most of whose members read for the Post-graduate Certificate in Education. An important element of Cambridge life is residence within the University in order that its members may associate closely for a prescribed number of nights each term. This is known as "keeping term," and so your first need is to gain admission to Hughes Hall as your college, and second, to gain acceptance by the University's Department of Education as your academic base.

Hughes Hall occupied a Victorian mansion some distance from the "Backs," the tourist mecca, crowned by the Gothic glories of King's Chapel, Queen's, Christ's, Magdalene, Trinity, and other colleges hallowed by history. Set within a verdant garden adjacent to Fenner's Field, second only to Lord's as the capital of cricket, what it lacked in medieval charm was made up for by modern plumbing. Established in 1885 to train women for the teaching profession—Hughes Hall was named after its first principal, Elizabeth Phillips Hughes—it was the oldest of five graduate institutions, co-educational, with 25 fellows, 35 senior members and 110 graduate students specializing in education.

Its president, Richard D'Aethe, tall, trim, tweedy, swiftly bridged the Anglo-American gulf with a story about a conference called by General Eisenhower to brief his British and American staff on final arrangements for the imminent Normandy invasion. "That is the schedule," he concluded, and asked if there were any questions. A British officer raised his hand. "General Eisenhower, Sir, why do you say *skedule* instead of *shedule?*" "Because," Ike answered, "I never went to an English shool."

D'Aethe who, like myself, had attended Harvard, ticked off some significant differences between our two countries' systems.

> You prefer large institutions, we lean to the small. Rather than lecturing hundreds of students, we recommend they read a book. An American professor faces large classes. We favor a one-to-one tuto-

rial relationship between supervisor and student. Your colleges revolve around the classroom and the curriculum. Our colleges are living places for social interaction, without curricula, courses or other activities that interfere with human engagement. Course work is left to the University. Your courses earn so many credits with which you "compile" a degree—a BA followed by an MA, capped by a Doctorate. Here a degree with first-class honors at the BA level is all one needs in the way of credentials—plus of course, professional performance. American performance is often judged by "publish or perish." We don't expect professors to build reputations on their books. Rather than a Ph.D. earned after several years spent in study and a dissertation that no one reads, we prefer to invest all that time and effort in some down-to-earth occupation. This is not to say our system is better, but that the two are different. Each would profit from a humanistic approach, studying problems common to both, learning what is emerging, and how each system is adjusting.

I thanked Dr. D'Aethe for his candor, inadvertently making my first *faux pas*. "I am not a Ph.D.," said the president, "but of that generation that didn't need a doctorate to get ahead." But, he mused, "the American way is coming into England and I daresay my successor will have earned that distinction."

My room overlooked a grassy expanse rolled and ready for the white-clad bowlers and batsmen who faced each other on the pitch. The dining ritual ordained breakfast at eight—beans on toast and tea. Lunch at one—bubble and squeak, toad in a hole, a cornish pastie eased along the alimentary canal by a cascade of custard. "Hall" or dinner at seven—meat, fish, sprouts, and more custard. At the head table D'Aethe presided, flanked by faculty, visitors, and dons from other colleges whose services to Hughes Hall earned them invitations for a compensatory meal. Conversation dwelt on gardening, gossip, chitchat far removed from the Falklands where trouble with Argentina was brewing. D'Aethe explained: "Dining together has priority over almost every other aspect of the educational experience. It is what distinguishes the English from the German system which discounts personalization. We don't allow business, problems, academic affairs to interfere with the pleasure of intimate association, the quality of life as distinct from its daily distractions. In seeking the meaning of English higher education, maybe that's the message."

The Department of Education of Cambridge University cowered across the street from the Fitzwilliam Museum whose formidable facade dwarfed the humble houses occupied by the department. I was apprehensive as I walked to my first meeting with Paul Hirst, the director. In our correspondence preceding my acceptance by Hughes Hall I sensed an absence of enthusiasm. "This Department," he had written, "is a small institution concerned with the initial training of teachers apart from a very minor element of higher degree study and our links with schools are exclusively for the purpose of teacher training. We would, of course, do all that we could do on an individual basis but it is only right you should know the very considerable limitations on what we could provide." The letter sounded inhospitable and, as I mounted the steps of 17 Trumpington Street, I flinched at the prospect of meeting the austere individual the letter proclaimed.

I could not have been more mistaken. A feisty man in his early fifties, Hirst brimmed with the milk of human kindness. Over coffee he explained his hesitation as stemming from fear that Cambridge might not meet my expectations.

> It is a law unto itself, exemplifying outrageous self-satisfaction and conceit. All the evils of English education are here. Fifty percent of Cambridge students come from Eton, Winchester, Rugby, and other independent schools. It typifies the tyranny of a system that produces and perpetuates England's social unrest. In that sense it might justify your presence, but overall you should have a broader picture than Cambridge presents. My fear is that Cambridge is so seductive as to seal you off from less opulent institutions mirroring more realistic aspects of Britain's distress. Anyway, welcome to Cambridge and how can I help?

Assuring Hirst that I would foray as far afield as might be necessary, I believed Cambridge would best serve as my base, largely because of his own diagnosis of its condition. Hirst agreed and suggested that I pursue my Puritan interests at Emmanuel College while he arranged a schedule responsive to my request.

Facing St. Andrews Street, a bustling royal road, Emmanuel College presented a faded stone facade behind which, across a grassy quadrangle, loomed a handsome clock tower flanked by arcades that led to one of Cambridge's loveliest gardens. Established in 1584 to provide the church with a preaching ministry;

named after Immanuel, Hebrew for "God is with us" and the eponym given by the prophet Isaiah to the boy, Jesus Christ, whose birth he predicted; becoming by 1617 the largest Puritan college in the English universities, it was from here that John Winthrop, John Cotton, Cotton Mather, Jonathan Edwards, and other pillars of Puritanism exported their orthodoxy from Old England to the New. Here reposed records of events that impelled them to flee England and set up a "Citty upon a Hill" where, unrestrained by wicked kings, Catholic clergy, and "relicks of popery" contaminating the Anglican church, earthly dominion and government of God achieved harmony within a Biblical State.

Deeply imbedded in English history lay the seed from which sprang America's schools. Indeed, education in the United States of America may be said to have begun at the moment in 1533 when Henry VIII impregnated Anne Boleyn, prompting the king to demand from Pope Clement VII an annulment of his marriage to Catherine of Aragon. Refused by Clement, Henry renounced obedience to Rome and established the Church of England whose Archbishop, Thomas Cranmer of Canterbury, granted the divorce, setting off a train of misadventures leading to the English Civil War, the decapitation of kings, and the persecution of the Puritans.

Puritan is derived from *puritani,* a term used in ancient Rome to describe religious deviants, and revived in Queen Elizabeth's reign as a nickname for Protestants who wanted to restore the Christian church "pure and unspotted" by popery. In 1559 Elizabeth, desiring domestic tranquility to achieve political and economic ambitions overseas, issued Acts of Supremacy and Uniformity. Restoring royal leadership of the Anglican Church, they required all Englishmen to attend orthodox services prescribed by Thirty Nine Articles retaining rituals from the medieval church and other ceremonial forms of worship—incense, organ music, ornate art. Denounced by Puritans as an Anglican "compromise" with Catholic superstition, the articles were resisted. Puritans swore allegiance to a Covenant with God, asserting that God had pledged Himself to abide by certain human ideas in return for man's acceptance of Scripture as rational, consistent, a fountain of reason. Puritans were to obey not the Queen, but what the Gospel taught.

Elizabeth acted to curb dissent. Courts of High Commission

issued decrees against unorthodoxy, removed ministers from their pulpits, inflicted punishments ranging from excommunication to death. From such persecution the Puritans fled, first to Holland and thence to the Zion on the bleak New England coast. Among them were no fewer than thirty-five graduates of Emmanuel whose initial impulse, once shelter and sustenance were secured, was to found a college akin to their alma mater in Cambridge. On October 28, 1636 the Massachusetts General Court passed an act establishing America's first institution of higher learning. Named after John Harvard who endowed it with his library, its purpose was to ensure the provision of "a learned clergy" and "a lettered people."

Although crowning the colony's educational achievement, Harvard did not account for its extraordinary performance in producing "a lettered people." "It being the chief project of that old deluder Satan to keep men from the knowledge of the Scriptures," an act was passed in 1642 requiring every town with more than fifty homesteaders "to endeavor to teach by themselves or others their children and apprentices perfectly to read the English tongue." Lest the intent of the act be overlooked, Cotton Mather pounded home two essentials of Puritan pedagogy. One, the key to understanding the Scriptures was each individual's ability to read. To Cotton it was not "back to basics" (plural) but to the *one* basic (singular): reading. "The children," he preached, "shall LEARN TO READ [Cotton's capitals] the Holy Scriptures and this as early as may be. . . . When the children can READ . . . cause them every day to READ the Book of Life. Have them to *remember* what they READ. Make them repeat the answer in the Catechism with all Exactness. Be not satisfied with hearing children patter out by ROTE like parrots."

The second essential of Puritan pedagogy was the audience to which this counsel was aimed. Parents, not schoolmasters, bore responsibility for their children's ability to read. "First of all, O Parents," he proclaimed, "this matter chiefly belongs unto you . . . none are so much concerned as PARENTS to look after it. There are parents who so neglect their children that at the Last Day, their miserable children will cry out OUR PARENTS HAVE BEEN OUR MURDERERS." And to children Mather said: "Count it a privilege to be taught anything."

Puritan parents did not dissipate childrens' attention over a multitude of texts, few of which, in the actual event, were available. From the first a child's focus was on the King James Bible in colloquial English, favored over Latin not only for Latin's Catholic connotation, but because English was a utilitarian tongue essential for earning a living—like the Scriptures, a primary purpose of Puritan education. "Teach your child well a profitable calling," Mather advised, "and make your sons beneficial to a human society."

Such were the origins of American education. Reading was the aim. Parents were the teachers. The home was the school. Most households, in addition to the Bible, had a wooden frame to which a piece of paper was affixed containing the alphabet, nine digits, and The Lord's Prayer. Called a "horn-book," it made no distinction between letters and numbers; the child absorbed both in the process of reading so that arithmetic, rather than a separate function, was unified within the reading process. Children advanced to catechisms—the Socratic method of questions and answers to test their understanding embodied in John Cotton's *Spiritual Milk for Babes* and onward to the *New England Primer,* famed for its poetic approach to alphabetization. Beginning with "In Adams's fall / We sinned all," it ended with "Zaccheus he / Did climb a tree / His Lord to see."

Fathers were fined for failure of a child to read. Nor were children absolved of their obligation to learn. Puritan moral theology declared children's hearts to be "dungeons of wickedness." Even infants were "sinners, doomed to perdition, depraved, unregenerate, damned unless redeemed by Puritan piety." To Jonathan Edwards "unrepentant children are young vipers and infinitely more hateful than vipers." Massachusetts law condemned unruly children to death, and no maxim was more observed than "spare the rod and spoil the child."

Emmanuel College made many things clear about America's past and present. Much I had been brought up to believe was wrong. Puritans did not dress in black and white but were given to gaudy raiment. Many drank to excess and could be ribald in behavior. Massachusetts was an oligarchy ruled by elders of the church; democracy was as alien to Puritan purpose as Catholicism, and historians who credited Puritans with freedom of religion could not have been more mistaken. Waves of religious extremism that inundate America have a Puritan connection.

Sanctimonius Puritans became Yankee traders. New Englanders worshipped "not God but cod." Religion waned; reading waxed. Literacy laid the basis for popular participation in colonial affairs. It whetted appetites for books transcending the Bible. Printing plants prospered. Bookshops burgeoned. Seventy years after the Plymouth landfall, Boston was second to London in the production and purchase of books. Written in the simple English that every farmer, fisherman, merchant, and sailor could understand, books fed a hunger for knowledge unsatisfied by Scripture.

Ability to read led to self-education. Interest whetted in whatever subject—science, philosophy, geography, politics, economics —each individual followed his bent with an unfettered mind. Be it by Bunyan's *Pilgrim's Progress,* Bacon's *Advancement of Learning,* Paine's *Common Sense* or the *Federalist Papers,* the way was paved to Revolution, the Constitution, a "More Perfect Union"— and a system that forsook the family's role in education and placed it in the school.

What would Cotton Mather make of modern education? From homesteads to schoolhouses. From parents to pedagogues. From horn-books to television. From Emmanuel College to Immanuel Kant. From the *New England Primer* to *Dick and Jane.* From one basic, *reading,* to a curriculum containing every problem with which parents and politicians cannot cope—sex, smoking, driving, dope, alcohol, AIDS, abortion, making out, and making money.

Amid the change, only kids remain constant. Now, as then, they are "dungeons of wickedness, vipers, depraved, unregenerate, and doomed to perdition."

30

What Scotland Yard Doesn't Suspect . . .

Cambridge University
England, 1982

Of Hughes Hall's fifty-eight candidates for teaching certificates, thirty-seven volunteered for interviews. Nine described themselves as "working class," another nine as "middle class." Only one was "upper class"—mother and father both doctors of medicine. Another eighteen were from families that had moved up economically since World War II, but who clung to their working-class roots. The following responses are suggestive of the outlooks among teacher trainees, as distinct from doctoral candidates:

As a one-time drop-out, decided I had a lot to say to potential rejects. I understood them, could talk to them and help them.

Decided to be a teacher. See myself in education as a reformer; as a
teacher of deprived people. I'm for total abolition of the Clarendon
Nine.* My worry is that many working class people will reject a
chance to learn even if it is offered to them. I want to change that.

To learn about a culture to which you feel antagonistic one must
join it for a year. Cambridge has strengthened my ideas about
inequality in education. My intention is to change the system. Like
Lenin I have my head in the clouds to see what lies at my feet.

Education has to change. Unemployment a growing factor. How
do we teach someone to live a life without work? New look is essential. Schools will have to adjust. You can't destroy the system but
you can tinker with it, replace a few people, alter things year after
year, get radical change through moderation. I'm not drawn to
moneymaking. What I want is a better educational system, a better
Britain, a better world.

I love kids and being in a classroom. All I want to be is a successful classroom teacher—not to change system or the world. I can
make teaching more enjoyable with drama, child participation,
group work. Believe in compromise with subability kids, get on
with them, not lose my temper and lay down the law. Many kids are
late bloomers. Wrong to base their lives on "O" levels.

As Paul Hirst had predicted, doctoral candidates at Cambridge
were rare. I voyaged far afield—to London University's Institute
of Education, to the Universities of Birmingham, Manchester,
Liverpool, Bristol, Leicester and several other cities—to compile a
total of twenty-six interviews of which these suggest content at the
doctoral as distinct from the teacher trainee level:

Chose teaching for all the wrong reasons. Wanted to be close to
my husband who was working for a Ph.D. Seemed a convenient
classic female subsidiary role and it didn't work out. Accepted for
Post Graduate Certificate of Education (PGCE) at Cambridge. Dis-
covered I didn't like children en masse. Wanted to tell kids what I
thought was exciting and worthwhile but spent my energy keeping
them quiet. Have a hearing problem and couldn't hear amid classroom noise. Didn't feel I was being myself in classroom—bad for me
and for the children. What to do next? Supervisor and husband

---

*"The Clarendon Nine" are England's ancient "public schools": Winchester, Eton, Harrow,
Rugby, St. Pauls, Merchant Taylors, Shrewsbury and Charterhouse. Actually private, they
were called "public" because they were open to boys from all over England, rather than tied
to any town.

advised a PhD in research. Am doing dissertation on women in book trades in 19th century. My secret ambition is to establish myself as a writer on girls' education from mid-19th century to present. Whole area of womens' studies is embryonic in Britain. Hundreds of years of masculine domination make Englishmen unused to women. University can't lose its maleness. I want to improve condition of women in higher education. I'm a feminist because looking at womens' history I know that women have been badly done by men.

Grandfather a general in the army. Father heads a corporation. Family linked with traditional aristocracy. My education all first class, Eton and Oxford. Radical break for me to become PhD. A decisive step away from private to public education. I don't keep up with old boy network. Neither Eton nor Oxford worked for me. They are enmeshed in ideologies not right for world we live in. Much revolt in sixties. Subculture had consequences on people like me. We became existentialists, socialists, communists. I didn't drift into education. My tactical position was to abolish Public Schools but main issue was to change British society with education as my focus—establish a theology, a left wing stance, a different pattern of ideas, build a network among Heads of Departments over three generations, all ideologically idealistic. Our hope is to do it through teacher consciousness. PhD is key. For Department to stay in business it needs people with PhDs to work students seeking higher degrees.

Others add:

On motivation, to be candid, I simply want something to do. A PhD grant gives me more than an unemployment benefit.

Why a PhD? I was offered money to go on studying and had to find a reason not to take it. I didn't find a reason and here I am.

I'm doing my PhD as the ultimate justification for goofing at Oxford. I don't have self-knowledge to understand my motive. A lot of letters after my name is of no use to me except to teach abroad where foreign governments are impressed by doctoral degrees. I'm into a PhD to be sure I can go abroad again. I have no social purpose. Put me down as an Hellenic man, not an Athenean. I don't clearly conceive of the world as being reconstituteable leftwards or rightwards in any way that will turn out to be proper.

Why a PhD? There is an element of truth in that I'm a fugitive from thirty adolescents—from tensions of the classroom—from frustration caused by necessity to enforce discipline rather than to teach. Too much administrative work—marking registers—only two or three kids out of 30 learning anything. These justify my desire to escape into higher education. As a schoolteacher you can't influence the system. Publication is possible only for a PhD—helps to get a better job. No pecuniary rewards. Reward is freedom from emotional stress of coping with 30 adolescents.

Working for a PhD makes sense. I get a basic grant of £2300 per annum, plus tuition fees, plus travel plus an extra increment of £150 per annum for each year I've worked, plus £250 per annum for age if you're over 27. Altogether I get £3290 per year while I'm working on my PhD. Also as a deputy resident in a student house I get a rent reduction.

The PhD is a matter of working one's self into a good job within a state-supported institution that through tenure gives one life-long protection from the market economy. It's like joining a good club set up to perpetuate the isolation of its upper class membership, or a religion with a secular priesthood that has taken over the schools, holding high the torch of French enlightenment and revolution but actually looking out for number one. However you look at it—a club, a religion, a cop-out from real life—the ticket of admission is a PhD.

What Scotland Yard doesn't suspect is that there's a revolution going on in Britain. Working class stiffs like me with doctoral degrees will one day capture DES (Department of Education and Science). The Clarendon Nine will go, if not by legislation, then by education. A new ruling class will be brought up in Britain by a new kind of public school that we PhDs will run on a Marxist model.

Between teacher trainees and PhD aspirants, a deep division. On one side, concern for classroom and kids, a desire to serve without regard to power, money, status. On the other, less concern with classroom and children, more a desire to escape them. Less yearning to impart knowledge, more an intention to use education as a tool to change society. Less reference to professional pride and responsibility, more to changing the status quo by mobilizing professional power. Less a commitment to use government grants to improve their professional qualification, more an admission that state subsidization of PhD study is better than being on the dole. Less a crusade to improve state-maintained education, more a vendetta against what is seen as the archenemy of British democracy: the independent schools. Overall, with differences due largely to circumstances peculiar to British society, not unlike the doctoral interviews at Harvard that respondents had withdrawn from publication.

What to make of this system that separates plodding sheep from greedy goats? A principal in a London school sighs.

> The doctoral degree is the handwriting on the English wall as on the American. It's only human for some people to reach for more pay and power. It also makes sense to recognize the need for competent policy-makers and administrators. Someone has to run the show, and better to put them through a program that whets their skills than to neglect the need for upper-level preparation for upper-level jobs. But that shouldn't blind us to the flip side—that teachers hate being bossed by bureaucrats who have copped out of the classroom. Just as generals can't win wars with mutinous troops, principals can't educate with sullen teachers. The answer? As in an effective army, pick officers from the best and bravest of the privates. Examine motivation as much as intelligence. Base strategy and tactics on their close collaboration. And be sure there's as much pay, perks and medals for the troops in the trenches as for the higher-ups in headquarters!

There is an ancient English axiom: "History is littered with the remains of those who have searched for the hissing gas leaks of education with the lighted matches of uninformed ideas." Probing the Puritan past and the PhD present, I sniff the scent of hissing gas.

31

How Japan Won the War

University of Kyoto
Japan, 1984

As a soldier, in 1945, I returned to the Imperial Palace where decades before I had been drenched at the emperor's garden party. It stood intact amid the rubble of the surrounding city, guarded by a GI from the First Cavalry Division. Smitten by the symbolism of an American soldier standing at the summit of Allied ascendancy, I walked up to him and pointed to the palace. "Right behind you lives a man for whom millions of Japanese gave their lives, believing that Hirohito is a direct descendant of the Sun God. That's a lot of history and a lot of lives, including Americans. And so I wonder what you must be thinking in such a place at such a time." "Well sir," he said, after several seconds of silence, "I'm thinking that my feet hurt and I want to go home."

Not far from the palace, in the headquarters of SCAP, Supreme Commander of the Allied Powers, an event occurred second only in importance to the victory itself in its impact not alone on Japan but on the unfolding future. Douglas MacArthur asked the War Department to send American experts to advise him on problems relating to education. Twenty-seven savants were selected as members of the United States Education Mission to Japan. They arrived in Tokyo on March 5 and 6, 1946 and remained in Japan for twenty-five days, working closely with the Civil Information and Education Section of the General Staff.

The mission's report became the basis for the reform of Japanese schools. Because education is credited with much of Japan's leap from the ashes of World War II to the cornucopia it has become, no aspect of my inquiry into education's ills meant more to me than what the United States Education Mission accomplished in paving Japan's postwar path. It was therefore with a special sense of anticipation that I received from Dr. Tetsuya Kobayashi, chairman of the Faculty of Education of the University of Kyoto, an invitation to study the school system believed by many to be better than any other.

Only one who had witnessed the abyss into which Japan had fallen could appreciate the height to which it had climbed. More than eight million Japanese had been killed or wounded in the war. More than two million dwellings and four thousand schools were destroyed. Factories, farms, markets lay in ruins. People scavenged green locusts to fend off starvation. Japan faced immolation on such a scale as to wipe out a sizable part of the surviving population.

Now, less than forty years later, Tokyo teemed with ten million men, women and children bigger, better dressed, busier than any earlier Japanese generation. The famed bullet train, *Shinkansen,* whipped me to Kyoto in less than two hours past a blur of rice paddies and parking lots packed with Hondas and Toyotas. Kyoto, spared by allied bombers, glowed in Japan's rising sun, each tiled rooftop of its thousand temples sprouting TV antennae. Kyodai, once a diminutive university overshadowed by imperial Todai, University of Tokyo, now boasted more Nobel laureates than any other institution in the islands. Here I was greeted by Dr. Kobayashi whose English was excellent, his hospitality hearty, and his historical overview such as to place in perspective both the significance of an American soldier standing at the portal of the Imperial Palace, and the performance of the United States Education Mission to Japan.

The Mission's performance cannot be judged without some understanding of the system it sought to correct. Japan's educational system emerged a thousand years ago from religious rudiments, its teachers monks to whose temples came the sons of Samurai, the warrior class, to learn Buddhist scripture, Confucian ethics, and Bushido, martial arts. In time feuding clans led by local lords came under the control of a single family, the Tokugawa, and an embryonic system of centralized instruction united the nation. As had Puritans in New England, so did the Tokugawa Shoguns make reading the single basic subject taught in *Terakoya,* parish schools. Every five families comprised a group, *goningumi,* led by an elder responsible for its obedience to authority. Orders from above were circulated in a register which demanded that the head of at least one of the five households be literate. By Imperial decree: "There shall be no community with an illiterate family, or a family with an illiterate person." As for the Samurai, the Shoguns laid down the rule: "Learning to the left, and arms on the right." For a soldier to be unlettered and ignorant was impermissible.

Literacy flourished. Pedagogy became an esteemed profession. Children were taught to "follow the teacher at a distance of seven feet so that they shall not even tread upon his shadow." As a national identity developed, so did awareness that Japan was threatened by foreign foes. In July 1853, the arrival of Commodore Perry's warships in Edo Bay aroused the people to their peril. Authority, wrested from the Tokugawa, centered in Meiji, an energetic young emperor who made an oath before the Celestial Gods and Terrestrial Deities, fixing Japan's future course: "Wisdom and knowledge shall be sought all over the world in order to establish firmly the foundations of the Empire."

Missions set out, searching for foreign practices with the most promise of successful transmission to Japan. To President Ulysses S. Grant a delegation appealed for assistance in setting up common schools needed for universal elementary education. It returned to Tokyo with a cargo of readers, desks, blackboards, and chalk bought in Boston for replication in Nippon's new schools. Exemplifying the lengths Japan was willing to go in breaking away from its authoritarian tradition, progressivism as practiced in the Oswego State Normal School in New York was brought back as the method on which its new schools would be modeled.

Other Yankee influences inspired the Japanese. Trousers, baseball, ice cream, sewing machines found favor, as did English. "Treaty Port Teachers" and "Water-front Professors" set up shop in Yokohama, forerunners of a flood of American missionaries imbued with the belief that no better system existed anywhere on earth to bring truth about God and Man to heathen populations. Among the first and foremost was William Elliot Griffis, a Rutgers theology graduate brought to Japan to establish a scientific school on the American principle. Griffis' book, *The Mikado's Empire,* describes his experiences at the onset of the Meiji era and provides insights on educational motivation not unlike those disclosed by PhDs I interviewed at home and in England. Uncertain of what he wanted to do with his life, Griffis was drawn to Japan because the salary—$3,600 per annum, plus house, a horse, free postage, domestic help, and a month's vacation—was better than he could earn in America, enabling him to travel, study theology, collect material for a book, support his indigent parents, carpet the floor of their house, and recuperate from an unrequited love affair.

On the secular side, men like David Murray of Rutgers, as the first national superintendent of schools, introduced American curricula, translated *McGuffey's Reader*s, and otherwise westernized Japanese schools. Marion Scott, a grammar school principal from San Francisco, headed the first normal school set up for teacher training. Inevitably, certain eccentricities peculiar to American education crept into the curriculum. Japanese pupils studying geography had to memorize mountains, rivers, flora, and fauna in each of the American states—not unlike the insistence on American geography as the SS *Universe* encircled the planet. English was taught by a method that made students "mindlessly imitate meaningless sounds uttered by the instructor," reminiscent of the Silent Way as taught in the Peace Corps. Imperial Tokyo University prided itself on its American professors, some of whose students assumed presidencies of such influential institutions as Waseda, Keio, and Kyushu universities. Others staffed the burgeoning bureaucracies of a nation rushing toward a date with destiny. That destiny was foretold by William Clark whose advice to his students in Sapporo Agricultural School would be followed by generations of Japanese youth obsessed by his admonition. "Boys," he said, "be ambitious!"—and so they were.

American input helped fulfill the early intention of the Meiji regime. The country's schools opened to all segments of society. The ability of every Japanese child to read raised windows of opportunity formerly the privilege of princelings. Now commoners could enter the lower ranks of the civil service and army. An aversion to arithmetic was overcome. Where once a nobleman deemed it "abominable that innocent children should be taught numbers, the instruments of merchants," mathematics achieved status as one of "the six Confucian arts." *Encouragement of Learning,* one of many books widely read by a literate public, contended that "all the people of the country, whether noble or base, whether high or low, must feel that they have a personal responsibility for the country."

The American pendulum, however, swung too far. Progressivism was anathema to classical Confucianists who valued filial piety, loyalty, and obedience to authority. Alarmed by student misbehavior, *shushin*—the indigenous moral code embodying patriotism, duty, discipline—was invoked. "Books dangerous to national peace and injurious to public morals" were banned and the Ministry of Education warned teachers that "it must be kept in mind that what is done is done not for the sake of the pupils but for the sake of the State." To compel compliance, moral training, thought control, and military drill were stressed. *Bu,* the oak leaf signifying military might and *bun,* symbolizing learning, intertwined, became the badge of Japan's uniformed students.

Eroded by such attitudes, American influence waned at precisely the point when educators everywhere were entranced by Germany's conquest of France. Occurring in 1870, it coincided with Japan's search for initiatives that reinforced its Shinto-Confucian philosophy. *Japan's Militant Teachers,* by Benjamin C. Duke, reveals how

> American ideals of education, shaped by Christian traditions and the western frontier and emphasizing individualism, humanism, and local control, were no longer considered appropriate for an Oriental country experiencing the painful transformation from a feudalistic base of Tokugawa times to a modern state under Emperor Meiji. *The Japanese leaders in the late 1880s thus made one of the most crucial decisions in the history of Japan: The model for Japanese education, as well as for many other institutions of the nation, including the 1889 Constitution, would henceforth be German, not American.* (Italics mine.) The Herbartian educational

ideal employed in Germany, a nation whose history, literature and traditions formed the foundation of the country's educational curriculum and moral teachings, appealed to the Japanese leaders as an ideal combination of moral training and the acquisition of knowledge. . . . The Imperial Rescript on Education provided the moral, philosophical, religious and patriotic foundation of Japanese education: the pattern of education was thus determined until the end of World War II. It was to be a highly centralized system based on the principles of elementary education for all and secondary and higher education for the intellectually able, with technical streams being added later in separate schools as Japanese industry developed. It was to emphasize Western technology and science, and Japanese culture and traditions based on Confucian hierarchical relationships. Its teaching methods were based on the Herbartian five-step process, which appealed to teachers seeking the most efficient means of teaching systematically a great deal of information and factual knowledge in the shortest possible time. . . . Normal schools were administered as quasi-military institutions, scrupulously designed to indoctrinate the principles of nationalism through a strict program of physical, moral and mental training of future elementary school teachers who were, in turn, to inculcate these ideals in the young during compulsory school classes. Since all graduates were liable to military service, it was deemed proper that military gymnastics and drill in the German model should be taught for three to six hours a week. A high-ranking military officer was assigned to administer the Tokyo Higher Normal School.

Imbued with belief in ancestor worship, divinity of the emperor, duty to the state, enforced by thought control, and fortified by the German military model, Japan conquered Korea, China, Russia, and took on the United States. As did Germany, it met defeat.

At which moment, enter the American Education Mission. Victory achieved, it was now the opportunity of America's educators to conclude a brutal war with an act of wisdom. After just twenty-five days devoted to a study of a system many centuries old and deeply ingrained in an oriental people, the mission submitted a sixty-page report to Douglas MacArthur, reordering Japan's schools from kindergartens to tertiary institutions. It rested on three premises. One, the evils of Japanese education. Two, the virtues of American education. Three, renunciation by Japan of its prewar practices and adherence to an American model.

The evils of Japanese education condemned by the mission

included its provision of "one type of education for the privileged few and another for the masses." "Disregard for differences in ability and interests of pupils." "Prescription of textbooks, examinations and inspections preventing teachers from exercising professional freedom." Education officials "with little or no professional preparation or experience in the classroom." In consequence, "Japanese children could not distinguish between fact and mythology, between the real and fanciful, in a scientific spirit of critical analysis." Examinations consisted of items to be forgotten as soon as papers were graded. *Shushin,* the ancient moral code of conduct infected children with false notions of discipline, duty, and correct behavior. Japanese students were "ill prepared for the world of reality."

American education, the mission averred, was unblemished by such evils. A paradigm of pedagogical perfection, it derived its virtues from its allegiance to democracy, liberalism, and freedom. The mission defined democracy as "deviation, originality and spontaneity."* Liberalism was "the sunshine under which the unmeasured resources of childhood will bear rich fruit." Freedom was "the atmosphere in which the best capacities of the teacher flourished." Japan must henceforth accept these as conditions essential to educational reform. *Shushin* must give way to the means whereby American youngsters achieve their exemplary behavior: a social science curriculum, plus participation in sports, clubs, and other extracurricular activities. Not content with extolling American pedagogy, the mission reminded Japanese women that "to be good wives, they must be *good,* and that to be 'wise' mothers, they must be *'wise'.*" (Italics are the mission's, not mine.) "Goodness," the report pontificated, "does not come from narrowness, and wisdom is not a hothouse plant." Capping a veritable vulgate of such homilies, the report admonished the Japanese to abandon *Kanji,* Japan's traditional language and substitute *Romaji,* a method of writing Japanese in Roman characters corresponding to English.

In its flowery rhetoric, self-righteous mendacity, and utter insensitivity to the nature of its captive audience, the mission's

---

*Deviation is defined by Webster as: "noticeable or marked departure from accepted norms of behavior." Originality as "freshness of aspect, design, or style. The power of independent thought as constructive interpretation." Spontaneity as: "Voluntary or undetermined action or movement." That these characterize American education seems somewhat dubious.

report mirrors malignancies within its membership. The American system it apotheosized existed mainly in the mission's imagination. The exercise of professional freedom by teachers; regard for students' abilities and interests; relief from regurgitative examinations; quality education for the masses rather than for a privileged few—these were consummations devoutly to be wished, rather than American realities. Bestowed upon a defeated foe, they enabled the Japanese—a disciplined, intelligent, industrious people—to employ the gifts with which they are so generously endowed, and confided to an enemy an educational recipe denied to ourselves.

Obedient to the occupation's authority, they waited it out. Sensing certain qualities that could profitably be applied to themselves, they demonstrated Japan's peculiar propensity: imitation in their hands achieves originality. Just as Japanese adhesives are stickier than Scotch tape, so were certain aspects of American education adopted and improved in Japan. Parent-teacher associations, for example, which often produce more havoc than harmony in American communities, cement in Japan a covenant between parents and teachers that virtually guarantees good performance by its pupils.

Proscribed from ever again engaging in military adventures, Japanese energies centered on mastering skills for their economic revival, and for the realization of hegemony through industrial rather than military means. Japanese schools were transformed into training institutions, producing efficient technologists, engineers, artisans, and salesmen who carry Japanese products to the far ends of the earth, accomplishing with order books what their forebears failed to do with *kamikazes*.

The occupation's magnanimity was monumental, its methods mild, its effects broadly beneficial. But rather than enhancing the aura of chivalry with which MacArthur's consulship was clothed, the Education Mission debased it by its denigration of an ancient culture and exaltation of its own. Its claim that the virtues attributed to America's system in 1946 were "painfully hammered out in practice"—long before Little Rock, Selma, and several Supreme Court decisions—was patently dishonest. That after only twenty-five days in Japan, America's preeminent pedagogues reordered another nation's schools seems the height of hubris. Not to mention that, in the process, they gave away the store.

And so it should come as no surprise that no sooner was the occupation ended than an ecdysiast Japan shed, garment by garment, the alien raiment with which it was garbed, and began a process presently intensified by an ad hoc commission appointed by the prime minister to re-Japanify the nation's schools. Once again, the Rising Sun flag is saluted, and *Kamigayo,* the national anthem, sung.

As the mission's report reveals, and as tension between the two peoples affirms, little has been learned since World War II. Then the issue was territory. Today it is trade. Before Pearl Harbor, Japan boasted six imperial universities, thirty state colleges, innumerable schools of engineering, commerce, and education. As for America, its universities ranked among the best in the world, and no nation in history spent so much money on public instruction. Yet Tokyo and Washington hadn't a glimmer of an idea of each other's anxieties, aspirations, intentions. The two peoples tested their muscle in a war to the causes and consequences of which both were blind.

Giants in the laboratory, the factory, the marketplace, pygmies in paideia, the two peoples grope once again with forces neither is educated to understand. Vast populations are waste products of school systems mandated to discipline, indoctrinate, and train, rather than to educate. Both manufacture marvelous machines, drunkenly driven to dire destinations. Neither has structured an educational enterprise to prepare its citizenry for the exercise of reason and the pursuit of peace.

32

Gaman, Secret of Japanese Success

Kyoto, Japan
1985

A few vignettes may suggest the character of Japanese schools. First, a sergeant in the U.S. Army serving in Japan describes how a Japanese elementary school differs from an American:

> My wife is Japanese. When our son Jeff turned six I took him to the DOD, the Department of Defense school for servicemen's children on our base. Jeff took a placement test and was tracked into the lowest of three groups. He didn't do well, hated homework, faked feeling sick so as to stay home. My wife went to school to get a fix on the problem. The teacher couldn't identify Jeff until my wife pointed him out. "Oh yes," the teacher shrugged, "he's the kid who can't read." Forty children in the class were tracked in three groups.

Blue group was doing 3-digit division. Green group was doing addition and subtraction to two numbers. Red group, Jeff's, had ditto sheets in addition. Teacher gave most of her time to the blues, mostly officers' children. As an enlisted man, I had no idea of what it meant for Jeff to be a red. Only now did I learn that the quality of a kid's education in DOD depended on his father's rank.

We took Jeff out of the DOD and placed him in a Japanese school, very strict, no questions about rank, no tracking. All the kids worked together, mainly on reading. As soon as the teacher sensed Jeff's problem she paired him off with a good reader. With coaching Jeff caught up quickly, became bilingual. When he was sick his teacher came to our house to help Jeff with his homework. My wife belonged to the PTA in both schools. In the DOD it was kind of a contest, parents and teachers placing the blame on each other for poor performance. Not so in the Japanese PTA. Teachers and parents were partners in furthering the kids' progress. Those *Kiyoiku-mamas,* "education-mothers," wrote notes drawing the teacher's attention to any problems. Like reading the newspaper, the child didn't understand why Nakasone owed his position as prime minister to the fact that he was president of the Liberal Democratic Party. Could the teacher please explain the relationship between the LDP and the Diet? She did.

American kids are bussed to school. Japanese kids assemble at a designated corner and walk to school together to teach them responsibility for each others' safety. American kids wear their street shoes in school, and sanitation is the responsibility of a janitor. Japanese kids place their street shoes in a cubicle inside the entrance and put on a pair of clean clogs. Third and fourth graders dust shelves, wipe windows, mop classroom and corridor floors; older boys tidy the toilets.

In the DOD teachers have trouble bringing thirty kids to order. In the Japanese, the class of forty children stand, bow to the teacher, and submit to an inspection of fingernails, hair and cleanliness of their clothing. The teacher sets the lesson and leaves the children to manage by themselves, the brighter boys helping the backward. The entire class goes forward together, with no one left behind or promoted over others. Classes concentrate on "the language of the nation"—the 48 *hiragana,* 48 *katakana,* 1,945 *kanji* or Chinese characters, and the English alphabet. There's no way so many characters can be learned except by rote memorization, recitation and repetition. It isn't creative, but it does enforce study habits and ensures one hundred percent literacy.

At noon DOD children gather in a cafeteria where meals are

served by hired help. In the Japanese school food is served by students. The children wash the dishes, scrub their teeth, exercise outdoors, and return for two hours of science, arithmetic, art and music. Every kid plays an instrument—flutes, harmonicas, triangles or bells—altogether, an orchestra. The schoolday ends with monitors asking whether anyone has something on his mind—questions, complaints, problems. Quarrels are aired and kids apologize for misbehavior. Then students and children exchange bows, say *sayonara* and head for home and lots of homework. Jeff's doing okay, and our only worry is how he'll do in an American school when we're posted back home.

Next, an American woman married to a Japanese.

I belong to the Foreign Wives of Japanese Association—mostly American women married to Japanese men. From the moment a child is conceived, the couple faces a crucial question: how do we educate our child? Panic sets in, tears are shed, there is no easy answer. If a child grows up in Japan, it must live by Japanese rules. That means pre-schooling in *yochien,* kindergartens with thirty or forty children. Very rigid and regimented. Children are told "hands on knees. Hold scissors. Cut, cut, cut." Each child learns to cut exactly like every other. In the sandbox the group builds a mountain. My daughter dug a tunnel through the mountain and was scolded by the teacher. "You must build a mountain, not dig a tunnel. You must do what we all do, not what you want to do." That's called *gaman*. [Many Japanese would define *gaman* as patience, or strict obedience to social norms.] Every child learns *gaman*—never, never, never do anything different from the group. Like one day the class went for a swimming lesson. My daughter wasn't wearing a regulation swim-suit. She was not allowed to swim.

First grade elementary starts with a shopping spree, uniforms, backpacks, pencil boxes and pads. Mothers weep at the opening ceremony speeches about each child's duty to serve Japan. Classes concentrate on reading. Very methodical, the tortoise and hare principle, slow but sure, the same page turned over every day in every school all over the land, lock-step teaching, rote learning, memorization, repetition, no one moved ahead, no one left behind. Schools set the rules and parents obey. Households are governed by the child's rising, dressing, going to school. No one dares whisper while he does his homework. Nothing matters as much as that he pass exams, climb the next rung on the ladder to a job with Toshiba or Suntory.

It's like the U.S. Marines. First you break the individuality, smash the spirit, cow the mind. Then you put the pieces together the way you want. Make the man a cog in a fine fighting machine. Make the child an obedient workaholic. Let there be no doubt about it. The system works. Test scores are the highest in the world. But it doesn't answer a gnawing doubt. Is that what I want for my child? Is her self-worth more precious than *gaman*? Is there anything sadder than a child never knowing who or what she is except a piston running smoothly in a well-oiled engine? The system may be okay for Japan, but not for our daughter. My Japanese husband agrees. We're coaching her at home so that she remains a human being, able to enter and survive in an American school.

Next, a secondary school. Over it hangs the menace of university matriculation. The ghost of Wilhelm von Humboldt haunts the halls. Everyone in uniform. Prussian punctilio. Do or die for the next exam. *Shiken Jigoku,* "Examination Hell," exudes heat. Teachers turn grim, students sullen as the tempo accelerates from art and music to math and science. Seventy percent of high school students sacrifice afternoon play, holidays, and summer vacations for supplementary study. In addition to tax-supported public schools, 100 thousand *juku,* cram schools, are underwritten by families whose education-related household expenses consume 10 to 20 percent of monthly income. Students pay priests to pray for their success in acquiring an educational pedigree, solely by which standard applicants are judged by prospective employers.

Subjects not susceptible to examination are not taught. Computers are rare. A principal explains: "Computerization is not included in university entrance exams, so there is no need to teach it." In an English class instruction is in Japanese. The reason: "Entrance exams test reading and writing in English so we do not stress ability to speak." An English textbook contains palindromes such as "Madame, I'm Adam," and sentences such as "I don't think that that that that that boy used in that sentence is wrong." Yet, having solved the palindrome, parsed the sentence, and passed the course, the student cannot direct a stranger to the railroad station. Teachers make no bones about it. "It's more important for a Japanese to read technical books in English so that he can apply its principles to his company's manufacturing methods than it is for him to converse with an American—unless, of course, his job calls for that ability, in which case he undergoes intensive training in conversation." As do elementary schools, secondary schools stress *gaman.* "Do as you are told. Conform. The nail that sticks out gets hammered down."

Democracy, the entitlement of every child to education, yields to meritocracy, the entitlement of only those who pass exams to enter higher education.

At the university level, interviews with doctoral candidates have a familiar ring. Here is one that, in its fidelity to the norm, says something central to the PhD phenomenon:

> As a high school student I didn't know what I wanted as a career, only that I wanted to learn, pass exams and enter a graduate school ensuring higher status. I decided to become a doctor. I failed the entrance exam. The only openings were in agriculture and education. I didn't want to be a farmer, and that left me with only one choice, education. In the absence of any other career, I chose it.
>
> Education, to me, did not mean a primary or secondary school where teachers must cope with children for forty hours a week. That would be too hard for me. I really don't like children. My preference was comparative education, the sociology of education, education at the research rather than the teaching level. My ambition was to become a professor and enjoy *kyuko,* time off from campus, escape from classes, a life of independence, pleasure, prestige. I was lucky that the Occupation introduced the American system creating a hierarchical structure in education. It made entrance into higher education dependent on degrees. In Japan today we have 150 institutions offering Master and Doctoral degrees. Credentialism has become the way to escape the classroom.
>
> As an associate professor, I earn less than my classmates at Tokyo University who entered law, banking, industry. But I have the security of a civil servant. I am protected for life against the risks of the marketplace. In ten years I will be eligible for a pension, and I will quit education. Actually, Japanese higher education is a pretty empty thing. Students don't expect much from the university. Neither do the big corporations which have their own training systems. Training, not education, is the aim of Japanese schools from kindergarten to the university. The average Japanese is not an educated man. He is a man who plays *pachinko,* a pin ball machine, and reads *manga.*

Manga are Japanese comic books. More comic books are read in Japan than in all the rest of the world combined. Close to 2 billion copies are sold every year, as compared with about 150 million in America. More paper goes into this production than into toilet tissue. About one third of all books and magazines bought in Japan are *manga*. A typical *manga* may run from 300 to 600 pages, thicker than the Tokyo telephone directory. Content ranges from rape, sado-masochism, ritual suicide to physics-made-easy, gourmet cooking, and business management, with the balance tipped heavily toward sex. A business executive sitting beside me on the train to Kyoto sets aside his copy of *Kinnikuman* "Muscle Man," and explains. "I work very hard. My mind is tired. For relief I read *manga*. Perhaps I should be reading Shakespeare, Tolstoy or *The Tales of Genji*. But what I hunger for is sex, violence, fantasy. We Japanese live hard lives. In *manga* we find escape."

A high school girl flicks through *Margaret*, 492 pages of cartoons for girls aged ten to twenty. "I think *manga* are beautiful," she says.

> As a Japanese girl I cannot be aggressive. I am not allowed to fall in love or have sex with boys. So I find relief in such a story as this. A girl falls in love with a boy. He is a drummer, with a foreign hair style, and he has a girl friend. One day they meet, laugh, touch each other, kiss. There is jealousy, fighting, scolding, undressing, making love in more ways than I could ever imagine without *manga*. What I can never do in real life I experience in comics. Without *Margaret* my life would be very dull.

Experts differ about Japanese education. In one view:

> "European rigor, American scale, Japanese intensity—these words capsule education in Japan, possessor of one of the world's most advanced and successful school systems. As a result of the examination system Japan acquires a large reservoir of well-trained people with a substantial core of common culture, people who are curious, teachable, disciplined and sensitive to humanistic and civic concerns."

Critics disagree:

> With little time to do anything else but study, students arrive at the university broken in body and soul. Some are shattered. They have spun themselves out and have no taste whatever for learning. At all levels there is a tendency for teaching to be dull and wooden. Lazy once they receive tenure, professors occupy an ivory tower, remote from society, students and one another. Japanese education is summed up by the student who asked his professor: "From the viewpoint of my academic career, would it be better for me to become a Marxist or a Keynesian?"

How to arbitrate opinions of experts? The simplest solution might be for the United States to attack Japan, to lose the war, and to await the arrival of the Japanese Education Mission to America. It too might investigate American schools for twenty-five days, advise us to replace English with Japanese, urge us to achieve wisdom, warn American women to be good, introduce *gaman,* and otherwise provide us with pedagogical perfection.

33

Educational Wonders Down Under . . .

The University of Sydney
Sydney, Australia, 1985–1986

My cup runs over. Two invitations arrive, one from the University of Sydney in Australia, another from the University of Canterbury in Christchurch, New Zealand. Jammed into the straitjacket of a jumbo jet, I wonder what sort of schools have the offspring of England's outlaws spawned? Before America's revolution, the riff-raff in Britain's overcrowded jails had been shipped to our colonies and sold into slavery. With independence, the United States barred its doors to these "criminal classes." In consequence, a "First Fleet" set sail from England in 1788 with 759 felons and, after a voyage of 14,000 miles, deposited its convict cargo in Sydney Cove. What systems of education have sprung from such inauspicious seed?

Hardly was my jet lag overcome than headlines in Australia's rough and tumble press revealed the depths to which antipodean education had sunk. "Why Our Universities Are Failing!" cried the cover of the weekly *Bulletin*. "Education Crisis Comes to A Head!" fulminated the *Financial Times*. "Teachers Blamed for Disillusioned Students," asserted *The Australian* which, in its weekend *Focus,* featured "The Crisis on Our Campuses." "Tertiary Colleges Can Drive Students to Suicide!," a sidebar added. According to the University of Sydney's student newspaper: "Faculty of Arts a Disaster Area . . . Like a Badly Leaking Nuclear Reactor!"

Seemingly, I had flown from frying pans sizzling in the United States into an academic inferno. Only the sublimity of Sydney's harbor, the allure of its opera, the hospitality of International House where I was quartered curbed an impulse to fly back home to Hawaii, avoiding exposure to so virulent a pedagogic plague— an impulse that, obeyed, would have denied me one of the happiest of my educational adventures.

Quite quickly I learned that the infirmities of Australian education were widely attributed to an absence of money, a standard excuse offered in America. From salary scales to cleaning classrooms, it explained ossification of the staffing structure, rundown in equipment provision, neglect of key research. Reliant on a fixed portion of the commonwealth budget, higher education was locked into a bureaucratic bind. At secondary levels, a 60 percent dropout rate; graduates unable to think, solve problems, make decisions, or prepare an employment application. Teachers overworked and underpaid, addicted to didactic methods of chalk and talk, teach and test.

Ridiculing so bleak an assessment of Australia's plight, one noted columnist wrote of God's intervention: "Hell is so overcrowded that it is about to be closed. 'Fortunately,' the Almighty reveals, 'there is now a place so appalling, so dreadful and so wretched that it will put the fear of Me into the most hardened sinner. I refer, of course, to Australia!' "

Any sense of dread the press instilled vanished as I ventured across the street from my lodging on City Road to the University of Sydney. Carved above its granite gate the motto—*Sidere mens eadem mutato* "Our spirit the same under another sky"—hinted of Cambridge, reborn beneath the Southern Cross, an impression affirmed by a handsome hybrid of Victorian and modern masonry fragrant with fresh-mown grass and carefully cultivated gardens. My office in Madsen Hall, complete with coffee urn, frig, and a cafeteria around the corner, offered amenities beyond my experience and expectations. Friendly faces appeared at the door with invitations to a shivoo at the Faculty Club to down some plonk with the dags, unless, of course, I was a wowser. Or to a barbie in Kiribili across the Coathanger to sample the snags. Don't clubber up, I was advised, and don't get off at Redfern or you'll run into a barney.

It took some time to assimilate Aussie solecisms. At first, indeed, I was offended when strangers called me "mite," an aspersion on my size. Not until I learned that "mite" meant "mate," signalling a stite or state that binds all fair dinkum diggers in fraternal bondage did I accept the hospitality so plentifully proffered.

"Shivoo," I gathered, meant a party, "plonk" was wine, and a "dag" was someone whose untidy appearance suggested lumps of excrement adhering to a sheep's behind. A "wowser" was a teetotaler, a "barbie" a barbecue, "Coathanger" a term for the harbor bridge from Sydney to the suburb of Kiribili where "snags" were sausages. Informal dress was *de rigeur*, as implied by "don't clubber up," and "getting off at Redfern" referred to sexual intercourse interrupted on the tram terminating at a Sydney slum where "barneys" or scuffles were common.

Once mastered, the argot of "Oz," as "the lucky land" is called, revealed the wit and warmth of a wonderful outback. A calaboose become a colony, a colony become a nation, a nation of fifteen millions tucked off in mid-Pacific, here, writ large, were the annals of education, from Virgil, Homer, and Caesar to Menzies, Whitlam, and Hawke. It was as if the theory advanced by Spencer, Comte, Freud, and Hall—that a child "recapitulates" within itself the evolution of the human race from prehistoric times to today— was acted out within the educational experience of Australia.

Vast, rugged, seagirt, the continent matches America in size and diversity. I bussed to Brisbane, Melbourne, Adelaide, rode the Indian-Pacific express to Perth, in Alice Springs glimpsed aboriginal education, and in Armidale, at the University of New England, by great good luck encountered James Bowen whose article for the Bicentennial Issue of *Discourse,* the Australian Journal of Education, had just been typed. Jim, a stocky, mustached man with an Aussie gift of gab, confided a copy of his paper entitled

"Education, Social Class and Privilege: European Influences and the Australian Response, 1788–1988" from which, with his consent, I herewith borrow.

As in other lands settled by Englishmen, Irishmen, and Scots, Australia inherited its educational system from the mother country. At the time the decision was taken to send its outlaws to Australia, Britain was ruled by a decadent monarchy. George III was demented, George IV a sexually scandalous glutton, William IV incompetent. Equally degenerate were England's schools. Oxford and Cambridge produced a privileged class, mandated to govern by divine authority. To its ancient independent schools, "the Clarendon Nine," flocked sons of gentry who monopolized higher offices of the royal court, the Church of England, the House of Lords, the army and navy, the bench and bar, the systems of schooling. From these citadels of spurious scholarship, "education" trickled down to common grammar schools established to produce a clerical class of paper pushers, number crunchers, and clerks who, living as servitors on the fringes of privilege, relieved their masters of such disagreeable duties.

Australia's early governors and military administrators sought to recreate an elitist social structure which they ruled. Acquiring vast tracts of land tended by indentured laborers, they set themselves on the path to power. Simultaneously, ex-convicts spread across the continent, established a "squatocracy," converted a continental jail into a colony of homesteaders. Gradually an urban commercial bourgeoisie emerged, prospered, and resisted so-called "exclusives" seeking to legitimize their control of the colony. Thus, within the first fifty years of the new settlement, the class consciousness, privilege, and conflict characterizing the old country were transferred to the new, with a school system in the image of England's.

The University of Sydney, established in 1851, was an exclusive institution, its first professors imported from Oxbridge, its first book the *Greek Lexicon,* its first purpose the production of "those belonging to the higher grades of society." As farmers and mercantile classes acquired wealth, a network of elitist private schools came to dominate secondary education. "We want schools of the type of the English public schools," said the Anglican Bishop of Sydney, "to train our boys of the upper and middle classes, and to be feeders for the more advanced education of the colleges." In such a situation, public education had hard sledding. Various codes were enacted by legislatures to provide minimal literacy for an industrial work force. The Catholic clergy supported parochial schools to offset Protestant public schooling, but authority resided in the private sector.

Back in Britain the private sector, challenged by social, political, and economic changes transforming Europe, sought some way to maintain Oxbridge and the Clarendon Nine as bastions of privileged power. It found it in Hellenism. As Greece came to justify the elitism of English education, so came it to infect its antipodean offspring. Hundreds of years, thousands of miles separate swagmen, diggers, drovers, and dags from Atheneans and Romans. Yet here, on this "fatal shore," the vast panorama of pedagogy is portrayed, a sorry story redeemed by Aussie mirth and melancholy.

Nowhere, by no one, is the tale better told than in James Bowen's book, *A History of Western Education* (St. Martin's Press). Education in Athens, it confirms, meant teaching privileged boys—*pais* means boy, and girls are excluded—to govern disenfranchised masses and slaves. From it comes *paideia,* the Greek word for education. Elementary schools—the word *school* derives from the Greek *schole,* meaning "leisure," reserved for the rich—taught children of the privileged class reading, writing, reckoning and religion. *Grammatikos,* grammar schools, trained adolescents in syntax and literature. Schools of *rhetor,* rhetoric, turned older boys into *politikon zoon,* "political animals" or politicians. *Curriculum* was Latin for "a course to be run," winners constituting a meritocracy as opposed to a democracy, and was based on the humanly relevant studies that equipped elites to manage society in confirmation of their inherited authority. The *New Testament* added religious emphasis to the meritocratic process, insuring that only those with linguistic ability in Latin and Greek could rightly rule. God ordained "a great chain of being" whereby aristocrats were born and educated to preside over lower social orders. Latin became the tool by which church, government, the learned professions of medicine and law distanced themselves from lower class levels of vernacular literacy.

"Hellenism," Jim Bowen writes, "offered an ideal vehicle for the ideological formation of a ruling class. Nothing could be better than Plato's *Republic* with its doctrine of an elite of intrinsic merit

—a golden class of guardians, born to rule, with a detailed program of the ascent to a vision of the ultimate Good." Thucydides and Herodotus sanctified the ideal of aristocratic ascendancy. The Peloponnesian and Persian wars were read as modern allegory; that tiny Athens could become a maritime power and achieve empire was a lesson not lost on lads who manned the British navy. That the battle of Waterloo was won on the playing fields of Eton owed much to English admiration of Greek blood sports. Competition of crews on the Thames invoked Odyssean dreams of Britannia ruling the waves.

Such borrowings by Britain from the Athenean past imfluenced Australia, leaving vivid marks on education, games, and sports. Not until British blundering in two world wars exposed the inadequacies of English education and class stratification did Australia develop a sense of national identity and educational autonomy, and break its bond with Britain.

Only, alas, to fall prey to the Prussian. Among the foremost of Australia's early educators was Dr. John Smyth who studied at Heidelberg, Leipzig, and Jena. Smyth brought back to Melbourne's Teachers College, of which he became principal, the experimental psychology of Wundt, the depth psychology of Freud, the differential psychology of Binet. Text of his course was *Adolescence* by G. Stanley Hall, that eminent American Germanophile who Smyth is said to have met in Leipzig. "The really significant importation," Bowen adds, "was latter day Herbartism —a dreary system of mechanized instruction that became entrenched in Australian pedagogy and persisted in teacher training colleges until the 1950s and even 1960s"—much as it has in America.

Mainly, however, it was from American wellsprings that innovation flowed into the lucky land's schools. In 1922 the Montessori method applied by Helen Parkhurst in Dalton, Massachusetts, was brought to Sydney's Darlington Practice School. For a while pupils became "Daltonites to the last one!" but enthusiasm waned as Aussie teachers, discontent with the loss of their authority, let progressivism lapse into lockstep drudgery.

The Winnetka Plan devised by Carleton Washburn in Winnetka, Illinois, aiming at the encouragement of initiative and self-expression, won a brief foothold in Perth until a financial depression did it in. In a replay of my own experience in New York City's

schools, William Wirt's Gary Plan arrived in Victoria, propelled
by the conviction of the state's chief inspector that "once adopted,
the platoon organization will prove as successful with us as it has
been in the land of its origin"—a prophecy self-fulfilled. Nor was
Australia spared "The Project Method," born of John Dewey's
contention that in times of social change, children be taught methods of thinking applicable to problems they would later confront
—an experiment that "came and went as a temporary craze in
some schools in the 1930s." W. H. Kilpatrick of Teachers College,
Columbia, sold Australia on his "Four Steps—purposing, planning, executing and judging"—economizing on Herbart's Five, but
lasting nowhere near as long as his German predecessor's. The
theory of inherited superior intelligence as popularized by Edward
Thorndike, and the process promoted by the Educational Testing
Service at Princeton, New Jersey, were employed by the public
school system as devices for selecting a favored minority to be
taught in specialized schools in competition with the private sector. Oz, in short, went all out on America's educational enthusiasms.

    Thus it was that little digger guinea pigs underwent the yo-yo,
hula-hoop, Mickey Mouse crazes that, in America, masqueraded
as "education." Indeed, one Australian, Peter Board, director of
New South Wales Education, fused Herbartian, Deweyian, Wir-
tian, Kilpatrickian, and Thorndikian ideas into an invention
called Brighton-le-Sands, after its location on Botany Bay. Its
declared intention: "to place responsibility on the children for the
management of various school interests, to be increased with each
advancing class." Greeted with great acclaim for its fine facilities,
its freedoms, its Rousseauian faith in the goodness of the child,
Brighton-le-Sands seemed a progressive's dream come true until,
as the district's population grew, as class sizes swelled, and as Australian imps proved less angelic than Peter Board promised, it
turned into a nightmare. Confronted with classes of seventy larri-
kins over whom they had no control, overtaxed teachers reverted
to chalk and talk, teach and test. Brighton-le-Sands. Born 1917.
Died 1922.

    After World Wars I and II conservative governments gave way
to labor. Old English, Irish, and Scottish stock was leavened by
continental Europeans and Asians. Although geographically remote from centers of super-power struggle, Australia's factories,

farms, and mines underwent economic ups and downs, and nuclear testing in nearby New Caledonia reminded it that nowhere on earth is mankind immune to immediate immolation. As everywhere else its schools are in crisis.

Many are disconsolate. In Jim Bowen's opinion,

> The salient feature of Australian education in 1988, the Bicentennial Year, is that class divisions have hardened, rather than weakened. The great initiative of the wartime Labor government under John Curtin and Ben Chifley who established the Australian National University and thereby began the process of Commonwealth funding for education, has been steadily subverted in the succeeding decades by conservative forces. The current economic structure of Australia bears little imprint of the struggles of the past to establish an equitable, democratic society.

Others, rarely sanguine, nevertheless exhibit an earthy, cynical outlook, imbued with humor somehow summed up in the story of the Aussie mother who knocked on her son's door.

"Johnny," she said, "it's time to get up." Johnny didn't answer. A little later she knocked again. "Johnny, get up, you've got to go to school." Johnny mumbled, "Oh mother, I don't want to go to school. I don't like the teachers and the kids, and the teachers and kids don't like me!" "All the same, Johnny, you've *got* to go to school!" "But why, mother, *why* have I got to go to school?" "Because," mother answered, "you're the principal!"

My own judgment is distorted by pro-Aussie prejudice. No school system can be all that bad, I believe, that produces such wonderful people—a highly subjective, unscientific standard unlikely to be accepted by others, including Australians, but one that may say more about the performance of schools than other academic criteria. As the Australian educational experience mirrors the inanities and insanities of pedagogy from past to present, so do Aussie teachers reflect the "up yours mate go fuck a duck" attitude appropriate to so absurd a history. They seem, by and large, to be a balanced lot, cocking a quizzical eye at all the hocus-pocus of complaint, and snapping a cynical salute at the politicians, bureaucrats, ideologues under whom they labor. Rarely does one meet a martinet, a self-seeking scrounger, an apodictic know-it-all pushing some nostrum for educational acne, or promising an X-ray insight into the mysteries of the mind. The PhD propensity subdued, neither publishing much nor perishing, attentive to research but given more to instruction, many adhere to a peculiarly Australian principle—a love of life, a zest for living. Better to enjoy a book, sail a boat, kick a ball, back a horse, barbecue a snag, and gulp a beer than run an obstacle course of unremitting labor, dropping dead in the traces.

On a planet where Americans see their "nation at risk, drowning in a rising tide of mediocrity"; where Japanese idolize mammon; where Soviets attune their schools to the *Internationale;* and Britons prepare for lifelong dependence on the dole, Aussies seek to live life in a spirit of mateship rather than hardship. Whether, in the harsh international competitive climate that prevails, they can survive and prosper remains to be seen.

It is, however, neither my judgment nor any other that matters so much as that of young Aussies. Wherever I went in Oz I queried kids about how they felt about their schools, their teachers, their future. To cite a few written replies:

> I have just turned 16 and I feel my education has not prepared me for the outside world. It is upon the shoulders of my generation that the world's fate will rest, for at the push of a button total world annihilation could result. What if education has not prepared us for the pressure and we crack?

> The education system is designed to get students to decide what rut they are going to spend their life in and to stay in that rut and be *happy!* Steady job, steady hours, steady life—maybe go on a party occasionally and get drunk but they have got to stay in that rut. People who don't stay in ruts society labels undesirable. So the education system is controlled by society and society won't acknowledge what it is. They're afraid they might not like what they see.

> Simply, I believe there will never be world peace until an effective education system has been established in every corner of the earth. With such a system there should be a world curriculum. This, of course, would vary from nation to nation, but ultimately revolve around the concept of world-citizenship and teach every child to love every man on this earth as a creature of God.

> Teachers are filling us full of facts that we can put in exams. Is there not something wrong with a system where it is possible for those lucky enough to be born with photographic memories, to be able to do better than others?

In high school you are faced with the fact that soon you will have to face the world by yourself and you are always reminded that you must always think of your future. But how can it be our future when our future may not even exist? This is the type of question we are faced with by the threat of nuclear war. I thought growing up was meant to be fun. But it's not. It's a lot of hardwork, pressure, exams. There's no time for us even to think of ourselves, and how to cope with a future that may never be.

Young Aussies echo their age-group all over the world. One boy was black, broad-nosed, shaggy-haired—an aboriginal, Australian equivalent of our American Indians, now a minority in their own native land. "When the white men came they poisoned our wells. Like animals, instinct warned us not to drink the water. So it is with education. We smell something sick in the schools, a system that's pious and patriotic, but leads to wickedness and war. Until schools are rid of that poison, kids instinctively resist it, and that's why we misbehave, drop out, and get into trouble."

34

The Best
Little Schoolhouses
in the World

University of Canterbury
Christchurch, New Zealand 1987

This article appeared in the June 6, 1987 issue of New Zealand's leading weekly magazine, *The Listener:*

KIWI SCHOOLS: THE WORLD'S BEST
New Zealand's child-centred education system impresses as achieving a level of excellence unmatched by any other.

New Zealand's schools are best, but only on a comparative basis. As so many Maoris, Marxists and feminists attest, the

schools suffer from every malady to which education is heir—
social, sexist and ethnic discrimination; elitism; poverty; poor
pedagogy; bureaucratic bungling; caning; irrelevant curricula that
stifle student interest and induce inertia; draconian assessment
that bars disproportionate numbers of New Zealand youth from
access to higher education. Doubtless other evils could be added to
the indictment with abundant evidence to sustain their severity.
Nevertheless, perceived from a global perspective, and reflecting a
purely personal bias, New Zealand's schools achieve a level of
excellence unmatched by any other.

The verdict rests on two reasons. One is that if some Kiwis
think their schools are bad, it is because they have not attended
others overseas. Second, New Zealand, more than any other
nation, bolsters my bias towards child-centred (but not child-dom-
inated) rather than state- or system-centred education. Like all
biases, mine is subjective, unscientific and, in this instance, at
odds with others who believe that education must begin and end
not with what the child wants and needs, but what the state, the
sect or other sacred institution asserts children must learn to perform their duties as responsible adults. Child-centred education is
identified as the academic arsenic that poisons society's wells. Illiteracy, non-numeracy, sexual license, drug abuse, vandalism and
other crimes are attributed to progressive-education enthusiasts
whose permissiveness has carried to excessive lengths Rousseau's
dictum that a child needs only to be loved to attain enlightenment.

Agreeing that much progressive experimentation has verged on
the insane, I nevertheless cling to my conviction that, for all their
ills, schools sensitive to a child's nature, needs and interests are
more likely to produce a sentient citizenry than those patterned
after the 19th-century Prussian model from which almost all Western (and Japanese) systems are cloned. It is therefore likely that
only those who endorse the view that society is best served if
schools meet the needs of the child rather than those of the state
will be persuaded of the excellence of Kiwi education.

This, of course, invites the question of whether or not New
Zealand education is indeed child-centred, in what respect and to
what degree as compared with others. A few observations to
affirm my opinion:

1. Whereas in other countries children enter school at the
beginning of a year or term as "cohorts"—a word other systems

employ to reduce individuals to anonymous increments of incoming objects to be taught—each New Zealand child celebrates its fifth birthday with admission into the company of its peers. Instead of flooding into classrooms in numbers beyond a school's capacity to cope, each entrant is accorded the teacher's affectionate attention, the classroom appears as a pleasant place, and the educational experience is off to a promising start.

2. Children work at producing their own products; they learn how to extend their own learning; they are monitored carefully by teachers who promote them as fast as they are able.

3. Reading is recognised as the single most important element in the teaching-learning process. Force-feeding techniques that make books obstacles to be leaped on the way to dreaded examinations are avoided. Teachers and parents aim at enjoyment rather than pressing for performance. Early on, learning comes under the child's initiative and command, releasing teachers to assist others in trouble. *Kiwi boys and girls, in consequence, score higher on international reading comprehension and literature tests than any other children in the Western world.*

4. More children's literature is available per capita than in any other nation. Books satisfy Kiwi kids' hunger for adventure, relaxation and self-instruction. As elsewhere, television menaces New Zealand's traditional love of reading, but anyone who visits a public library on Saturday mornings when youngsters are out of school senses that New Zealand's appetite for the printed word and picture remains hearty.

5. That a nation with fewer than four million people should produce teachers internationally ranked beside Froebel, Pestalozzi, Montessori and Dewey says something of significance about New Zealand education. Sylvia Ashton-Warner's books— *Teacher, Spinster, Bell Call, Incense to Idols*—are widely acclaimed for their sensitivity to a child's insights and outlook. Teachers, she taught, must have the patience and wisdom to listen, to watch and wait until the child's line of thought becomes apparent, and to set the creative pattern in which these forces will naturally flow. Her writing reinforces the image of a strongly child-centred strategy all the more remarkable for the small, remote society from which it springs.

6. New Zealand's schools are ecologically oriented. Forays to forests, lakes, mountains and sheep-filled meadows are staples of

primary and secondary school curricula. No other state-supported schools are so extensively equipped for such excursions. Bedding, tents, cooking utensils ensure that many, if not all, New Zealand children are made aware and appreciative of their country's natural splendour and of their personal responsibility to ensure its survival.

7. New Zealand teachers seem less burned-out than their ilk in other countries. They enjoy more autonomy, less "work-book" regulation, greater opportunity to improvise and to adapt the text to the child rather than vice-versa. The craving for credentials that lures the best, brightest and most ambitious to graduate schools is less obsessive. Few seek sanctuary in administrative sinecures; few covet advanced degrees for the better pay, power, prestige and perquisites that a doctorate delivers; few fanatics seek pulpits to propagandise and indoctrinate rather than to educate. Able and dedicated instructors remain at the chalk-face content to be teachers.

8. Research in New Zealand remains clinically close to the classroom, responding to the need for more knowledge in such hands-on areas as curricular revision, teaching techniques and assessment. It does not, as elsewhere, ascend into the stratosphere or overshadow instruction. Nor does pressure to "publish or perish" separate professors from their students. Lacking a large-scale publishing industry, New Zealand is necessarily eclectic, importing the best from overseas. Because imports are expensive, New Zealand librarians are selective in their acquisitions. Thus economies are turned to advantage; libraries are better able to serve the child-centred interests of researchers, teachers and students.

9. Impressive is the testimony of parents and children in a position to contrast school experiences here and overseas. To cite one mother:

> We have three kids from 8 to 15. They were happy, healthy and doing all right in Christchurch schools until my husband's boss sent us overseas. Very quickly we knew they were in trouble. Sarah, the eldest, loved to read, write and act in school plays, but maths were not her dish. She'd come home in tears because her teacher said she was stupid. When I explained to the principal my daughter was a reader rather than a maths type he said, "Sorry, it's maths that matter, not reading books." All three children lost their self-confidence, became surly, began to misbehave. My husband quit his job and we

returned to New Zealand. Everything has changed. Sarah is again a happy girl who loves school, excels in sports and publishes stories in the school paper. New Zealand schools are not for principals, pedagogues, the Minister of Education. They're for Kiwi kids.

10. New Zealand's telephone directories are illustrated not by professional artists, but by school children. The 1986 Christchurch cover has a picture of the post office entitled "My People, Our Place", painted by Elizabeth McKelvey, Form 7, Avonside Girls High School, winner of a secondary school art competition. Creativity is encouraged in Kiwi kids. Somehow, that says it all.

True, New Zealand has problems. Its agricultural economy is vulnerable. Job scarcity places Kiwi kids in jeopardy. Though they lead the Western world in reading, they do poorly in math, and a major effort is under way to repair this deficiency.

What New Zealand exemplifies is the child-centred focus of its schools. Examined in historical depth and global breadth, state-centred school systems—from Sparta to Spain, from Prussia to Russia, from Hannibal to Hitler—have always and inevitably induced xenophobia, boundless ambition and bloody war. Harbouring more life-enhancing aspirations and satisfactions, New Zealand seems an island of sanity amid a storm-tossed sea of Bhopals, Chernobyls and misguided missiles. The child-centred schools of this diminutive antipodean David set an enviable example for suicidal Goliaths whose scientific prowess is unmatched by the wit to wield it wisely.

It is doubtful that so optimistic an estimate of Kiwi education will satisfy politicians, industrialists and technocrats. Perhaps, indeed, it has been overstated. Better to conclude that were I condemned—God forbid!—to climb again the long, steep, hazardous hill from kindergarten to college, it would be Kiwi schools I would opt to attend.

With this estimate of Kiwi education I agree.

In fact, I wrote it.

35

"Nigger"

Wist Hall
September 1987

Fall semester begins. Unlike the spring semester's engaging empha-
ses on history, autumnal approaches embrace Social Foundations
and Philosophy of Education, subjects infinitely more demanding
of disciplines with which I am not endowed. These courses contain the very essence of a process that decides candidates' ability to
pursue careers as professors, policy-makers, administrators, and
other principals in the educational endeavor. If the ills of education are to be traced to their source, participation in these more
rigorous regions of the doctoral rat race seems essential.

Dr. Royal Fruehling, a scintillating anthropologist with an ear-
nest, ingratiating manner, lays it on the line. We are to read a book
entitled *A Strategy of Decision* whose authors, D. Braybrooke and
C. L. Lindblom describe a strategy called "disjointed incremental-

ism" by which an issue can be moved from problem solving to policy making. Faced with a problem, the "strategy" posits certain alternatives to be considered, mainly incremental changes in the status quo:

> Analysis and evaluation occur in a long chain of amended choices, in the course of which consequences are considered, adjustments made, a reciprocal relationship established between ends and means. Analysis and evaluation are oriented toward remedying a negatively perceived situation, rather than toward reaching a preconceived goal.

I search this "strategy" for whatever it may convey as to what is meant by "disjointed incrementalism"—words that swiftly signal the inanities of academic English. Wisely, Dr. Fruehling couples the Braybrooke book with *The Troubled Crusade, American Education 1945–1980* by Diane Ravitch. (Her *The Great School Wars* exposed what lay behind my difficulties in New York City's P.S. 171, earlier recorded.) Dr. Fruehling asks that we cite evidence from Ravitch that supports or rebuts the theory of disjointed incrementalism, looking at government actions, court decisions, student riots, and other crises in America's schools.

Ravitch zeros in on racism. "While some issues in American education waxed and waned . . . the problem of racial inequality in education grew in significance with every passing year." If anything was disjointed in American education, it was this ingrained kink in America's schools. And so I wrote:

> Ravitch describes the tensions, violence, conflicts and fears that infected relations between the races, north and south; the south's efforts to stonewall federal efforts at desegregation; the Plessy v. Ferguson decision of 1896 which upheld the constitutionality of a Louisiana law segregating rail passengers by race; Rosa Park's refusal to relinquish her seat in a Montgomery Alabama bus to a white rider; the Brown decision of 1954 declaring state-imposed racial segregation in public schools unconstitutional; Southern Manifestos decrying the Brown decision as "a clear abuse of judicial power." Her chronicle is rich in 'increments' so 'disjointed' as to arouse wonder about the sanity of the democratic system in ordering its educational arrangements. What follows is an effort

to put Ravitch's superb historical account in a personal perspective that sorts out "jointed" and "disjointed" increments as one individual perceives them. [At this point, Dr. Fruehling notes: "Here I think you have redefined the assignment." Which, in an effort to pump blood into this astringent exercise, indeed I have.]

When I was a boy, brought up in New York City early in this century—a first generation American who badly needed someone on whom he could look down—that someone was a "nigger" who, despite the fact that *his* ancestors were born in America, and *mine* in Europe, was less American than I. The first Negro I knew was the janitor of the tenement we occupied, an illiterate man who stoked coal in winter, and installed awnings over our windows against the summer sun. My sister was warned to give him wide berth, because it was a sad fact of life that blacks lusted for white female bodies. We called them niggers, coons, jigs and jigaboos because it was by such sobriquets that they were known in Minstrel Shows and other entertainments in which they played banjos, jigged and otherwise behaved like buffoons—the ultimate insult being that blacks were really whites with fuligenous faces. Minstrels yielded to Amos 'n' Andy, among the first blacks—actually white—to make it big in radio, along with Stepin Fetchet and other comic characters addicted to fried chicken, chitlins and watermelon. The amused contempt with which blacks were held was unrelieved by prize fighters like Jack Johnson, New Orleans jazz, or an occasional poet like a classmate of mine at City College, Countee P. Cullen.

When, in World War II, I was mustered into the army, black and white troops travelled in segregated trains to Camp Lee, Virginia, where draftees served in segregated regiments. In part this was due to blacks' poor educational qualifications. Most were employed as truck drivers, grave diggers and laborers that denigrated both their competence and their courage.

As editor-in-chief of the army's newspaper, *The Stars and Stripes,* it was my task to remind readers that our fight *against* fascism was, at core, a fight *for* freedom, equality, social, political and economic justice. The disparity between our ideals and our actions mocked the purposes for which the war was fought. In a series of editorials, I strove to publicize the issue. To quote one, illustrated with a thumbs-up photo of a black GI:

Let's Set the Post War Pattern

About one soldier in every ten in this man's army is a Negro. Wherever you go—from the beaches to the front—you see these lads doing their stuff. Which leads up to the story of three GIs—white boys—who were caught on the road one night with the gas needle of their jeep angling toward the zero mark.

They made several bids for refill without success—until they pulled into an orchard where a Negro medic outfit was dug in for the night. Piled in a neat stack under a tree were about 30 jerricans, all empty. Empty, that is, except for the few drops that always stick inside the neck of a GI can.

Well, those Negro GIs came out of their holes and tilted the empties into one can. By the time the 30 cans were wrung dry there was enough gas in the jeep to get to the next dump.

"Don't mention it" was what the Negro sergeant said as the GIs resumed their journey. But the decent things Joes do for each other *should* be mentioned. They ought to make things a little easier when we go back home.

It drew the second largest soldier mail in the *Stripes'* history, almost all favorable. Eisenhower himself, asked at a press conference in Paris his opinion of the Negro soldier, replied: "I draw no distinction between white and black GIs. They are *all American soldiers,* they did a great job, and just as together they won the war, so together can they win the peace."

It was an awesome moment, the end of a frightful war, a time to apply its lessons before social, economic and political pressures put blacks "back where they belonged." With one veteran out of every ten a black, entitled by service and sacrifice to a fair shake, never before in the American experience was the climate so ripe for racial reform.

That climate was chilled when, the war in Europe at an end, a group of educators-in-uniform arrived from the Pentagon to describe the GI Bill. As earlier mentioned, *The Stars and Stripes* had the task of publicizing the gigantic educational undertaking, and a special briefing session exposed these educational officers to our questions. Our black reporter, Allan Morrison, asked what provision was being made for Negro veterans. Would the same pre-war conditions prevail, excluding Negros from higher education, consigning children to inferior schools, and otherwise treating blacks as second class citizens?

"Not at all," he was assured by an affable officer. "All such matters will be dealt with at local levels, in accord with what each community believes best to insure opportunity for each and every veteran."

Morrison said this offered little hope for Negro soldiers returning to the south or to northern ghettos where local custom guaranteed that blacks would suffer discrimination. The officer was adamant. "Not at all," he repeated. "The GI Bill is as open to nigras —I mean Negros—as it is to whites."

Let us now return to Ravitch and to the strategy of "disjointed incrementation." The record she reveals describes a variety of means well orchestrated and directed toward opposite ends. At the federal level, executive, legislative and judicial efforts to desegregate schools. At state and local levels, their frustration by racist politicians, judges and public, expressing with enormous unity, clarity and physical force the determination of Southern states to maintain the antebellum status quo. The United States, in short, was disjointed by federal, state and local increments radically at odds on race.

If any segment of American society seemed to be capable of perceiving this racial disjointment in historical, philosophical and future-oriented perspectives, it would be educators—men and women academically conditioned to bring reason, order and intellect to problem resolution. None better than they could replace 'disjointed incrementalism' with 'well-jointed' sanity.

Yet, oddly, it was precisely within this privileged sector of society that the situation was negatively perceived, with consequent fragmentation of the national effort toward racial reform. Rather than standing at university gates and welcoming blacks with open arms; rather than inviting combat veterans to pool their experiences in programs to prevent future wars; rather than creating curricula with an international overlook that affixed eyes on global problems demanding racial accord as prerequisites to their resolution, pusillanimous presidents, fissiparous faculties and the nation's educational apparatus as a whole discouraged black enrollment, or viewed it with puzzled confusion, or capitulated to whatever pressures were applied by aroused, antagonistic and unruly elements of the population, including students.

Thus was a precious, once-in-a-lifetime opportunity lost. Confrontations at Columbia, Cornell, Kent State and other institutions brought education to its knees. Martin Luther King, John and Robert Kennedy, Medger Evers, students, black and white, lost their lives. And black soldiers came home to America, took off their uniforms, and once again became niggers.

Dr. Fruehling comments on the paper: "You have chosen an imaginative and wholly legitimate vehicle by which to execute the assignment. However, such a vehicle requires some other innovations if the relationship between the narrative and the attributes of "disjointed incrementalism" are to become clear. They are not self-evident. Required would be some specific reference at various points, or, if the narrative is to be kept intact, a brief analysis at the end."

This paper earns my first B.

Praised as "imaginative," "creative," "interesting," and "well-written," all my essays thus far seem somehow to break an undefined barrier governing graduate performance. As best as I can make it out, this barrier seems to be intolerance of any tendency a student may have to wander off the academic reservation, entering into territory not governed by the curriculum, the syllabus, the lesson plan, the book. If any increment is more disjointed than such persistent discouragement of original experience and personal immersion in problem perception and resolution, I can't imagine what it is.

36

A Social Cancer Menaces Education

Wist Hall
October 1987

Dr. Fruehling provides us with twenty-five pieces from the Honolulu press focusing on a dispute between the Hawaii Department of Education (DOE) and Hawaii's Filipino community that, after ten years, remains unresolved. Filipinos complain that although they number 12 percent of Hawaii's population, they hold less than 3 percent of DOE jobs, whereas Japanese, comprising 29 percent of the state's population, fill 59 percent of teaching and 67 percent of administrative positions. The DOE contends that merit (undefined) supercedes ethnicity in hiring procedures, and that teacher turnover is too slow, vacancies too few, to improve the situation.

Dr. Fruehling asks us to extract from the newspaper articles examples of how the policy problem has passed through phases of "problem-sensing," "conceptualization" and "specification," with evidence that six analytic procedures have been applied: "forecasting," "policy alternatives produced by forecasting," "resultant recommendations," "information produced by recommendations," "monitoring of the consequences of such recommendations," and "evaluation of information and policy performance produced by evaluation."

Additionally, four questions are posed: "Have the several stakeholders in the issue used ethnographic, evaluative and normative approaches for producing information and reasoned argument?" "According to what criteria can we determine whether or not public actions are right or wrong?" "Can we determine truth or falsity of normative ethical claims?" "What is the source of ethical knowledge?" Answers, we are advised, demand knowledge of meta-ethical theory involving cognitive and noncognitive types that, in turn, depend on familiarity with epistemic and nonepistemic subjectivism. Among the sources we must explore are a book by George Knight entitled *Issues and Alternatives in Educational Philosophy,* and another, *Taking Sides: Clashing Views on Controversial Educational Issues,* by James Noll.

To extricate us from this epistemological quagmire Professor Fruehling has designed a chart, here reproduced, entitled "Policy Argument Activity (in Education)." It establishes a procedure we must follow: Information leads to Qualifier and Policy Claims which must be sustained by Warrants, Rebuttals, and Backings, resting on a Value or Ethical Basis (authority, parallel cases, known motives, analogy, explanation, intuition, and rules). Six modes on which correct answers depend are Idealism, Realism, Neo-Scholasticism, Pragmatism, Existentialism, and Behaviorism. Knight adds a seventh mode to the cited six, "Analytic Philosophy," which alleges that "the broad sweeping statements of philosophers are nonsense."

I am, quite clearly, an "Analytic Philosopher." Did the idiocy of my quest for a doctoral degree demand demonstration, nothing could better confirm it than my simplistic responses to Dr. Fruehling's complex questions. Dodging the rhetorical roadblocks, avoiding the deontological, teleological, axiological, and practical normative minefields, and defusing the cognitive epistemic booby

POLICY ARGUMENT ACTIVITY (IN EDUCATION)

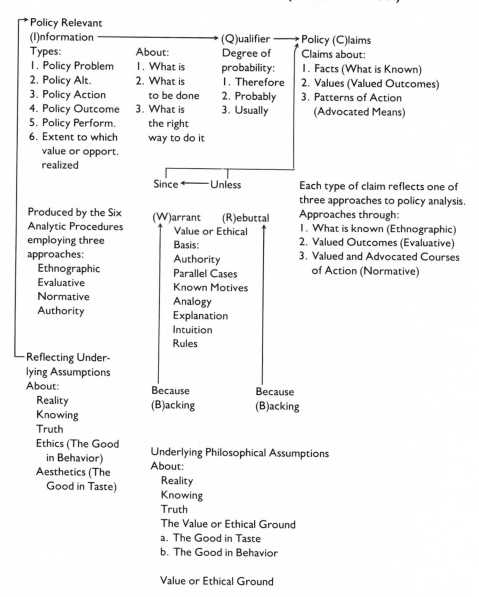

Policy Relevant
(I)nformation ————————————→ (Q)ualifier ——→ Policy (C)laims

Types:	About:	Degree of probability:	Claims about:
1. Policy Problem	1. What is		1. Facts (What is Known)
2. Policy Alt.	2. What is to be done	1. Therefore	2. Values (Valued Outcomes)
3. Policy Action		2. Probably	3. Patterns of Action
4. Policy Outcome	3. What is the right way to do it	3. Usually	(Advocated Means)
5. Policy Perform.			
6. Extent to which value or opport. realized			

Since ←——— Unless

Each type of claim reflects one of three approaches to policy analysis.

Produced by the Six Analytic Procedures employing three approaches:
Ethnographic
Evaluative
Normative
Authority

(W)arrant   (R)ebuttal
Value or Ethical
Basis:
Authority
Parallel Cases
Known Motives
Analogy
Explanation
Intuition
Rules

Approaches through:
1. What is known (Ethnographic)
2. Valued Outcomes (Evaluative)
3. Valued and Advocated Courses of Action (Normative)

Reflecting Under-
lying Assumptions
About:
Reality
Knowing
Truth
Ethics (The Good in Behavior)
Aesthetics (The Good in Taste)

Because
(B)acking

Because
(B)acking

Underlying Philosophical Assumptions
About:
Reality
Knowing
Truth
The Value or Ethical Ground
a. The Good in Taste
b. The Good in Behavior

Value or Ethical Ground

Our class is asked to resolve a dispute between Hawaii's Filipino community and the Department of Education by following the procedure formulated by this chart.

traps infesting a problem that for ten years has resisted resolution
by the DOE and the Filipino community, I affirm the following:

1. The issue rests on whether or not DOE is in compliance with
Supreme Court decisions banning racial discrimination. It is a
legal or juridical rather than an educational issue.

2. The Filipino community is a "Special Interest" concerned
with financial and other advantages accruing to its members
through employment by DOE. DOE is a "Vested Interest" protective of its autonomy. Neither is a "stake-holder." The dispute is a
confrontation between two entities, each so intent on its own
advantage as to obliterate the only true "stake-holder" in this
issue.

3. The sole "stake-holder" is the child. Unless the child is seen
as central to any legitimate educational issue, whose interests
supercede all others, the issue itself is flawed and unworthy of ten
years of academic attention.

4. The pile of chips comprising the "stake" of a poker player, or
the salary stipend of a DOE employee, differs from the "stake" of a
student. The life-chances of a child take precedence over Lady
Luck or the ambitions of an adult job applicant. That any ethnic
group asserts a greater right than has the object of education, the
child, is as grotesque a distortion of the real policy problem as is
DOE's self-defensive reaction.

5. DOE's failure to introduce an educational element reflective
of factors favoring the interests of the child suggests a singular
inability to identify educational issues and resolve resultant problems on historical, geographical, cultural and pedagogical principles rather than on legal, ethnic, economic or other grounds that
lie more within the realm of politicians, lawyers, bookkeepers,
and bureaucrats than of teachers.

6. Filipinos inhabit an archipelago consisting of 7100 islands
falling into three groups: the Luzon, the Visayan and the Mindanao. Depending on where he or she is born, a Filipino speaks one
of 75 different languages, of which seven are of major importance:
Tagalog, Cebuano, Ilongo, Waray-Waray, Ilocano, Pampango
and Bikol. (As a Peace Corps Volunteer, I served in Bohol and
spoke Cebuano, a language virtually useless outside the Visayas.
Only the *lingua franca,* English, draws Filipinos into a common
linguistic web such as exists in Hawaii.)

7. What then best serves the interest of a child of Filipino or any other ethnic origin? Who does the Filipino community wish to add to the DOE roster as a teacher? Why? To provide employment for Filipinos, or to educate children? If the former, is education adequately served? If the latter, what benefit accrues to a classroom by virtue of his or her presence? What language does he or she speak; how does his or her cultural background fit the local Filipino and Hawaiian framework; how are children advantaged by indiscriminate employment of teachers on other grounds than merit? How is merit defined—other than as the efficacy of the child's educational experience?

8. Rather than expending ten years of time and energy in quasi-legal contention, might not DOE develop a program centered on the child, capitalizing on Hawaii's ethnic diversity, encouraging children of different backgrounds to exchange songs, stories, slang, sports that dispel ethnocentricity and enrich sterile curricula so overly dependent on texts?

To Dr. Fruehling's four questions I reply:

1. To the first question—have the several stakeholders used ethnographic, evaluative and normative approaches—I reply that since the child cannot use ethnographic, evaluative or normative approaches for producing information and reasoned argument, the question is unanswerable.

2. The only criterion by which rightness or wrongness of a public action (in education) can be determined is its impact on the child.

3. The truth or falsity of normal ethical claims can best be determined by examining their responsiveness to the educational interests of the child.

4. What is the source of ethical knowledge? God only knows what is meant by "ethical knowledge," to say nothing of its source. But since children depend on adults for beneficial educational input, ethics subsume action in the child's behalf above all others.

Be it Mindoro, Masbate, or Mindanao from which Filipinos came to Hawaii, all honor Jose Rizal who wrote *Noli Me Tangere* "The Social Cancer." There is a social cancer that menaces American education. Educational issues cannot be resolved by tortuous procedures, pseudoscientific pretensions, and a glossolalia so argotic and arcane as to caricature ivory-tower jive. Whereas doctors and lawyers speak to each other in a vocabulary deliberately designed to exclude outsiders, the educator's dialogue is with the pupil, the parent, the public at large. The language of this exercise can do incalculable damage to such a dialogue. And the labyrinth through which we are led to problem nonresolution does disservice to teachers, to children, and to the community.

In *Issues and Alternatives in Educational Philosophy*, George Knight writes: "Mindlessness is the most pertinent and accurate criticism of American education in the twentieth century. Educators have been more concerned with motion than progress, with means rather than ends. They have failed to ask the larger question of purpose, and *the professional training of educators, with its stress on methodology, has largely set them up for this problem.*"

I sense myself "set up" by this assignment.

Dr. Fruehling responds:

No, I'm not sure that that is a fair assessment. I think the methodological model that we are working with is intended to be a means for combatting mindlessness and for better identifying a problem and proposing and implementing a thoughtful, purposeful policy action. It also enables the assessment of that action in terms of the unrealized needs and opportunities that instituted the problem originally. Included are unrealized need and opportunities of children as well. If they are excluded from consideration it is because they are increasingly devalued in our society. We forget that they are the client group on which the entire educational edifice rests. I won't argue with your assessment of the jargon.

No professor is more humane, more sensitive to student's problems, and more expeditious in offering assistance than Royal. We agree that I accept an "incomplete" for the remainder of the course, and devote the rest of the semester to a problem I deem more educationally significant than the Filipino–DOE dispute. Credit will depend on whether a paper I write satisfies Dr. Fruehling's standards.

I re-examine Dr. Fruehling's chart. Other students in the seminar have mastered its twists and turns, gained good grades and, presumably, after graduation, will apply this approach to problems they will encounter as policymakers and principals in the public schools. Why am only I unable to apply it to problem resolution? How, I wonder, are problems solved? By an academic strategy like this "Policy Argument Activity"? Or by immersion, observation, participation?

I review the major learning experiences of my life. A bum on the Bowery. A prisoner in an army stockade. A GI at the front. A Peace Corps volunteer in a Filipino village. An itinerant in India, Indonesia, Africa seeking at the source the realities of life as most people live it.

I resolve to cut classes for a week and move to Waianae where, it is rumored, Hawaiian education is at its worst.

37

The Worst
Little Schoolhouses
in the World?

Waianae, Hawaii
November 1987

Were the *Guinness Book of Records* ever to rate education, Waianae on Oahu's lovely leeward shore might likely boast the worst little schoolhouses in Hawaii—even, perhaps, compared with Britain, Japan, China, Australia, Africa, the Soviet Union, and other systems I have studied—the worst in the world. Test scores bottom out below all others in the islands. Most pupils fall beneath the national norm; few achieve above the national average. In reading, writing, arithmetic none perform so poorly. Absenteeism is endemic; Waianae High School leads Hawaii with

21.1 percent of students truant every day. Juvenile crimes ranging from murder, rape, and arson to fist-fights and felony produce more police arrests and Family Court referrals than in any other district. Fewer boys and girls complete high school or go to college. Fewer find employment in other than poor-paying entry-level jobs, or advance to more prosperous positions. Adolescent pregnancy, alcohol abuse, drug addiction go hand in hand with academic failure and early dropout. With over half its population full- or part-Hawaiian, of whom more than 50 percent are on welfare, Waianae arouses wonderment about how a state as blessed as Hawaii can sustain a system with schools so sick as Waianae's seem to be.

To learn what was wrong with Waianae I spent a week in its elementary, intermediate, and high schools. I met with principals, teachers, pupils, parents, police, and employers. I attended classes, examined text books, ate in cafetoriums (they serve both as cafeterias and auditoriums), browsed in libraries, loitered in toilets, inspected playgrounds, gridirons, and graffiti, and otherwise sought understanding of Waianae's woes. With neither an academically sanctioned hypothesis to prove, nor a theory to be validated by statistical study, my search was unscientific. I approached Waianae with an open mind, curious rather than critical, seeking simply to make some sense of so sad a situation.

"Good" and "bad" are largely matters of personal perception. A "good" about Waianae is immediately apparent. Waianae is not a city slum in which population pressure, pollution, and urban ugliness foster crime. Quite to the contrary, its natural and man-enhanced splendor is so abundant as to draw multimillionaires, celebrities, and sybarites to the magic of its mountains, the lushness of its valleys, the beauty of its beaches. Makaha, on its fringe, is a surfing center of the world, a fact not lost upon "Seariders," as Waianae's kids are called. Paradoxically, Waianae's assets diminish its efforts in education. The pull of the Pacific is more powerful than the classrooms of its schools.

While its elementary and intermediate schools are bright, orderly and attractive, gloomy beyond words is Waianae High School, a landscape littered with sinister concrete keeps and wooden shacks needing little more than the watchwords *Arbeit Macht Frei*—"Work Makes Freedom"—to duplicate Dachau. Classrooms dark, dingy, too hot for human habitation. Toilets few, strongly scented, without soap, towels, tissue. Bells clang at hourly intervals; 1,800 inmates race to other rooms before doors are slammed in their faces, or furtively dawdle out of sight until another dismal schoolday is done. Staff confined in dimly lit dens, bedlam echoing through wooden walls covered with the current motto—RESPECT—a precept at odds with so squalid a setting.

Yet again, within this architectural atrocity, another paradox. In no other schools have I encountered teachers more dedicated to duty. To stay where they are needed, to cope against odds, to give Waianae's boys and girls the last full measure of their knowledge, energy, and devotion—no definitions go farther than these to distance Waianae's teachers from others who prize pay, prestige, perquisites above tutorial obligation. Products themselves of an imperfect educational process, some may lack subject mastery or teaching technique, but such deficiencies are recompensed by the care they lavish on their charges. One teacher speaks for many others: "I've been here for twenty-two years and you couldn't pay me to teach anywhere else. Nowhere are problems so severe, and nowhere are teachers more needed who really care about kids."

Leading to yet another paradox, the kids. Delinquents by any statistical standard who in any ordinary school would be deemed beyond redemption, here in Waianae they are objects of affection, approbation, and respect. In one teacher's words: "We have some bananas, but most kids are priceless diamonds in the rough. Unlike sneaky students in other schools they don't hide their true feelings behind good behavior. They're not conformists, and that can cause trouble, but they're upfront, honest, close to nature. We have big problems in Waianae, but it's not the kids so much as the community."

Next paradox, the community. Here, long before golf greens carpeted the valley, Waianaeans tilled the soil and fished the waters. Here, in 1826, a New England missionary named Hiram Bingham wrote: "A man in the region was sent to tell us what he knew, but his efforts to enlighten us proved the ignorance, darkness, imbecility and confusion of the heathen mind." Such a sentiment scarred "heathen" self-esteem, a wound deepened by the Great Mahele that legalized transfer of land from public to private hands. Only seven farmers in Makaha Valley filed for fee simple titles to their *kuleanas* (properties). Foreigners expelled local families from their farms and fisheries. Today, a few miles down the road, Japanese build a hotel, condo, and golf club complex. Says a local citizen: "More jobs for our kids as chambermaids, busboys, short-order chefs. What other future do they face in Waianae, the fast-food capital of Hawaii?"

According to police, a legacy of theft, vandalism, and violence causes Waianae's crime. Poverty, unemployment, broken homes, single parenting take their toll. Latchkey kids get into trouble. Others are brought up to believe that the alien invasion sanctions antisocial action. Parental and peer pressures devalue *haole* (white person) education, standard English, book-learning that disparages Hawaii's heritage. It is hard for schools to overcome resentments so ingrained.

But, paradoxically, beneath the criminal crust most Waianae parents care about their kids. One mother explains:

> In 1979 forty families formed a Waianae Coast School Concerns Coalition. We were tired of Waianae's rotten reputation and determined to show our children were just as good, bright and able as any others. We wanted to become involved in the children's learning, help with homework, make tests fairer to our kids, end social promotion—pushing up pupils from class to class only to learn at graduation that they couldn't read or write. Well, we're told that tests are none of our business. We're lectured on "behavioral objectives," "affected domain," "assertive discipline" and other gobbledegook that drives us up the wall. They want us to stuff envelopes, chaperone field trips, donate cookies, punish our kids for the schools' misbehavior. Parents are fed up, burned out, the Coalition is down the drain along with PTA and every other effort we make to beat the system.

And so, yet another paradox, "the system," an entity consisting of the state government, its Board of Education, elected officials who regulate the Hawaii Department of Education. Additionally, the Governor's Conference on Education and, importantly, the University of Hawaii's College of Education that certifies most of the principals, teachers, and administrators who staff the public schools. Unlike those in other states, Hawaii's is a centralized system without neighborhood school boards to localize education. Hawaii's system, moreover, is tied into a national network. To receive federal funds and enable graduates to enter mainland institutions, its schools must meet academic standards set by the Western Association of Schools and Colleges. Waianae High School, for example, must submit an *Appraisal** establishing its equivalency with other schools. Thus Hawaii is drawn into and its Department of Education deals with difficulties that increasingly agitate a fretful nation—the shortfall of its public schools as against the successes of Japan, the Soviet Union, and other countries.

No clue to Waianae's plight seems so persuasive as the DOE's role as specified in Waianae High's *Appraisal*. It affirms that

> the State Department of Education establishes the philosophy, goals and objectives for public education in Hawaii. Due to the centralized system of education in Hawaii, the major areas of needed improvement are determined by the Superintendent and approved by the Board of Education. The educational objectives at Waianae High School are derived from and consistent with those of the DOE. The Governor's Conference on Education also affects the school's prioritizing of stated objectives. *For instance, considerable emphasis is being placed upon vocational education where in the past reading was emphasized.* (Italics mine.)

Replacement of reading by vocational education sets in train a sequence of responses in on-site interviews with administrators, teachers, students, parents, and employers. A consensus exists that reading is central to all instruction; that inability to read predetermines failure in other subjects; that reading enables students to discern their interests and aptitudes, keep up with their course work, choose careers, and undertake their own education. In one teacher's opinion: "Unless a person can read a manual well enough to follow instructions, or read a newspaper well enough to vote, he or she is handicapped as a worker, a citizen, a human being. That the system sees auto repair or wood-turning as more essential than reading says all one really needs to know about what's wrong with education in Hawaii."

A registrar adds: "So many programs mandated by DOE demand compliance that elementary and intermediate schools can't concentrate on reading. We have kids coming into high school struggling with their ABCs. It's too late for remediation.

---

*The Waianae High School *Appraisal* (Form C) for 1986, submitted to Leeward Oahu District Office, DOE, consists of 241 pages of questions asked by the Western Schools and Colleges Association, and answers by an Accreditation Committee set up by the High School representing faculty, academic departments, associated services, students, and community.

Those who can't cope fall behind, get frustrated, quit. Result: truancy, dropouts, delinquency."

A police officer: "Almost all the kids we pick up are either illiterate or close to it. As youngsters they start out with stars in their eyes, but if they can't make it in school, they can't make it in society. In the slammer it's too late to learn to read and write."

A parent: "My kids come home from school. I ask where's your books? What about homework? My kids say they're not allowed to bring home books. Too heavy, too big, too few, cost too much money. So no books. No homework. No reading. Only TV."

A teacher corroborates the parent's complaint: "Too true and tragic. Here's our history text, *America: Its People and Values,* Heritage edition, Harcourt Brace, 832 pages (The Oahu telephone book for 1987 consists of 708 pages). Plus a supplement, *Sources in American History.* Together they cost about $45, weigh about six pounds, not exactly what you'd call light reading. We have so few we keep them in class so they can't be taken home, stolen, or used for homework."

An English teacher adds: "Our textbook is *Focus on Literature: America,* Houghton Mifflin, 674 pages, full of fancy pictures, mostly meaningless, too expensive, another backbreaker the very size of which discourages reading. What we need are enough smaller, cheaper books so that every child has a copy to read for fun and homework. It sometimes seems DOE and publishers conspire to discourage reading."

An employer (resort hotel): "We're obliged by union contract to give preference in employment to Leeward applicants. If there are two qualified candidates, I must select one from Waianae. But job applicants can't read instructions, fill out forms, talk understandable English. I ask what work would interest them. They don't know. Their horizons are very limited. It's as if they've never read a newspaper or cracked a book."

A librarian: "Our Searider library has 22,000 volumes. We subscribe to over 100 periodicals. Whatever interest a student has, there's a book or magazine to feed it. The problem isn't books. It's readers."

Waianae High's library is the finest facility in the school, air-conditioned, clean, and spacious. From its shelves I select fifty books at random and check usage. Examples: *Japan Today* (Forbis, catalogued 1976). In ten years, thirteen readers. *Zen and the*

Art of Motorcycle Maintenance (Persig, 1974). One reader in thirteen years. *All Things Wise and Wonderful* (Herriot, 1976). Four
readers in eleven years. *Adolf Hitler* (Dolan, 1981). One reader in
six years. *On Reagan* (Duggan, 1984). Six readers in three years.
Mailer, A Biography (Mills, 1982). Eight readers in five years. Of
fifty books, thirty-three have never left the library.

A student: "I'm into food service, retail clerical, that kind of
stuff plus all the shit I must take for graduation. There's no time
for reading books. Even if there was, why bother? You don't need
books to work for Taco Bell, McDonalds, Pizza Hut."

Elementary teacher: "Don't knock Pizza Hut. It sponsors the
National Reading Incentive Program. For every book a child reads
I paste a sticker on this Pizza Hut chart. With five stickers the child
gets a free pizza. Corporations really help us with such incentives.
Chevrolet gives us reflectors for Halloween. Scott swaps coupons
from their paper products for computers. Hawaiian Air has a contest for kids to color pictures. Winners get a free trip to Disney-
land. Funny that businessmen use Skinner and Watson teaching
incentives while the DOE sits on its ass."

Among service station managers, a consensus: Waianae kids
aren't "educated." In one manager's words: "Here's *Mitchell's
Automotive Manual*'s section on air suspension: 'The air suspension system is an air-operated, microprocessor-controlled suspension system. The system replaces the conventional coil spring and
provides automatic front and rear leveling.' Okay, that's a standard instruction every mechanic needs to know, but if he can't
read it, he can't fix it. I don't expect a boy just out of school to be a
first-rate mechanic, but if he can't read, or make change, or talk to
a customer, I don't keep him. He's back on the beach, into drugs,
booze, sex, you name it."

I study Waianae High's *Course and Registration Guide*. Graduate requirements are English, covering literature of America and
Europe from Beowulf to modern times, four credits. Social studies
include world history and cultures, U.S. history and government,
European studies and geography, with one basic course in Hawaiian, four credits. Science embraces biology, chemistry, human
physiology, two credits. Another two for math. Asian, European,
and Pacific languages include nine courses each in French, Spanish, Japanese, and seven in Hawaiian. "Practical and industrial
arts" cover everything from agriculture to home economics—alto-

gether about 100 subjects are taught in the four year cycle, of which about half are academic and half vocational.

A consensus: Designed to meet standards set by the Western Schools and Colleges Association, it is essentially a conventional mainland curriculum. A few concessions are made to Hawaii history, language, animals and plants, but, by and large, Hawaii's natural, physical, cultural characteristics, its close ties to China, Japan, the Philippines, and other Pacific islands from which its population largely comes are neglected. So are opportunities inherent in its ethnic composition, economy, and strategic position in the Pacific. Dictated by DOE, the curriculum obligates Waianae High to "develop competencies in writing, speaking, listening, comprehension, computing, decision making, problem solving," etcetera. Unrealistic in scope and means of accomplishment, objectives are not met. A strong tilt toward Europe, an inappropriate absence of Asian inclination, depreciation of Hawaiiana and neglect of reading—these reflect DOE's disposition toward mainland equivalencies rather than toward the nature, interests, and needs of Hawaii. The College of Education is also faulted for its failure to prepare teacher trainees for Hawaiian realities, resulting in "culture shock" as they cope with classroom conditions.

A teacher: "It isn't really a curriculum so much as an obstacle race, a series of hurdles a boy or girl must jump. We coach them all we can but Waianae kids are Seariders, not runners in an academic rat race. They stagger, struggle, fall behind, give up, drop out, or finish a twelfth grade course at a sixth grade level. Having to clear the track and make room for the next heat of runners, we deliver diplomas to youngsters who can't read and write."

A teacher: "The curriculum is a collection of credits, four English, two math, etcetera, big blocks that bump into each other six periods a day, squeezing students and teachers between the cracks. Bells ring. Classes shift. Doors lock. Rolls are called. Before much teaching takes place the hour is over. Too many subjects, too little time. No focus on the few things that are really important. Depending on who's running the Board of Education and their hobby horses—'character formation', 'computing', 'decision making', 'appliance repair', that's what we're supposed to teach."

A parent: "What's a Beowulf?"

A consensus exists on language. A parent: "DOE wants to

stamp out pidgin. That's like someone in France telling schools to stamp out French. Pidgin is our language. Unless they respect the way we speak, we can't respect what they teach."

A parent: "Believe it or not, my kid was studying French. I asked why French? Who speaks French in Hawaii? Teacher threw up her hands. 'DOE says every Hawaiian kid must learn a foreign language.' And so I ask again, why French?"

Manager, resort hotel, Makaha: "Half our guests are Japanese, sometimes up to 80 percent. What we need are employees with Japanese language competence. It seems sensible for Hawaii's schools to produce such people, but Waianae kids speak only pidgin. Unless the public schools from elementary on up give students a vision of the bigger world out there, kids are locked inside a prison. So that our Japanese guests receive the same courtesies here in Hawaii that Americans do in Japanese hotels whose employees speak English, we're setting up Japanese classes for our people in guest-related jobs."

An administrator: "Okay, we've got the message that Japanese is important. So we've set up some token courses for seniors. Out of 1,800 students in Waianae High, about 170 get a smattering of Japanese. Unless DOE gets serious about the situation, recognizes that a large part of our population has a head start in Japanese, that thousands of our tourists come from Japan, and that no state in the union enjoys our opportunity to link Asia and America through language, teaching Japanese is just a joke."

A businessman: "Here's an article from *U.S. News and World Report:*

> Pacific Rim, America's New Frontier. The prize is breathtaking: a booming market of 1.5 billion potential customers. The Pacific Century is how some now see the next hundred years. The center of gravity is shifting from the transatlantic relationship toward the Pacific basin and Japan. South Korea, Taiwan, Hong Kong, Singapore have become miniature Japans. Over the past decade average compound growth rate in these five miracle countries has been 8.2%—roughly three times that of the European community.

Why don't our schools seize the opportunities this opens to Hawaii? I'm not for turning our schools over to the Visitor's Bureau, Hilton or the Bank of Hawaii, but it seems strange that no one has figured out an educational strategy that fits Hawaii's position in the Pacific into the big picture."

A consensus on school-community relations: They don't exist or are hostile. The Waianae Coast School Concerns Coalition and PTA are either dead or dying.

A teacher: "We wanted to establish grade level standards, inform parents why their children were failing, and let parents decide if they wanted their child to be promoted. A terrible hassle ensued over class retention and social promotion. I'm afraid we teachers have been taught to talk over parents' heads with our jargon, and the anger this arouses is beyond belief. It goes back to the UH College of Education where as trainees we are pumped full of high-sounding gibberish only educators half-understand."

A parent: "I go see the teacher and ask how my boy is doing. Okay, he's doing good, teacher says, not to worry. He gets promoted, but he hates school, he wants to quit. I go see the teacher. She says she's sorry, my boy is academically disadvantaged, what he needs is correlating basic skill activities with vocational training. *Oh shit!*"

My thoughts drift back to Japan, to *kyoiku-mamas,* "education mothers" whose bond with teachers virtually guarantees the success of Japanese students. I talk with Waianae's students, and read what they have written in their journals:

> The most important thing to me is my mother, father, brother and sister. My mother loved me a lot but we are broken family. My father, brother and me here in Hawaii. My mother was in Philippines. I like to go back to my mother. Its hard for me to live with my stepmother. Because she blames me that I ate her cookies. And then she yelling me because I never help to do something. And every time she and my father was fighting because of me and I don't know what happen they fight and I dont know what did I do to them. And then my father said I go live with my aunt.

> I'd like to change a lot of things in our school and in the world too. The first thing I would change in school is our lunches because our lunches are stale and we eat lots of leftovers. [I lunched in cafetoriums and found the food fresh, generous, inexpensive, and edible.] In the world I would like to change the United States and Russia. I would like to have peace between these two, why should I study if soon I will be dead? I would like to change lots more but there are too many to change.

> I don't know how to read. But when I try to read in front of a class and when I make a mistake the other people laugh and I get a funny feeling inside of me. And as soon as the teacher say that we

are going to read out loud then I tell her I have to go to the toilet because I don't want to read.

If I get married I would want to have a very handsome and rich husband. I would like a very big and beautiful wedding. I would want to be in gold and white, have lots of gifts, and continue the marriage with a beautiful honeymoon.

When I grow up I want to be governor of Hawaii, travel to Japan and smuggle in jewelry. Or be a judge and make money gambling. I want a lot of money because it can buy me lots of things like clothes, girls what I mean by girls is that when you have money they really like you.

I'm from LA, it's my first year in Waianae. It's different from California, kids here aren't serious about school, they don't know anything except Waianae, they think Waianae is the world, the teachers try so hard but the kids don't really listen. Most have never even been to Honolulu. Once they got off the bus they'd be lost.

A local lawyer also puts Waianae's problem in a personal perspective.

I'm born and raised in Waianae. In school I studied Dick and Jane, rivers and mountains of the mainland, snowmen, Peter Stuyvesant, Roger Williams. No relevance to Hawaii except to say our ancestors were lazy, we should be glad Americans came and saved us from ourselves. We rebelled. Such was our anger that we turned it against ourselves. Anger was and is the spirit of the land that causes our crime rate. My classmates went to prison. I went to college on a $200 scholarship, studied political science, became a lawyer, who, like you, asks what's wrong with Waianae? How can we build schools in which our kids learn to respect themselves, talk with their own grandparents, move ahead of the *haoles* and Asians to the front of the class instead of dropping out? How can kids be happy in schools that recycle them into *haoles?* Either give us schools that make Hawaiian culture viable in the modern world, or give us the resources to set up an alternative system that restores Hawaiian pride, abates our anger, enables our children to dream.

At odds with all the evidence is Waianae High's self appraisal. It describes an almost perfect academic institution. One learns that

the curriculum meets needs of students who plan to continue education at college or trade school. A high percentage of credits earned by WHS students indicates adequacy in meeting needs of college prep students. College Board and SAT test scores improve, reflecting efforts of units set up for this purpose. Overall, academically, most of WHS's needs are met by a favorable teacher-student ratio of 26, and by greater input by faculty members into the school's master plan. Teachers, counselors, administrators have continued their professional growth over the past six years. Library facilities enjoy steady increases, 9.3% in circulation, 22.2% in usage. The growing number of resources available indicate that the library is generally meeting the curriculum needs of most of the students and teachers.

More wishful thinking:

Counseling services help students prepare for competency exams in basic skills. Health services provide a safe and caring environment for ill, injured and troubled students. Attendance services report that students' daily/hourly attendance is notated and appropriate action taken. Severely alienated students are served by an off-campus Alternative Learning Center. Tutorial services are provided potential dropouts. A Pre-industrial Preparation Program helps disadvantaged students to pursue vocational careers. A Reading Center offers one-on-one instruction to needy students. A Quick Kokua Transition Center provides career, employment and related services in such areas as sex, physical substance abuse, interpersonal, peer and family problems, coping with grief, runaway problems, suicide and teen pregnancy.

True, dedicated professionals strive to render such services, working against appalling odds, without resources commensurate with the problems they confront. Effort and efficacy do not equate.

The *Appraisal,* one suspects, does what "the system" wants and expects it to do. It whitewashes Waianae High's performance, conceals its problems, satisfies the Leeward Oahu District Office's appetite for approval, lulls the BOE and DOE into bureaucratic lethargy, deceives the Western Schools and Colleges Association, and earns for Waianae High accreditation it does not deserve. Concealing reality beneath a face-saving facade, it deflects DOE and BOE from confronting and correcting their errors. Thus—and this is the ultimate paradox—it perpetrates and perpetuates an evil that condemns Waianae's kids to inferior education.

My week in Waianae ends. I take leave of the service station managers, the cops, the Pizza Hut and Taco Bell emporia, the principals, parents, employers, the self-sacrificial teachers and the kids. It takes no special expertise to sense what's wrong with Waianae—an almost total mismatch, a culture-clash between "the system" and the society it is supposed to serve. And the tragic human tendency to paper over problems, cosmetize blemishes, and otherwise bury the bad beneath an elegiac tombstone.

Dr. Fruehling, appreciative of my research effort, grades the paper B. That leaves only one more hurdle to be jumped—the Philosophy of Education.

38

The Critique of Pure Cant

Wist Hall
October 1987

Professors Barry Bull and Victor Kobayashi teach Philosophy of Education. Bull, a Hollywood-handsome young man out of Yale embodies every quality of an excellent teacher—energy, loquacity, enormous enthusiasm for his subject. Kobayashi, resembling a whiskery cherub, graying, with oriental eyes that radiate wisdom, balances Bull's bounce with a laid-back stance and an arsenal of insights at odds with Barry's. The semester starts out as a dialogue between the two teachers. This suits the students, as mystified as am I by the content of the course, exemplified by the philosophy of Immanuel Kant, the German giant before whom generations of thinkers on the human condition have humbly bowed—conspicuous among them, American educators.

The class sits transfixed as Barry drives home the key to Kant, the Categorical Imperative, intoning each word as if the Ten Commandments, the Sermon on the Mount, the Oath of Allegiance were revealed in one transcendental truth. *"Act,"* he announces, *"only as though the maxim of your action were by your will to become an universal law of nature."*

As Dr. Bull stresses each syllable of Kant's edict, memories invade my mind. The growl of Prussian *panzers* converging on my ass. Swastikas somehow symbolizing the gutteral gibberish of Heidegger and other Nazis who hallowed the holocaust. Of Adolf Hitler who did indeed act as though the maxim of his will became a universal law of nature, dooming millions to death in Auschwitz, Dachau, Belsen, Buchenwald—categorical imperatives, each and all.

"Bullshit," I blurt. The pun is unintended but it sharpens my point. "Instead of praising that Prussian prick, he should be drawn and quartered!"

Stunned by my outburst, the class is quiet. Then, like champagne bursting from a bottle in which, too long, the bubbles have been imprisoned, laughter, exclamations, a clatter of conversation erupt, overcoming the awe that has for so long silenced the seminar. Whatever is wrong with my anti-Prussian prejudice, and however the violence of my views evinces the poverty of my scholarship, an educational breakthrough has occurred. Barry Bull thanks me for shifting the burden from his back, inviting students to invigorate the teaching-learning process by active, vocal, impassioned participation. I am warned, however, that so outrageous an attitude will not wash unless the essay I write supports my stand; otherwise a penalty may yet have to be paid.

And so, entitled *The Critique of Pure Cant,* this is my essay, based on our text, *Foundations of the Metaphysics of Morals,* by Immanuel Kant:

Doctors have not established the cause of my collapse—overly assiduous study, heat exhaustion, onset of Alzheimer's—but on October 5, 1987, at 4:45 p.m., in room 201 of Wist Hall where my seminar on the philosophy of education was in session, I went into convulsion, frothing at the mouth, and uttering unintelligible outcries. I recovered consciousness in a large, bleak room, its barred window admitting just enough light to reveal a strange collection of characters in 18th, 19th and early 20th century attire, all male, and silently intent on some mental image that gave purpose to the masturbation in which they were engaged. A rich aroma suffused the air—of sausage, sauerkraut and *Konigsberger Klops,* delicious little liver dumplings cooked with capers. Music —a medley of Wagner, Strauss and Horst Wessel—issued from some unseen source. In attendance were two white-clad orderlies named Hans and Fritz—both oddly reminiscent of my philosophy professors, Barry Bull and Victor Kobayashi—the hallucination, of course, symptomatic of the insanity by which I was seized.

Responding to my question as to where I was, Hans said it was the *Allgemeine Krankenhaus* in Konigsberg, a little city in eastern Prussia, "What you Americans call a 'funny farm.' Here it is the Philosophers' Ward." "Why," I asked, "does everyone masturbate?" "Because," said Fritz, "philosophy is strictly a male disorder. There are no female philosophers. Only by giving themselves to masculine introspection, without wives, mistresses or other feminine distractions, can they concentrate on themselves and achieve the onanistic orgasm they are otherwise denied."

Beside me sat a hollow-chested leprechaun, less than five feet tall, busily engaged in the manipulation induced by whatever fantasy filled his mind. Suddenly he stood up and started to pace up and down. As though upon a signal, everyone glanced at their watches and nodded with satisfaction. "Right on time," said Hans, "he never misses!" "Who," I asked, "was this person whose punctuality inspired such respect?" "It is Kant," whispered Fritz. "Immanuel Kant! Immanuel is Hebrew for *Gott mit uns* (God with us), the Prussian motto. Born here in Konigsberg in 1724. By religion a Pietist, by profession a pedagogue, and, as you see, very punctual, very precise, very Prussian!"

Noting my presence, Kant halted, bowed, held out his hand. "You *must* join me on my daily stroll. You *must* share my expertise in metaphysics, astronomy, meteorology, mathematics, logic, moral philosophy, physical geography, fireworks and fortifications. Also I am an oracle on the lawfulness of vaccination. I issue edicts on all these subjects which men of wisdom *must* obey."

Heeding Kant's command, I synchronized my steps with his and listened as he laid the foundations of the metaphysics of morals.

"All Gaul was divided into three parts, and so is philosophy—physics, ethics and logic. You *must* agree that each part requires a man particularly devoted to it so that the empirical and rational are not mixed up by bunglers who call themselves free thinkers. Philosophy *must* begin with *a priori* concepts, however confusedly or insufficiently determined, so as to avoid shutting themselves up within a circle of words!"

Sensing myself shut up in a circle of words, I was about to ask how confused and insufficiently determined concepts could escape such a fate. But Professor Kant clearly did not suffer fools gladly. Silence seemed my wisest course as he repeated: "Where everyone is a jack-of-all-trades, the crafts remain at a barbaric level."

Impressed by the diversity of Dr. Kant's talents, I asked how a jack-of-all-trades like himself managed never to bungle and reduce them to a barbaric level. Dr. Kant dismissed my doubts with the sheer authority of his answer. "The metaphysics of nature *must* be put before empirical physics, and a metaphysics of morals *must* be put before anthropology. These prior sciences *must* be purified of everything empirical. Everyone *must* admit that a law *must* imply absolute necessity. He *must* concede that the ground of obligation here *must not* be sought in the nature of man, but sought *solely* in the concepts of pure reason, and that every other precept which rests on principles of mere experience *must never* be called a moral law." Stamping his little foot to reinforce each *must,* Professor Kant concluded: "He *must* admit that the command 'Thou shalt not kill' does *not* apply to men only, as if other rational beings had no need to observe it."

Such certitudes banished any doubt in my addled brain as to Dr. Kant's omniscience, but I could not help asking what rational beings other than man did the Herr Professor have in mind to whom the command 'Thou shalt not kill' might be applied? And why must a precept as universal as experience *never* be called a moral Law? Disdainful of the stupidity displayed by my first question, Dr. Kant dwelt on the second. "Because it is in fact *absolutely impossible* by experience to discern with complete certainty *a single case* in which the maxim of an action rested solely on moral grounds and on the conception of one's duty. *We cannot by any means* conclude that a secret impulse of self-love, falsely appearing as the idea of duty, was not actually the true determining cause of the Will!"

The Will! Dotty as I was, even I came to comprehend its importance. As Professor Kant rather apocalyptically put it, "*Nothing* in the world—indeed *nothing* even *beyond* the world—could *possibly* be conceived which could be called good without qualification except a *Good Will!* A *Will* good in itself can be produced only by pure reason, manifested in actions done not from inclination but from duty." Professor Kant pointed at Hans and Fritz who, as usual, were engaged in tending to the needs of their patients: "There are many persons like them so sympathetically constituted that they find inner satisfaction in spreading joy, and rejoice in the contentment of others which they have made possible. But I say that, however amiable it may be, that kind of action has no true moral worth!"

"But Dr. Kant," I made bold enough to ask, "what if I see a hungry child and offer it bread? Has not such an act true moral worth? What better example of good will exists than to feed a hungry human being?" "Example!," thundered Dr. Kant. "Imitation has *no place* in moral matters, and examples serve *only* for encouragement! They can *never* justify our girding ourselves by example and our setting aside their true origin which lies in reason!"

As though a bandage was torn from my eyes, I suddenly saw the error of my ways. The day I helped a blind man cross a crowded street! The dimes I dropped into Salvation Army kettles at Christmas! The hours spent beside a sick friend's bed, easing not his pain but my own—spurious gestures that hid my selfish intent! Never again, I vowed, would I ever behave so basely.

Not until one day, on our stroll, did the profundity of Professor Kant's proposition reveal itself in all its radiant beauty. Passing a bedraggled wretch with a yellow star of David embroidered on his breast, Dr. Kant whispered "*Juden!* A Jew! Nothing would be achieved on behalf of Jews as long as Jews are Jews. As long as they have themselves circumcized they will never be members of civil, bourgeois society."

Herr Kant's insights dispelled a prejudice to which I had for too long been prey. How mistaken to have mourned the holocaust! How liberating to have pure reason cleanse my mind of cobwebs of compassion! "Judaism," Dr. Kant continued, "is a pseudo religion subjugating man to external statutory laws, a worldly State. The term euthanasia as used in early stages of philosophy does not imply death out of merciful attitude but a disappearance out of the inner forces of the entity in question. Jews bear society far more harm than good. They are vampires of society!"

It was at this point that Herr Kant professed the principle of "The Categorical Imperative." "If an action is good only as a means to something else, the imperative is merely hypothetical. But if it is thought of as good in itself, and hence as necessary in a will which of itself conforms to reason as the principle of the will, the imperative is categorical. There is only one categorical imperative: *act only as though the maxim of your action were by your will to become an universal law of nature!*"

How right had Hitler been! Jews are vampires of society. They bear society more harm than good. Euthanasia does not imply death out of merciful attitude but a disappearance out of the inner forces of the entity in question. The holocaust was nothing less than the elevation of so simple a maxim to a universal law of nature.

Swept away by the impeccable logic of this remarkable man, I struggled for words to express my appreciation. "It is not alone the laws you lay down," I cried, "but their universality that I admire— the knowledge you possess of other peoples, other places, other cultures. Please, Professor Kant, tell me your opinion of America!"

"Ach, Amerika!," Kant exclaimed. "Americans are incapable of civilization. They have no motive force, for they are without affection and passion. They are not drawn to one another by love, and are thus unfruitful. They hardly speak at all, never caress one another, care about nothing, and are lazy. Americans are incapable of governing themselves and are destined for extermination."

"Tell me," I begged, "about your travels in America that led you to such correct conclusions!" The Professor, for once, seemed puzzled. "My travels? *Ach ya,* once it was I travelled from Konigsberg to Arnsdorf, sixty miles away. Aside from that, what need is there to travel when all one needs to know exists precisely here, in Prussia?"

I must admit that I was set back by this admission. Herr Kant had never laid eyes on a mountain, had never seen the sea. How could he have mastered physical geography? Never having married or fathered a child, how could he embrace the human race, to say nothing of femininity, comprising as it did half the human species? Never having been a soldier or engineer, how could he have fathomed fireworks and fortifications? Never a doctor, what worth his verdict on vaccination? By any earthly standard his answers to such questions would reveal this greatest of philosophers as a mountebank, a falsifier, a fraud. Except, as in a sunburst, did I see the light. Such genius was divinely ordained. A God-like creature, Kant's wisdom and goodness were not subject to empirical experience and examination, but entitled to belief because of his preternatural power. Even I, insane as I am, could comprehend how, moved by ideas generated solely within the boundaries of his Prussian domain and German brain, he produced a universal philosophy of such profundity!

Nor was Kant alone. Hegel and Heidegger also inhabit this Prussian loony bin. Hegel, whose genius is nowhere better revealed than in his immortal words: "Man by himself is historically nothing. The State is the divine idea as it exists on earth!" Hegel whose dialectical process led to Marx who inspired Lenin, leading to the Russian Revolution, and the enviable prosperity that has made the Soviet system the economic wonder of the world!

Heidegger raises his arm, swathed in a swastika, in salute. "The Fuhrer," he declares, "alone is the German reality, present and future, and its law!" Again, that magic word, the Law! The *Universal* Law. The *Categorical Imperative* all men of reason must obey. Together, Kant, Hegel and Heidegger shout "Heil Hitler!" Then we drink our beer, swallow our sauerkraut and consume our Konigsberger Klops. As always, they are delicious.

It is with deep regret, I confess, that the euphoria kindled by Kant did not endure. I think it was something he said, one day— that "we do not indeed comprehend the practical unconditional necessity of the moral imperative; that we can only comprehend its incomprehensibility, and that all one can fairly demand of a philosophy which in its principles strives to reach the limit of human reason is to admit that such reason is limitless."

After so great an investment of mental and pedestrian effort, I could not accept so empty a result. The hopelessness induced by this revelation brought me to the very brink of suicide, a fate from which I was saved by Kant himself. How well I remember his words: "A man who is reduced to despair by a series of evils feels a weariness with life but is still in possession of his reason sufficiently to ask whether it would not be contrary to his duty to himself to take his own life. Now he asks whether the maxim of his action could become a universal law of nature. In this case it would not exist as nature; hence that maxim cannot obtain as a law of nature, and thus it wholly contradicts the supreme principle of all duty."

How palpably true! How perfectly Professor Kant portrays the emotions of individuals so distraught as to place their heads inside ovens, or jump from windows, or slash their wrists. Before Ernest Hemingway pulled the trigger, or Marilyn Monroe took the pill, why did they not ask themselves whether their action was sanctioned by the categorical imperative and universal law of Immanuel Kant?

Though saved from suicide, I was declared incurable and discharged from the Philosopher's Ward. Hans and Fritz sent me on my way with a lunch box filled with little liver dumplings cooked with capers. From the world's finest philosopher came a friendly farewell: "Never, never in this world—never even beyond this world—must you ever forget the greatest of all Konigsberger Klops!" Signed: Immanuel Kant.

And so, here I am, home again in Hawaii, in the College of Education where Dr. Bull and Dr. Kobayashi seem rather unhappy to see me. Remarkable how much they resemble Hans and Fritz!

The reaction from Prof. Kobayashi, and endorsed by Prof. Bull:

> Your paper is creative, well written and has a nice sense of humor. If you had not attempted to make it a paper on Kant or on specific philosophic and historical figures, and made your paper a product of pure fantasy and imagination, I would have no quibble. However, you are doing a philosophy of education assignment, and using Kant, and ascribing certain ideas and thoughts to him, which are inaccurate and show little understanding of why he is such an important (rightly or wrongly) thinker in the history of Western philosophy. Would your allegations hold up in court, had Kant been alive and then sued you for defamation of character? I'm afraid not! Your paper may be effective polemics, but a very bad paper on Kant.

The very bad paper draws a C, dooming my degree. True, it reflects more fury than philosophy, but it *was* an *EdD*, not a *PhD* assignment. My passion had provoked discussion and snapped the seminar from its snooze. I plead that the equivocal C be reduced to an honest F, thereby clearly identifying the issue. Drs. Bull and Kobayashi, so to speak, recant, raise the C to B, and put the paperchase back on track.

I have taken liberties in quoting Kant, but the essay, I contend, portrays the dictatorial, arrogant dogmatism of the Prussian paragon. Italics have been added to indicate Kant's addiction to authoritarian emphasis. Kant's description of Americans is from Henry Steele Commager's *The Empire of Reason,* taken by him from Kant's lectures on Philosophical Anthropology at Konigsberg in 1722, as cited by Gerbi. Kant's comments on Jews are taken from Johan Friedrich Abegg who visited Kant in 1798, as cited in *Jews and German Philosophy* by Nathan Rotenstreich, a rich resource for other evidence of anti-Semitism in German philosophy. Heidegger's remarks are from the *Encyclopaedia Britannica.*

An aversion to implicating others in my academic crimes deterred me from citing George Santayana, Harvard's highly-regarded philosopher, but it comforts me to have him in my corner:

> The categorical imperative, not satisfied with proclaiming itself secretly omnipotent, proclaims itself openly ruthless. Kant expressly repudiated as unworthy of a virtuous will any consideration of happiness, or of consequences to one's self or to others . . . his moral doctrine was in principle a perfect frame for fanaticism . . . sanctifying beforehand every stubborn passion and every romantic crime. . . . Thus it is from Kant, directly or indirectly, that the German egotists draw the conviction which is their most tragic error. Their self-assertion and ambition are ancient follies of the human race; but they think their vulgar passions the creative spirit of the universe. Kant was the prophet and even the founder of the new German religion. . . . In the guise of an infallible conscience, before which nothing has a right to stand, egotism is launched upon its irresponsible career. . . .

39

"Footnotes"

A stout florid female knocked on my office door in the East-West Center where I was writing my thesis. A University employee, she supplemented her income by doing dissertations, and volunteered to turn my scrawl into a legible typescript. I leaped at her offer. Within days she was back with a draft of the first few chapters, fulsome in her praise for what I had written. But as my life continued to unfold, delight changed to disdain as she dumped the pages on my desktop.

"Garbage," she growled.

"What's wrong?" I asked.

"No footnotes," she answered.

Footnotes, she divulged, were what dissertations were all about. "It's not what you write that matters. It's what you've read that you can cite as the source of what you've written." How, I wondered, could I base the story of my life on any source other than myself?

"Sorry," she shrugged. "No footnotes, no dissertation. And no degree." Furious at my failure to heed her advice, the lady scurried off my sinking ship, forcing me to find someone able to finish my paper on a machine that matched her wretched Remington.

Dr. John Dolly, dean of the College of Education, was also upset by what he read when my thesis (a.k.a. the contents of this book) circulated among the staff. "The problem," he believed, "is basically with the underlying assumption that autobiography is legitimate as a doctoral dissertation. A good autobiography does not equate with a good dissertation. Both can be mutually exclusive." Complaining about the lack of a conceptual framework and a systematic tie to the literature, he pointed to certain procedural problems. "In the development of a dissertation, there is normally a prior agreement on goals and process. No such process was ever followed in your case. It never started with a systematic investigation of a problem that was clearly defined from the start. Without a single citation of a source in 300 pages, it evidences no more than your own experiences and opinions, and adds nothing to the theory of knowledge." It was, the dean declared, an unprecedented performance that faced the College with a *fait accompli*. "As a self-confessed conservative, it makes me uneasy."

Allied with the dean was Anne Keppel, director of womens' studies. Dr. Keppel's verdict was "Yes, your autobiography is interesting, readable, a remarkable life and a rousing good yarn, but a dissertation it isn't."

Both Dean Dolly and Dr. Keppel belonged to a body of five professors whose decision determined failure or success in the doctoral rat race. Unlike shrewder candidates who chose friends within the faculty on whom they could count to guide them from starting line to triumphant finale, I had deliberately selected four men and one woman least likely to let me get by with anything less than a superior submission. What I wanted was a rough, tough, no-nonsense, blue-ribbon jury that would measure the evidence by the strictest of standards. What I wanted was what I got.

As chairperson I had picked Dr. Melvin Ezer, a Harvard man who, heading Education Foundations, seemed certain to defend his department's integrity. Professor Ralph Stueber was associated with the Peace Institute; none better than he could evaluate my stand on this sensitive subject. Reuel Denney, co-author of *The Lonely Crowd,* commanded campuswide respect for his intellect, experience, and poetic expression. Dr. Keppel brought sexual balance to the delicate educational equation. Finally, by recruiting the College of Education's dean, I clinched my claim to a committee more rigorous than any other to validate or vitiate my doctoral ambition.

In the bruising battles that ensued, I rued my folly. Dean Dolly, a mountain of a man, was courteous, considerate, even kind, but obdurate in his opposition. Dr. Keppel, repeating *ad nauseam* that my narrative was not a dissertation, quit the committee. Her replacement, George Simson, editor of *Biography,* the authoritative publication in its field, differed with Dolly and Keppel. His comment: "Fascinating. I learned a lot. Your book is directly in line with the great 19th century tradition of the public servant. As an instructive survey of 20th century attitudes, experiences and ideas in education, it's invaluable to the non-pro reader. Experiential education in a world of intellectual stuffed-shirts makes an excellent theme." At two of Dolly's doubts he aimed unerring answers. There was no literature to which my essay could have a systematic tie. Generals, statesmen, actors, authors, everyone else wrote the stories of their lives, but educators were so secretive about themselves as to create a vacuum almost unfulfilled except for my confessions. As to the conceptualization Dean Dolly demanded: "What your thesis avoids—over-conceptualization—is what makes it strong."

Reuel Denney's verdict:

> Goodfriend's excellent dissertation makes many references to topics studied in my department (American Studies) with respect to both educational and non-educational aspects of American development. . . . His references to these matters contain no inaccuracy as to fact and no major problems of interpretation; and these references often contain important insights and reminders related to the social and cultural context of education in the U.S. This is notably true of his comments on the G.I. Bill, for example. . . . I *do* think there are some exaggerations and over-simplifications in his account of the German influence on American ideas of culture and education.

In Denney's view, however, "German thought since the Reformation and Romantic movement shared a major responsibility for the rise of Nazi antisemitism. This is a problem insufficiently addressed by educators . . . "Even now," Denney declared, "German guilt is emphasized by failures of Heidegger, Gadamer and others to apologize for their intellectual and moral mistakes in speaking up for Nazism." Believing that I weakened my case by failing to blame Christian institutions and communicants for the holocaust, Denney nevertheless contended that my dissertation did indeed constitute a significant investigation of the Prussian problem. Denney also denied that a good autobiography and a good dissertation did not equate. The problem was the tendency of too many dissertations to depend on other sources and citations for what their authors lacked ability to originate and substantiate themselves.

Dr. Stueber suggested that reflection on a long and interesting life contributed to the ongoing discourse on schooling and education. To the extent that these are highly personal as well as social and cultural, autobiography was an authentic approach and, in this instance, a contribution to understanding the interplay of peace, war, and education. As a veteran, I had put these elements into a moving personal account which he applauded. "Perhaps," he remarked, "we need to take Arthur's admonitions about nationalism in all seriousness and ask wherein precisely liberal educational theory is weak and what reformulations might be considered." As for the absence of footnotes, that, Dr. Stueber suggested, could be repaired by a preface dealing with the development of autobiography in an educational metaphor, with footnotes and other academic ornamentation.

Dr. Ezer produced a memorandum to the Graduate Advisory Council of the College of Education, dated April 3, 1987.

> Arthur Goodfriend is an 80 year old scholar who has a wealth of academic experience at various institutions. He is also the author of several books. He was initially referred to this department by the dean. The department voted to admit him to the doctoral program but because of his unique background it was suggested that an individualized program be developed for him. He is to complete a course in areas of departmental emphasis wherever there is a deficiency, sit for a comprehensive exam, make a presentation of his dissertation proposal, write a dissertation and defend it. While Mr. Goodfriend's program is irregular, we believe it to be justified because he is an extraordinary student. The characteristics of rigidity and inflexibility should not be employed when fashioning a program for extremely uncommon students.

Dr. Ezer affirmed that my paper amply vindicated the department's decision. The fact that this memorandum had been endorsed by Dean Dolly did not dissuade him from his stance.

It was a replay of my life. The teacher who tore up my tulip.

Latin and Math. Golf Links. The Silent Way. Caleb Gattegno, Geddes MacGregor, the New College fiasco—just one more collision between tradition, rigidity, jargon (them) and originality, flexibility, colloquial English (me). Or might it really be the other way round—wisdom, experience, scholarship (them) versus stupidity, anarchy, ego (me)? Of only one thing was I sure. One didn't get a doctoral degree from a college whose dean deemed educational autobiography a no-no. I threw in the towel, but Mel Ezer snatched it. "No way," he said. "Let's fight this to a finish!"

And so, in reverse, I stumbled the last steps of the Calvary. A year after my dissertation was begun, and long after its completion, I made my proposal. I wrote a preface based on an article by Jerome Bruner* with more footnotes than plums in a Christmas pudding. Borrowing from a bibliography of majestic length and depth, it certified my scholarship. I took and passed two comprehensive exams and several oral inquisitions. And finally, the "Defense."

The "Defense" was advertised in the *University Bulletin*, the public was invited, and a small audience attended my last-ditch effort to scale the summit of the academic Everest. Since no record exists, these questions and answers are abstracted from the actual event, and capture more the thrust of my thinking than the dialogue itself.

What ails education? German measles.

What are the symptoms? Excessive nineteenth century nationalism, insufficient twenty-first century globalism.

What is the cure? There is no cure; the disease is deadly.

Since when are measles deadly? Since they became a species of educational AIDS.

How did education contract AIDS? Education seems something of a whore, fickle, in bed one night with Rousseau, the next with Dewey, seducing one horny scholar after another, infecting each with a strain of insanity that sickened the kings, kaisers, commissars, and other sovereigns she serviced.

---

*"Life as Narrative," *Social Research* vol. 54, no. 1, Spring 1987.

Who passed on the virus? Fritzian philosophers who kantaminated the classrooms.

How could classrooms get "kantaminated?" By school systems serving the military-industrial complex to enhance the superiority of nation-states.

Aren't superiority in science, technology, industry, evidence of superior education? They evidence vocational training, not education.

What about the oath of allegiance, patriotism, courses that teach kids to be good Americans? That's indoctrination, not education.

Most experts think the answers to education's ills are bigger budgets, better pay for better teachers, smaller classes, longer hours, accountability, freedom of choice. Don't you agree? No. That's legislation and administration, not education.

But mustn't we educate children about sex, drugs, cigarettes and other problems? That's information, not education.

You mean we should not educate children about AIDS? Not until doctors themselves are educated; until then children can only be informed.

What better way is there for kids to become informed? By learning to read.

Why aren't kids learning to read? TV—and too many other subjects—sex, drugs, cigarettes—clogging the curriculum.

Who is responsible for what's wrong with our schools? Historically, American educators who went to Germany in the nineteeth century, admired the system, and brought it back to America. Today, pedants who, oblivious to causes and consequences, perpetuate the pestilence.

But do not today's educators warn of a nation at risk? It's not a nation that's at risk, but civilization, humanity, the planet.

Taxpayers hire experts with doctoral degrees to manage the school system. What's wrong with them? Too many are fugitives from the classroom who prefer pay, power, perks to teaching kids.

What's the answer to that? Elevate teaching above administration. Examine doctoral candidates on motivation as well as ambition.

As a Doctor of Education, what would be your prescription for better education? From Plato to Piaget, hundreds of prescriptions have mentally murdered millions of children caught in the crossfire of their conflicting theories. The last thing education needs is another prescription.

Doesn't that make your own theory rather weak? My theory is not weak. It is nonexistent.

Without a better theory, how can schools do a better job of educating anybody? Schools don't educate anybody. Literate individuals educate themselves.

Why do you want a degree in a profession so crazy and corrupt? The answer derives from the other side of education. Had I not undergone the paperchase for a doctoral degree, I would have missed the greatest intellectual adventure of my life. And no other human activity holds out more hope for the survival of civilization, and preservation of the planet.

It was a long, difficult day. When it was done I heard from Dean Dolly. "I see nothing," he wrote, "to warrant changing my position and feel I have done what I must do in terms of my own conceptual model of a dissertation. Obviously my colleagues on your committee disagree with my point of view and are in full support of your dissertation. This indicates that you've met the criteria established for doctoral degrees at this institution."

40

An Imperilled Planet's Plea . . .

A threatened planet pleads for education less responsive to the selfish needs of nation-states, more sensitive to its imminent extinction. Less dedicated to the dichotomy of the humanities and sciences, more aware that salvation lies in their synthesis. Less driven to making money by intensifying competition, more given to solving the planet's problems by cooperation.

Until parents, like Puritans, assume responsibility for their offspring, schools are houses of detention, littered with the societal debris dumped upon them, keeping kids on hold from post-infancy to late-adolescence, unleashing them as adults on a democracy that staggers beneath the burden of their ignorance. And, as the Aussie aboriginal affirmed: Until schools are rid of the poison that kids instinctively smell in the system, students will misbehave, drop out and get into trouble.

That civilization somehow survives is due largely to the devo-

tion, zeal and self-sacrifice of tried-and-true teachers. But teachers
—overworked, unappreciated, poorly paid, and devoured by the
demands of a sick society—cannot fulfill their primary purpose:
the production of people who read, who read widely, who reflect
deeply, and who enrich their reading with an abundance of experience.

Only when that role is returned to the school may teachers best
serve civilization, achieve peace, and preserve the planet.

ACKNOWLEDGMENTS

Since the intention of this exercise has been to identify education's ills, it may be best to admit at once that I, ordained a Doctor of Education by as estimable an institution as the University of Hawaii, may be, if not education's most malignant affliction, at least its latest. It therefore becomes difficult, even dangerous, to express gratitude to innocent individuals, thereby implicating them in whatever academic crimes this book commits.

It is thus with some misgiving that I commend my doctoral committee: Melvin Ezer, chairperson of Educational Foundations in the College of Education, who championed my cause through thick and thin, coaching me over the hurdles, and hooding me as I breasted the tape; Reuel Denney, co-author of *The Lonely Crowd,* whose worldly wisdom overcame academic overemphases; George Simson, editor of the journal *Biography,* who argued the case for autobiography in an educational metaphor; Ralph Stueber, among the most inspiring of my professors, whose connection with the Peace Institute concerted with my own interests. Two others, John Dolly, dean of the College of Education, and Anne Keppel, whose domain is womens' studies, deserve special commendation for their resistance to my dissertation, denying to the bitter end that autobiography is an acceptable subject for a doctoral degree. Which members of my committee best served scholarship, readers must judge for themselves.

Others to whom appreciation is owed are eminences in institutions who accepted me as a visiting scholar, providing hospitality, information, and advice that advanced or, depending on one's viewpoint, retarded research. At Harvard's Graduate School of Education, Francis Keppel, Paul Ylvisaker, and Israel Scheffler; at

Cambridge, Sir Peter Swinnerton-Dyer, Paul Hirst, and Richard D'Aethe; at the University of Kyoto, Tetsuya Kobayashi; at Sydney University, John Cleverley; at the University of Canberra, James Bowen; at the University of Canterbury, Graham Nuthall and Warwick Elly; at the University of Moscow, Professors Gafanova and Lubovsky; at the University of Leningrad, Professor Zelenev; and from Beijing Normal University, Yang Zhi-Ling and Lin Bing. To list the multitudes in many faculties who endured my probing would imperil other innocents; my gratitude may be better expressed by omitting rather than adding their names to what may become more a roster of disgrace than of academic honor.

Innumerable colleagues read drafts of the typescript, their cheers urging me on, their warnings neglected. Those so solidly tenured in their positions who my appreciation cannot possibly harm include Hayden Burgess, Leon Edel, Joan Fulton, Norman Geschwind, John Haak, Elaine Hatfield, Robert Hewett, Sasha and Henry Kariel, Keith Lorenz, Jack Maddux, Janet Nordyke Ohuchi, Graham Parkes, Edwin Penn, Richard Rapson, Marion Rasse, Pier Schwartz, Robert Straus, and Belle Zeller. My professors—Barry Bull, Royal Fruehling, Victor Kobayashi, Robert Potter and Ralph Stueber—truly tested my mettle, and endured my intractability with amazing grace. Masterminding the entire performance was Irene Oka, without whom Educational Foundations would be unfounded. For access to an office at the East-West Center I am deeply indebted to Sumi Makey.

The typist entrusted with my manuscript gave up in disgust, defeated by my handwriting, obscenity, and absence of footnotes. Two lovely ladies, Shirley Peacock and Rosemary Hilbery, rushed to my rescue.

Without the wisdom of Norma Gorst, freelance editor, and William Hamilton, Janet Heavenridge, and Iris Wiley, my editors at the University of Hawaii Press, the last vestige of my academic pretensions would have vanished.

Finally, that the University of Hawaii Foundation dares publish this tract testifies to its courage, and augurs an argument that hopefully may heal, not aggravate, education's ills.

AG

Honolulu, Hawaii
September, 1989

INDEX

ABOUT THE AUTHOR

Before World War II Arthur Goodfriend believed schooling was something to be endured because society so ordered. Not until the indelible sight and stench of Dachau, Belsen, and Buchenwald overwhelmed his senses did he associate such evil with education.

Born in 1907, he is a survivor of New York City's "school wars" and the Great Depression. As a writer for *The New York Times;* an editor of *The Stars and Stripes* in Europe and China; a foreign service officer in China, India, and Africa; a presidential envoy to Asia; a Rockefeller Fellow in Indonesia; and a Peace Corps Volunteer in the Philippines, the author began to focus his attention on the teaching-learning process. Drawn to the great universities of the world—Heidelberg, Harvard, Cambridge, Kyoto, Moscow, Leningrad, Beijing, Sydney, and others from whose heights doctrine descends to primary, secondary, and tertiary levels of education—he mingled with students, teachers, parents, and administrators, and himself filled each of those roles.

He questioned why education, however variously defined, was accused of failure to fulfill its function. Aware that to change the system he needed to join it, Arthur Goodfriend, at the age of eighty, embarked on a quest for a doctoral degree. He collided with the theories, methods, manners, and scruples of the academy and encountered deep-seated diseases afflicting our schools that nostrums, bandaids, and dollars cannot cure; but in December 1988 he received an Ed.D. degree from the University of Hawaii.

Goodfriend's twenty-three previously published volumes range

from Army military manuals to studies of intercultural communication and an analysis of New College, an educational experiment
tried at the University of Hawaii.

The author, also an artist, is extending his thoughts on education and the arts as an activist serving as a member of the University of Hawaii Council on Aging. His current activities as writer
and artist encourage other senior citizens to reflect on and to give
meaning to their life experiences.